Apartheid on a Black Isle

APARTHEID ON A BLACK ISLE

REMOVAL AND RESISTANCE IN ALEXANDRA, SOUTH AFRICA

Dawne Y. Curry

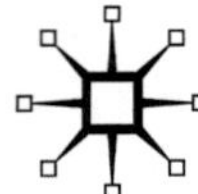

First published in 2012 by
PALGRAVE MACMILLAN®
in the United States—a division of St. Martin's Press LLC,
175 Fifth Avenue, New York, NY 10010.

Where this book is distributed in the UK, Europe and the rest of the
World, this is by Palgrave Macmillan, a division of Macmillan Publishers
Limited, registered in England, company number 785998, of
Houndmills, Basingstoke, Hampshire RG21 6XS.

Palgrave Macmillan is the global academic imprint of the above
companies and has companies and representatives throughout the world.

Palgrave® and Macmillan® are registered trademarks in the United
States, the United Kingdom, Europe and other countries.

ISBN: 978–1–137–02309–4

Library of Congress Cataloging-in-Publication Data is available from
the Library of Congress.

A catalogue record of the book is available from the British Library.

Design by Integra Software Services

First edition: November 2012

10 9 8 7 6 5 4 3 2 1

This book is dedicated to my mother, Ronnie, who taught me my first lessons on resistance.

Contents

List of Tables

LIST OF PHOTOS

Acknowledgments

This intellectual journey would not have been possible without my mother's love and encouragement. My mother's support was duly noted on numerous occasions, but especially when I told her that my picture with Nelson Mandela would proudly be displayed on the wall in between Martin Luther King, Jr. and the South African leader. She didn't even bat an eye, and said, "I'm sure it will." At the time I hadn't stepped foot in South Africa nor had I finished my doctoral program, but that didn't stop my mother from believing in me. Strangely enough, however, when that moment came on two occasions, I decided not to have the photo taken. I wanted the encounters to remain forever etched in my mind rather than produced as photographic images. It took me five years to accomplish that goal, as I had begun my explorations to South Africa in 1997. Under a fellowship from the Social Science Research Council (SRC) and the American Council of Learned Societies (ACLS), I tested the feasibility of my dissertation project. During that fellowship tenure I lived in South Africa for a year, and experienced Johannesburg's pulse, culture, and vibe. That stay began my lifelong love with the country and its diverse peoples and landscapes. I thank the SRC and the ACLS for giving me this opportunity to get my feet wet.

Other funders are due their acknowledgments. Several grants from Michigan State University (MSU) further afforded me trips to South Africa. A year-long Fulbright Hays fellowship sponsored by the United States Department of Education also provided me with the monetary and psychic space to conduct archival research and to record over a hundred interviews, many of which appear in this book. I also would like to thank the University of Nebraska-Lincoln (UNL) for supporting my research as a junior faculty member. All of these opportunities would not have been possible without the encouragement of my former advisor, who had me writing grant proposals during my second week at MSU. My colleagues and I all sat around a table at a coffee shop every week and constructively critiqued each other's work. That was a rewarding experience, and I thank you. My dissertation committee, David Robinson, Peter Limb, Darlene Clark Hine, Peter Beattie, and John Metzler, provided constructive feedback that assisted me when writing this book. I thank you for your ear, your encouragement, and your intellect during my odyssey at MSU. I would also like to thank Marshanda Smith, Nokuthula Cele, Mona Jackson, Leslie Hadfield, Assan Saar, Mary Mwiandi, and Hilary Jones for attending my dissertation defense and for representing the contingencies of MSU's Comparative Black History and African History programs.

Several people offered advice or encouragement in other ways. My colleagues at UNL, both in History and the Institute for Ethnic Studies, have shaped my scholarship and professionalism in profound ways. I am deeply indebted to Margaret Jacobs, who read several versions of this manuscript. Margaret was hospitalized but still found the strength and the time to offer constructive feedback. Her background in the North American West and Australia proved invaluable. I would also like to thank my official and unofficial mentors and friends: Carole Levin, Jeannette Eileen Jones, and Amelia Montes for their guidance, humor and tough love. Amy Nelson Burnett, Parks M. Coble, Victoria Smith, Vanessa Gorman, and others armed me with knowledge about teaching and the tenure process. I would also like to thank all those friends who offered emotional support : the Garzas (James, Jenny, Katherine, and Deborah), Linda and Perry Fauntleroy, Angela and Joey Lee, Bridget Goosby, and Kevin Palmer. These special people allowed me to enter their homes and their hearts and for that I am eternally grateful. I thank you for your counsel, conversations and laughter. Kwakiutl Lynn Dreher helped me out during a crucial time in the writing process. When meeting me at one of our favorite haunts to discuss my progress, I outlined each chapter, and Kwakiutl, who likes to make visuals, examined what she wrote and said with her southern drawl, "you got all that in one chapter? Girl, each one is a dissertation." That was a turning point for me because I thought that I had to write three additional chapters. After that conversation, I was able to pursue my work and under less stress! Thanks Wa. Billie Ann Davis, one of my dear friends, thanks for the "consultations," the love.

Family members also deserve their due. Momma Claudine and Daddy James were my "grandparents." I always checked on them whenever I was going to "town" and would often sit and chat. One time I interviewed Momma Claudine about her life as a midwife. I will never forget the story she told me about a mother who asked if her child was ugly. Momma Claudine said, "I tell you what, if its ugly I'll take it home and when it gets good looking I'll bring it back to you." Thanks Momma Claudine for being my grandmother, for your quick wit, and for attending my college graduation. Daddy James, thanks for slipping me that twenty dollar bill, when I was struggling, and for our talk about your first plane ride to Atlanta at the age of 90. I bet, you and Momma Claudine are both flying now. Their offspring Shirley Dunaway, Jeanette Cottrell, Maxine Carter, Denise Mazyck and Vanessa "Tinsey" Pope have each offered undying support and love by feeding me during Christmas breaks, by attending my doctoral graduation, and by just simply having their doors open when I came to Virginia to visit. I love listening to your stories about the past. Sometimes my sides never stopped hurting from all the laughter. My adopted "father and mother" Gus and Louise (Weazie) Dunaway never stopped loving me even when years past between us. Thank you all for that Virginia Northern Neck hospitality.

My South African contacts were as equally valuable. Thanks to Morwesi Dorothy Pitso for "our walks," and Lindiwe Tshabalala and Maisaka Mphahlele for securing interviews during my tenure as a Fulbright Hays Fellow. Nthabiseng Motsemme provided me with the opportunity to become a godmother and a better observer of South Africa's glorious and tumultuous past. Our Friday night talks on various subjects over home-cooked meals were always lively. All of the South African artists that I had the privilege of seeing perform: Gloria Bosman, Selaelo Selota, Paul Hamner, McCoy Mrubata, Judith Sephuma, Simphiwe Dana, and Blk Sonshine among other South African gems, thanks for entertaining me with your musical gifts and providing me with a way to relax after a hard day's work. Dr. Mark Mathabane, thanks for your inspirational visit to UNL and for further cementing my love for Alexandra.

I would be remissed if I did not acknowledge the public transportation system in Johannesburg, which made it possible for me to engage with the Alexandran community on a daily basis. Research would also not have been possible without the archivists at the National Archives of South Africa in Pretoria (Michelle), the Cullen Library Historical Papers at the University of Witwatersrand, and the Killie Campbell Library in Durban. Last but not the least, I would like to thank the Alexandran community for making this American feel at home in your beloved township. Thanks for granting me interviews and taking time out of your schedule to share your knowledge about one of South Africa's most riveting and vibrant communities.

These "accolades" would not have been possible had my mother not instilled the value of an education. Every day when I came home from school, I took my clothes off and did my homework at the kitchen table. Momma spent numerous hours with me going over vocabulary and math. She would always say "I don't know why they teach y'all all these new fangled methods. I learned this way." Her way, I must admit was a lot easier. I respected all the advice my mother gave me about school, until she suggested that I take typing in the tenth grade. I had no desire to learn this skill, in fact, I flunked several typing drills and even threw the evidence of my failures in numerous trash-cans. Practicing at home on my pica typewriter didn't help matters either until one day I decided that I was going to conquer typing. Instead of dreading the class, I began to listen intently to my teacher Mrs. Francine Waddy's instructions, "feet flat, one foot slightly forward, eyes on copy, begin," and off I would go to improve my typing speed. I think that at one time I got up to 60 words per minute with one or two typing errors. While it may have taken me to my college years to understand the value of this course, my momma always knew, and because of her and Mrs. Waddy I have an invaluable skill. No matter how many degrees I hold, I am still in awe and inspired by Momma who remains my mentor, friend, and confidant. Thank you Momma for your intellect, sense of humor, and candor.

APARTHEID ON A BLACK ISLE

In the 1950s, Richard Ngculu lived a relatively quiet life with his family in Alexandra, South Africa. Even though the apartheid government had designated families for removal, it spared the Ngculus the embarrassment, the shame, and the hassle of selling or renting their family home. In that space, Ngculu doted on his family, devoting all his attention to being a good husband and father. Ngculu was also an avid reader and a talented mechanic, who—by his own estimation— "performed miracles on some broken down jalopies."[1] He enjoyed plying his trade until the African National Congress (ANC) wooed him to join the organization and he forayed into a new "profession."

The ANC was founded as the South African Native National Congress (SANNC), a political body, in 1912. It took its current name in 1923. At the time of Ngculu's initiation and membership in 1963, authorities had raided a major safe house on the outskirts of Johannesburg where the police arrested 19 people, including future president Nelson Mandela. The ANC, the country's oldest nationwide black organization, took a major hit with its leadership incarcerated. This made Ngculu's recruitment more essential, as people like Oliver Tambo had skipped the country to run the ANC in exile. In the same year as the Rivonia raid, the Organization of African Unity (OAU) was established to end colonialism, abolish apartheid, and defend member nations' sovereignty.

While an unprecedented number of nations gained freedom in 1960, colonialism continued to dot Africa's map, as Zimbabwe, Mozambique, Angola, Guinea Bissau, and Namibia still fell under its oppressive yoke. If that was not enough, Africa also became entangled in the Cold War between the United States and the Soviet Union, with different nations falling like dominoes under Communist and American influence. Further, the South African government was not above invading neighboring nations to arrest or permanently silence opposition or using its neighbors and their stance on colonialism to curry favor. After deliberating at length (and taking into consideration Africa's colonial situation, South Africa's repression, and Alexandra's demographical changes), Ngculu finally pledged his allegiance to the ANC.

With the ANC guiding him, Ngculu went for military training in neighboring Swaziland. Within months, he moved up the organization's ranks and ended up as a weapons specialist. He trained recruits and assisted in forming small political units called cells. In fact, Ngculu helped to lead the assault against apartheid's injustices and inhumanity. In a rare interview months before his death, Ngculu explained how Alexandra's unique demographic and geographic characteristics enabled resistance to apartheid to flourish:

Resisting on a black isle meant that we had to become creative, using all types of resistance to wear down and defy the apartheid machinery that meant protesting in the streets, devising secret codes, using the armed units to advance the struggle and engaging in camouflage to keep up the appearance of normalcy.[2]

When he was not training recruits and helping them to form cells, Ngculu engaged in camouflage in another way. His house, which concealed weapons, seemed to the casual observer to be an innocuous mud brick structure lathered in gold paint and adorned by plants. The Ngculus even had a pet, and by all estimations from the outside, they were a typical Alexandran family: god fearing and hardworking. When I walked into their house in 2002, they had photos, mementos, and other expressions of love adorning the walls and the coffee tables. Two plush sofas and a table with refreshments greeted me as I entered the living room. I sat down and waited for their cue. Ngculu's wife, Sarah, began the conversation talking about marriage. I thought, "I am going to get a story about love and intimacy," since the couple was celebrating their twentieth anniversary on the very day that they decided to share with me, an American and an outsider. I also thought that a story about love would be an interesting way to introduce Alexandra—through the lens of marriage and weddings.

Just when Sarah had me spellbound with her story about how the couple had met, she started talking about Alexandra. It was only then that Ngculu, who had been noticeably silent, decided to speak. His baritone voice greeted and alarmed me. I assumed that he had done public speaking or had been an announcer on the ANC's underground station, Radio Freedom. Established in 1967 and headquartered in Lusaka, Zambia, Radio Freedom had broadcasted from four other African nations from staggered frequencies, but he said, "no my role was more behind the scenes, I was the local chemist, creating and dispensing chemicals."[3] I couldn't believe that this gentle man had performed such risky work, and on top of that, had hidden his secret from his family even though he had used their home, especially the kitchen, to perfect and "cook" his chemical experiments and to store weaponry. His wife always knew of his double identity but never let on while he was involved. In fact, she whispered this in my ear: "I knew he was part of the struggle. The dead giveaway was the trips throughout and outside the country, but I pretended not to know."[4]

In this single square mile hemmed in by Sandton, Kew, Bramely, and other White areas, Ngculu and other residents engaged in what was arguably the most multifaceted, inventive, and versatile strategy of resistance during the 1970s. *Apartheid on a Black Isle* brings to the fore the definitive but underappreciated role that Alexandra played in advancing human rights. Alexandra's documented records and its oral histories, gathered here for the first time, invite us to conceive of resistance in ways that established scholarly models fail to reckon.[5] This book examines the resistance not only in its manifestations of underground movements and student uprising, but, more importantly, in its relationship to the environment and environmental destruction and how these amplified dwellers' opposition to apartheid. Alexandra stood at the vanguard of protests throughout its one hundred—year existence from 1912 to 2012. Alexandra' s residents used bus boycotts, squatter movements, housing campaigns, education boycotts, and other protests to air their dissatisfaction with low pay, inadequate housing, police brutality, and segregated living conditions.

With Ngculu's testimony and court documents, my book, *Apartheid on a Black Isle*, proves that Alexandra was a major hub of clandestine activity. Ngculu's experience with the ANC's armed wing, Umkhonto weSizwe (MK or Spear of the Nation), founded in 1961, further sheds light on how Alexandrans interpreted defiance, remade the political environment, and carried on a sustained struggle against the state. He, along with countless others, protested during the 1970s, when it appeared that the government had successfully clamped down on overt protests. My book, *Apartheid on a Black Isle*, challenges the premise that a period of quiescence rested between more visible, conventional protests in Alexandra. The township's layout, makeup, density, and compactness shaped its response to government policy that banned the ANC and the Pan Africanist Congress (PAC) along with other political organizations following the 1960 Sharpeville Massacre, a peaceful pass protest that turned into a killing orgy. Like these organizations, Alexandrans resorted to clandestine ways to sustain the struggle, forming political cells of three to four people that worked secretly and independently of other units, even those existing within the same township. Other scholars such as Gregory Houston, Bernard Magubane[6] and Raymond Suttner[7] have addressed this crucial period but only a few historians have examined Alexandran activists. During the alleged period of quiescence in the 1970s, Alexandrans were hard at work opposing apartheid's many injustices. Not only did residents face demographic and physical changes to their landscape, they also used this decade to register this disquiet, by refusing to move, by participating in the underground movement, by finding alternative ways to mourn, and by joining in solidarity with Soweto during the student uprising.

While the highly contentious and violent student uprising punctuated the 1970s, the outcomes and contributions of this crucial period served as a prototype for how people memorialized apartheid and its inhumane effects in subsequent decades.

During the hearings of the Truth and Reconciliation Commission (TRC), when apartheid victims heard testimonies of perpetrators of violent crimes, participants seized the historical moment and its immense gravity to convey an array of emotions. They wept, pleaded, demanded justice, prayed, paused, thought, sweated, made requests,[8] and reconciled. While these actions exhibited fortitude and frailty,[9] testifiers used their narratives to cleanse the past, to accept the future, and to live in the present. They also revealed how the government restricted public mourning, and forced Alexandrans to create new traditions of remembrance during and after the 1976 student uprising.[10] If we take into consideration human emotions, then it was not out of the ordinary for township residents to lament, recount horrific stories, and reveal notions of death because the violent and repressive political state had remained the same from the 1970s to the 1980s, with apartheid officials steadily accruing deaths into their solvent account.

Testimonies not only underscore life in this turbulent environment, they also reveal ways in which Alexandra's residents memorialized decedents by creating different forms of obituaries. Through their experiences with death and property loss, Alexandrans reconciled with the soil, their ancestors, the township, the dearly departed, the bodily impaired, and each other. As a result, their reconciliations revolved, mutated, and intersected with the protests and resistances that they waged or the memories that they relived. Alexandra's protests also captured some of the tenor and temperament of global events.

As the world and Africa faced major changes, including OPEC's oil embargo (1973), Augusto Pinochet's successful Chilean coup (1973), Ethiopian leader Haile Selassie's ouster (1974), Rhodesia's second Chimurenga (uprising) (1972-1980), and America's exit from Vietnam (1975), South Africa and Alexandra faced external and internal pressure. The UN outlawed apartheid and held its proponents accountable for human rights violations through its Apartheid Convention of 1973. The world took another stab at this inhumane policy when the international community launched sit-ins, engaged in economic and sports boycotts, stormed the South African embassies, hosted exiles, and also issued sanctions. The South African government was an international pariah, and its day of reckoning was fast approaching.

As external influences impacted South Africa economically, politically, and culturally, tensions mounted within this powder keg. Eruptions occurred throughout the nation. Durban residents, for example, held a workers' strike in 1972. More behind the scenes activities also took place, or at least their public roles were not identified as struggle related.[11] When Martin Ramokgadi and other Robben Island political prisoners were released, they helped to form internal networks.[12] These structures developed and flourished during this period as the ANC sought to infiltrate and inundate the country with attacks on installations, railroads, oil refineries, and other soft and hard targets to bring the apartheid government to its political knees.[13] A more visible protest, the 1976 student uprising, swept the nation ferociously. And with the introduction of television nationwide in this year, Africans and the world could witness apartheid's inhumanity. Witnessing the killings of school-aged children aroused all kinds of emotions: some South African youth became so angry that they went into exile and joined the MK. This made places like Alexandra rife for recruitment, so much so that safe houses developed to cater to the ever increasing demands to form cells and extend the interior networks between townships and regions within and outside South Africa. Further compounding the tensions, in 1977, Africans lost a prominent antiapartheid activist—Black Consciousness (BC) proponent Steve Biko—who died violently while in police custody.

Alexandra's history paralleled these global and domestic events, as the 1970s ushered in a new wave of defiance within this iconic township. Its residents faced a stiff challenge to their existence. With the threat of forced removals looming over their lives, Alexandra's dwellers publicly issued a challenge to the apartheid regime when they used the media to plead their case. Not only did inhabitants publicly criticize the apartheid regime's brutality, they also engaged in a national campaign to end White rule. By dividing the township into streets and zones, Alexandrans used their enclosed space to their advantage and created cells throughout the township that linked up with other national and regional sites. Like their global counterparts, Alexandrans and other South Africans wanted social and political change. Instead of using the traditional ways to assess and access public outcries of defiance, *Apartheid on a Black Isle* shows how Alexandrans used the landscape, their bodies, and the media to resist within the strictures of apartheid and the insulated geographical terrain that they inhabited.

SITUATING *APARTHEID ON A BLACK ISLE* INTO THE SEA OF HISTORIOGRAPHY

Because of its rich and diverse history, Alexandra has blazed a trail on the intellectual and scholarly landscape. Its many resistance struggles highlighted the different incarnations of apartheid South Africa and Black township life. Scholars grappled with analyzing transport[14] and other subsistence issues, the Health Committee and its local governance,[15] the student uprising,[16] political organizations, and people's power and space,[17] among an array of other topics spanning the early 1930s to the twenty-first century. Many pages featured the all-encompassing forced removal process that hit Alexandra ferociously in the mid-1950s. Forced removals are attempts by a state or any powerbroker to displace people from traditional or ancestral lands or spaces of urban or rural habitation to implement policy that politically and geographically disadvantages, displaces, and dehumanizes subordinates.

Not just germane to South Africa, or Alexandra in particular, forced removals have occurred throughout history, as evident with Australia's aborigines;[18] with the United States' Native Americans; and even closer to South Africa, with Zimbabwean urbanites very recently.[19] Racial segregation, health concerns, conservation,[20] interracial cooperation, and slum-like conditions have ranked among the rationales given by governments to uproot people from their traditional lands or habitats. Residents of Johannesburg's Sophiatown and Cape Town's District Six lost their battles to protect their homes and businesses when the government destroyed these vibrant communities. By contrast, inhabitants of the integrated community of Durban's Warwick Triangle,[21] Cape Town's Glenmore, and Johannesburg's Alexandra fought off abolition. Alexandra accomplished this goal in 1940, 1943, 1950, and 1979.

Prior to 1979, and before government officials issued a reprieve, Alexandra was under major attack. Many forcibly left the township. A large majority, however, answered Dutch Reformed Church (DRC) minister Sam Buti's call to fight evictions and stay in their homes. Hailing from Brandfort in the Orange Free State (OFS), Buti moved to Alexandra in 1959, at the age of 25. Like Richard Ngculu, this third generation pastor led a dual life. On Sunday mornings, he rendered sermons supporting racial segregation, however, away from the pulpit he professed his allegiance to antiapartheid activity.[22] He was not only an outsider, but a person who represented Calvinism, the faith long adhered to by the White Afrikaner minority.[23] However, through his deeds and commitment, Buti ultimately won over his adopted community and emerged as the preeminent leader of the Save Alexandra Party (SAP) in 1974.[24]

During his quest to save this storied township, Buti used development as a tool. He engaged in civic duty long before it became fashionable in the 1980s. Besides communicating with childhood friend Minister of Cooperative Development (MCD) Piet Koornhof, Buti took to the streets and picked up debris. This was a practice that Alexandrans had long adopted when they had competitions for the cleanest yards and streets, but somewhere along the line, they had lost their community pride and Buti wanted to restore it. Buti also wanted Alexandra to attain parity with the White suburbs that encircled it. Nicely manicured green lawns appeared in White suburbia, as did other signs of urbanity and healthy living such as indoor plumbing and clean streets.[25] Alexandra by contrast had several families in one yard, hundreds of people using one water tap, and then to further add to their demoralization, they excreted wastes in buckets left by the road for night soil workers to deposit at a site that doubled as a cemetery. With no electricity or indoor plumbing, Alexandra languished far behind other townships comparable to it, let alone the White areas it sought to emulate.

Instead of focusing on leaders and their organizations, *Apartheid on a Black Isle* highlights those most intimately affected by the removal process and therefore provides a glimpse and analysis from below. When the state politically dispossessed Alexandrans and threatened or took their properties, they went through periods of denial, alienation, and economic hardships. Some even experienced bodily pain or died in the violence. Alexandrans had a direct relationship with the property, because as Buti maintained, " . . . some people here not only own houses, but the ground too."[26] Not only did ownership refer to the buildings that lay upon particular sites, it also incorporated the earth that sustained them. Land not only signified wealth, it and the river that snaked through Alexandra were mediums that allowed residents to commune with the ancestors. The forced removal process disrupted this relationship and threatened the very existence of the township's moral and social fiber by changing how people identified with their community. Before this demographic change occurred, dwellers could trace a family's history by their address because according to Caroline Nkosi, "We in Alexander used to know one another."[27] This pattern of familiarity was one of the special qualities that Alexandra possessed, and it was also one of the defining factors that influenced how Nkosi and other Alexandrans maintained the personal and communal histories they cultivated. All of these qualities was not lost on Reverend Buti who used his oratory skills, and his newly emigrated status to save the township's physical environment, the spirituality it nourished, the community ethos it sustained, and the geographies it defined.

Besides analyzing Buti's contributions, scholars such as Mike Sarakinsky, Philip Bonner, and Noor Nieftagodien have discussed in their respective works from "Freehold" to "Model Township"[28] to *Alexandra: A History* the structural and political impact of the forced removal process.[29] These scholars also address how much the forced removal process cost, how Peri-Urban exercised its authority, how people evaded the pass laws, and how the government deliberated on how it would reduce the population or restructure the township.[30] Building upon these studies, *Apartheid on a Black Isle* thematically interprets the forced removal process to discuss gender, space, and ageism. No matter how much Alexandrans fought, the apartheid regime affected their persons in profound, psychosomatic ways. When the government took away the only homes they knew, many Alexandrans experienced bodily pain and memorialized this ordeal corporeally. This also occurred during the student uprising, when dwellers lost loved ones.

Sparked by South Africa's inferior education system, this year-long revolt was a historical watershed. Education had long been a struggle in South African history. Going back to the 1953 Bantu Education Act (BEA), the government had closed down all missionary schools except for institutions run by Roman Catholics, the Seventh Day Adventists, and the United Jewish Reform Organization, which used their own finances to teach Africans.[31] The Act also enforced the separation of races in all educational institutions. Some religious schools resisted government edicts. Former exile Rose Innes Phahle's father served as a school director for St. Hubert's Catholic Mission School. According to Phahle, his father circumvented the law by allowing teachers to discuss African history and politics.[32] Teachers used debating as part of their hidden curriculum to politicize,[33] to educate students about the historical past, and to encourage them to interrogate the present.

Alexandrans also had the private Haile Selassie School, but the government closed its doors in 1953. On the day of the school's closing, police officials stormed the building, confiscated books, and pieces of chalk, blackboards, and other school equipment while several chairs remained in the rooms along with a pupil's raincoat. Longtime activist and street orator Josias Madzunya, who had taught at the school since its opening in 1948, was expelled and arrested along with three other colleagues while the police issued a summons for a fifth defendant. Days later, the police tore down the school.[34] With the closing of alternative schools, Africans were left with imbibing what the state deemed appropriate: learning how to serve in menial capacities, remembering the history of European and western civilization, not their own history, and . . . this was not only detrimental to Africans' well-being, it also hindered their intellectual growth. Yet, even with the passing of the BEA, the government was not through meddling in the educational affairs of Africans.

Despite worldwide condemnation, with the antiapartheid movement deeming South Africa an international pariah, officials busied themselves with further entrenching African inferiority. Authorities were so relentless in their pursuit that they mandated that students learn all subjects in Afrikaans. Students preferred learning in English because it was considered the language of liberation,[35] as many poets had adopted it during the late 1960s and the 1970s as part of the Black Consciousness Movement (BCM). Learning Afrikaans, however, was a different story. Africans were so adamant in their refusal to learn the oppressors' language that on June 16, 1976, students from Soweto's Isaac Morrison High School led a peaceful march to protest the imposition of Afrikaans. Police officers met the marchers, who numbered in the thousands, with heavy artillery, casspirs, hippos, and live ammunition. Shots were fired in all directions with one bullet felling teenager Hector Petersen. His lifeless corpse lay straddled in another fellow Sowetan's arms, as his sister ran alongside, crying in angst. Local professional photographer Sam Mzima captured this scene and immortalized the harrowing image that appeared in local, national, and international newspapers.[36] Not satisfied with the government's refusal to change this law or the way the state handled the protest, the revolt quickly spread from Soweto to other townships, including Alexandra, where it erupted two days later, on June 18, 1976.

Although the student uprising impacted hundreds of South African communities, certain characteristics link all the movements, whether sporadic or planned; these include police reprisals, a rising death toll, opposition to Afrikaans, lack of school fees,[37] inadequate education, subpar school facilities and overcrowding,[38] generational disputes, and a "join or else ultimatum."[39] Alexandra showcased all of these tensions and highlighted the interracial cooperation between Coloureds[40] and Africans.[41] White and Black women also joined forces when they formed an Alexandran branch of the nationally recognized Women for Peace (WP). This unique composition of middle-aged mothers spoke before parliament, and advocated on behalf of the youth. While substandard education sparked the student uprising, residents redefined the township's interior space by using the destruction of Chinese and Indian owned shops along with government-run beer halls and schools to resuscitate the movement. When Alexandrans committed arson, hurled Molotov cocktails or hijacked buses and rammed them into these buildings, they struck at the institutions of their oppression. Africans wanted to obliterate these "monuments" of apartheid authority from the landscape because they represented subservience, inferiority, and racialization. More than anything, these spaces imprisoned their spirits, and threatened their livelihoods, familial structures, and even their day-to-day existence. They also consumed their hard-earned wages.

As much as education, cultural consciousness,[42] and destruction defined the student uprising, so did death. It is in this way that *Apartheid on a Black* Isle builds upon while adding new layers to recent scholarship by Philip Bonner and Noor Nieftagodien that examines Alexandra's contribution to the student uprising. According to the official inquiry into the uprising, the Cillie Report, which covers events from June 16, 1976, to February 28, 1977, 39 Alexandrans lost their lives. Twenty-four died on the uprising's first day[43] from police gunfire, stab wounds, and ricocheted gunshots.[44] Though valuable for its content, the Cillie Report explains death in clinical terms by itemizing the decedents' age, race, blood alcohol level, date and place of death. Using that information but offering an alternative from the report, *Apartheid on a Black Isle* analyzes how survivors mourned and interpreted the passing away of loved ones. Alexandrans created their own language of mourning. Instead of using scientific terminology and autopsy photographs to immortalize the deceased,[45] Alexandrans painted oral canvases that framed death and their remembrance of it.

When apartheid officials regulated[46] funerals and burials, residents found other ways to grieve. They used the morgue, the streets, the police station, and neighboring countries to reflect and to carry out activities associated with death during apartheid, such as retrieving the bodies and finding information about loved ones.[47] These activities often occurred before or in lieu of funerals.[48] For this exploration, *Apartheid on a Black Isle* highlights the underappreciated role of women in the student uprising. Women participated emotionally (when loved ones died), physically (when they went to find decedents), and corporeally (when their bodies manifested their pain). Many took to the streets to find loved ones[49] in addition to throwing Molotov cocktails, chanting, singing, or engaging in destruction on behalf of the liberation movement. Some saw their loved ones pummeled against a rock,[50] shot in their arms,[51] or witnessed the blood stains,[52] they left behind. When loved ones died, survivors began to interpret why and how their children, siblings, or friends passed away. They also moved around to obtain decedents' bodies. These actions, the viewing of bodies and their reclamation, required mobility. People had to travel to fulfill African customs. They had to tell the body that it was going home.[53] Survivors were not the only ones to use mobility as a form of resistance. Richard Ngculu and other operatives also crossed national and international boundaries to advance the liberation struggle.

Documented underground political activity in Alexandra began in 1962—two years after 16 African nations had gained independence[54] and the infamous Sharpeville Massacre, which led to 69 deaths with scores injured. After the Sharpeville Massacre repression gripped the nation not only with the enforcement of curfews, it also affected cultural outlets. Government officials prohibited radio stations from playing the ever popular "Azikwelwa" (We Won't Ride slogan),[55] which highlighted the year-long 1957 bus boycott that began in Alexandra and catapulted local leaders, such as Josias Madzunya, into national prominence.[56] Following their banning in 1960, the ANC and the Pan Africanist Congress (PAC), among other political organizations, went underground, formed military wings, and established bases in neighboring countries and abroad. Places as far away as Ghana and Liberia on the African continent, as well as Europe and the Americas, served as hosts to ANC and PAC activists. The stories of ANC and PAC militants feature in many works as auto/biographies,[57] theorizations about the underground,[58] or reclamations that addressed women and their literary silences.[59]

Even with this variance, there exists a tendency to describe foreign exploits. With their respective monographs and films, Raymond Suttner *(ANC and the Underground)*,[60] Lynda Schuster *(A Burning Hunger)*,[61] Philip Noyce *(Catch a Fire)*,[62] and Lee Hirsch *(Amandla)*[63] have partially settled the score.[64] Each of these mediums adds to our discussion on how the underground movement evolved; however, some lingering questions exist. For instance, how did insurgents reach and leave their soft targets, how did cells function, how did operatives transport weaponry, and how did an urban landscape like Alexandra play a role? In *Apartheid on a Black Isle*, I answer these questions by discussing the following: how operatives used everyday household goods to transport weaponry; how they used camouflage to disguise themselves and the weapons they carried; how they created arteries both within and outside Alexandra to convey recruits and other personnel; and how they used nature to advance the liberation struggle.

Despite the township's long-standing commitment to resistance and the underground dating back to the late 1950s/ early 1960s, previous studies highlight Soweto or only allude to specific Alexandran leaders like Martin Mafefo Ramokgadi or the arrests the state made within the township.[65] This treatment discounts what Alexandra actually offered to the movement: an established base, safe houses, and an alternate ferrying arrangement. As a base and place of departure, operatives launched offensives from Alexandra or at least strategized and left the township to head to other areas where they recruited or learned more about cells. Through their networking, insurgents linked Alexandra to Soweto, Pietersburg, and other townships and regions across the country. Not only does the work explore the establishment of cells both within and outside Alexandra, the work also shows how operatives transported weapons. Alexandrans disguised weapons by placing explosives inside household items, and created the illusion that they represented innocuous articles rather than readymade bombs that could decimate entire communities. By showing this aspect of mobility, the work diverges from Raymond Suttner's study, *The ANC and the Underground*,[66] by exploring ways in which the home and its artifacts featured as tools of camouflage.

Apartheid on a Black Isle also charts new ground in its discussion on gender and the underground movement. Instead of simply pointing out the differences between men and women or making a specific point to highlight and reclaim women's contribution to history,[67] *Apartheid on a Black Isle* turns its attention to intra-gender politics. While some men dressed up as women or assumed female roles, they also fraternized during car rides or during military training as part of the initiation in the underground. These occasions provided the following opportunities: fostered male bonding, reduced concern about emasculation,[68] and created different ways to recruit. Car rides allowed operatives to dissemble even though they interacted within the public eye. Mobility not only fostered this exchange, it also added to the allure of being an operative. Without the ability to move from one place to another, whether by car or on foot, many of the operatives' missions ran the risk of abortion, failing, or reaping less success. Fueled by various methods of mobility, men and women, who participated in carrying camouflaged items to their designations, did so under the cover of darkness and light and also under the watchful gaze of an apartheid regime bent on entrenching its authority and silencing its dissenters. Through the stories of Alexandra's Black and Coloured populace, this book highlights the interface between public and private defiance. It shows how these two distinct categories meshed together to form interwoven patterns of resistance. Alexandra's volatility, versatility, and vitality made it one of the major centers of dissent not only in South Africa's history but also world history. Like its African counterparts, Alexandra also experienced its own form of colonialism with the apartheid regime. White officials made laws that segregated and sequestered the country's largest population, and rendered them foreigners in their native land.

Despite this political dispossession, Alexandra's vibrant history of resistance threatened apartheid officials, who constantly sought its abolition, harassed its dwellers, and cordoned off its peripheries. Alexandrans not only withstood these challenges to the township's sovereignty and its precarious existence, they also never cowered even during the 1970s, in a period when resistance allegedly dipped to an all time low. *Apartheid on a Black Isle* resuscitates, amplifies, and restores Alexandra's historical place during a crucial period in South African and world history.

Structure of *Apartheid on a Black Isle*

Divided into six chapters, *Apartheid on a Black Isle* unites three main themes: the forced removal process, the underground movement, and the student uprising. Chapter 1, " 'We Are Too Old, Where Are We to Go?': Forced Removals in Alexandra," explains how Alexandrans responded to government orders to relinquish their properties. During this key era, when the United States and the Soviet Union vied for pieces of Africa, Alexandra also experienced its own internal partition when apartheid officials destroyed homes to construct single sex hostels for migrant workers. Not only did Alexandra lose its family dwelling status, it also lost human resources. Partitioning impeded the township's organic growth, reducing the population and changing the physical landscape, so much so that people sold homes far below market value. Some dwellers refused to leave and milked the *Rand Daily Mail* and other media for their coverage. As a platform for the dispossessed, the printed media captured the forced removal process by documenting its tone, tenor, and themes. Homelessness, economic hardships, one-parent households, and sickness brought on by apartheid's brutality and violence highlight some of the structural and emotional pain that Alexandrans endured and immortalized.

Chapter 2, " 'Oiling the Machinery': Recruitment and Conversion in Alexandra's Underground Movement," brings to the fore the township's underappreciated role in subversive activity. In this chapter, I explain how everyday Alexandrans became operatives. They followed a distinct pattern toward organic professionalization[69]: they obtained political education, engaged in military instruction, and were sent out on missions to obtain arms, find recruits, or funnel money. They also experienced conversions. When prospects met along Alexandra's Jukskei River, they underwent a spiritual rejuvenation. Many operatives channeled the ancestors or viewed the experience as a political passage to manhood. These conversions also revealed ways in which operatives used nature and its environs to recruit, to inspire with freedom songs, and to form a fraternity among those present.

Chapter 3, "Secrecy, Camouflage, and Mobility in Alexandra's Underground Movement," shows that insurgents developed a meticulously planned ferrying system in Alexandra that took seasoned operatives and novice recruits within and outside South Africa to safe houses, targets, and training sites. Not only did operatives engage in local, national, and international travel, they also carried weapons across these same borders. Weapons appeared in canned food and other seemingly innocuous objects. As operatives took excursions to establish and maintain cells, perform reconnaissance, and launch offensives, they also exchanged and manufactured explosives and arms. Sometimes their missions, which had them traveling as near as Soweto (20 miles) and as far away as Pietersburg (180 miles), entailed detonating railroad lines or funneling money.

Chapter 4, " 'They Shouted Power': During the Student Uprising," explores how and why Alexandrans joined in solidarity with Soweto to protest against the imposition of Afrikaans as the medium of instruction for all Africans. Throughout this protest, Alexandrans registered their disquiet in the streets, where they used destruction as a tool of resistance. During the student uprising, symbols of apartheid faced destruction, as residents used this form of protest to set buildings on fire, to confiscate food and other merchandise from Indian and Chinese owned shops, and to throw stones at Public Utility Corporation (PUTCO) buses or hijack and ram them into stores. Alexandrans wanted to remove those structures that entrenched apartheid. Besides the Asian owned businesses, they also targeted government run bottle stores and beer halls for the aforementioned reason. While the apartheid regime erected beer halls and other dens of temptation, Alexandrans used razing as a form of moral retribution.

In Chapter 5, "Alexandra in Memoriam: A Celebration of the Lives Lost During and Beyond the Student Uprising," I argue that when apartheid interfered with funerals, dwellers found other ways to grieve, by visiting the sites of death and by reclaiming the bodies. People engaged in these activities because police officials often withheld information or falsified death records. Sometimes, loved ones simply disappeared. To find answers, survivors underwent *reclamation*, the process of finding missing or murdered loved ones or friends by combing the streets, and by going to the morgue, the police station, or the ANC Khotso House.[70] The bereaved also traveled to neighboring countries to witness the site of death and to obtain the corpses they so desired so that they could properly bury decedents.[71] These excursions and recollections enabled Alexandra's inhabitants to create obituaries that centered less on the person's accomplishments, but more on how they died.

Chapter 6, "Conclusion: David's Story," explores the ways in which Alexandrans attained catharsis following long periods of violence and numerous deaths throughout the township. This chapter ties together the themes that thread the work.

An Oral and Social Historian's Odyssey

As I sat documenting these stories, these assaults on humanity, I could not help but recall the intellectual odyssey that I had experienced. It all started with a South African history course as a first year graduate student. An Ohio University professor discussed the Alexandra bus boycotts and piqued my curiosity with this statement: "Someone here will want to know if the people in Montgomery, Alabama, knew about the people in Alexandra, South Africa." So, I said, "Did they?" and he responded, "I don't know." I thought about this possibility and wondered whether or not there was in fact a connection. I had studied African American history and was beginning to see things comparatively, so I requested to do an independent study paper, which allowed me to examine these historic protests in great depth. I didn't make this conclusion at the time, but will now by stating that the boycotting citizenry in each place complied with and resisted different forms of segregation. Alexandrans boarded "Black and Coloured" only buses whereas Montgomerians shared their transport with Whites with only a placard and ten seats (until the buses filled) dividing them. I also learned that resistance had many forms and that to further understand its permutations I needed to read works that incorporated the voice of ordinary Alexandrans. I turned my attention to author Mark Mathabane, who wrote of his coming of age under apartheid in the critically acclaimed *Kaffir Boy*.

As did Mongane Wally Serote's *To Every Birth Its Blood*, Mathabane's work captures the sights, the sounds, and the smells of Alexandra. Even with its geographical insulation, Alexandra developed as one of the more reputed places for cultural exchange. Music was such a prevalent force that Serote gave it voice in his novel. As the music ebbs and flows throughout the text, it depicts the harrowing reality of Alexandra—the stark poverty, the malnutrition, the density, and the poorly built infrastructure.[72] Whereas Serote used music to draw in readers, Mathabane allows this epitaph, which during apartheid appeared at the township's entrance, to evoke emotion and to introduce them to the apartheid South Africa that he witnessed and lived in:

WARNING THIS ROAD PASSES THROUGH PROCLAIMED BANTU LOCATIONS WITHOUT A PERMIT RENDERS HIMSELF LIABLE FOR PROSECUTION FOR CONTRAVENING THE BANTU (URBAN AREAS) CONSOLIDATION ACT 1945, AND THE LOCATION REGULATION ACT OF THE CITY OF JOHANNESBURG.[73]

This sign preys on readers' senses and sensibilities. It meant that no one born elsewhere could live there. As a result many families were separated. Oftentimes one parent lived in the reserves or some other part of South Africa or they occupied Alexandra illegally. Some laws required up-to-date passbooks to live in Alexandra, while during the forced removal process, others required documented proof of performing labor in Johannesburg for 15-plus years. Those rules, and others like them, coupled with the 30-plus words above, officially spelled "stay out."

Similar admonitions initially retarded my visit to Alexandra. Several people exclaimed, "Alex, it's not safe! It's a no-go zone. Don't go alone. I am a South African and I don't go to Alex." I heeded their warnings, until I decided that my visiting Alexandra would enhance my education, and my research. I later learned that my sojourns enhanced my street credibility. I gained "respect" because I walked Alexandra alone and traveled on the kombis, the public mini-van taxis mostly ridden by Africans and offering services to South Africa's townships and South Africa's cities. This all didn't happen on my first trip; it took several ventures before I lost my "virginity."

In 1997, I boarded a plane leaving East Lansing, Michigan, headed to Miami, Florida, en route to Cape Town, South Africa, for the very first time. Still in my 20s, I was somewhat nervous going there, as the only person I knew from South Africa was in Michigan. At the time, my doctoral advisor armed me with contacts, supplying me with a name and a place to stay upon arrival. We also had talks about race and what to expect. I put all of that training out of my mind, when I fell asleep following dinner and stretched out on three economy seats. I woke up hours and time zones later when the plane began its initial descent into Cape Town. Table Mountain and the Atlantic Ocean greeted me. These iconic markers provided my first glimpse into Africa, the place once identified as the Dark Continent and the White Man's Burden/Grave; heralded as the US/Soviet Union chessboard; and now proclaimed the Cradle of Civilization. To me, like many African Americans, Africa was my salvation, my homeland.

I was soon disabused of that notion. People didn't view me as African American or Black. In fact, there was no innate connection to me based on a shared history of oppression; instead, it was quite the opposite. This made for a sobering experience and clearly erased the reverie I had previously felt.

With my light skin, and short hair (I had shaved off all my hair and sported the then popular Sinead O'Connor look), I was considered Coloured. Under the apartheid regime, that term signified anyone with mixed ancestry. I soon learned that complexion didn't solve everything in this lived experience on race. Sound, nationality, geography, and language also played roles in determining blackness, whiteness, and Coloured identity.[74] Race is such a social construction that I thought that my informant, Carol Britz, whom I introduce further in Chapter 4, was African. I was quite wrong, as her mother tongue was Afrikaans and she identified as Coloured, the same racial categorization that she applied to me. In fact, Britz used an age-old definition of Coloured to insist that I had a White parent. Today, the term is highly contested,[75] yet, in everyday life, people still informally classify based upon older, obsolete ascriptions.

More than once, on this and subsequent trips funded by the Social Science Research Council (SRC), Fulbright Hays, and the University of Nebraska-Lincoln (UNL), people initially spoke to me in Afrikaans. I spoke and knew very little Afrikaans. The one phrase I equipped myself with was *Ek is 'n buitelander*, "I am a foreigner," but that didn't stop people from getting annoyed with me. Some pointed fingers violently, others lambasted me verbally. Part of me wanted to go home; another part of me recalled my own personal history. I couldn't escape my "new identity" no matter where I went. Even when I left Cape Town, and went to Alexandra, one man, who eluded an interview even after promising one, saw me and without me uttering a word, stated, "She's a Coloured but not from here." I don't know if my permeable identity had an impact on my excursions into Alexandra. I will say that it didn't impede me. From 2001 to 2006, I collected over a hundred interviews, the bulk of which I conducted during my Fulbright Hays tenure.

Before conducting the interviews, I explained the consent form. I discussed the following with regard to the project: purpose, procedures, risks, benefits, freedom to withdraw and ask questions, the right to confidentiality, the no compensation clause, and the right to receive a copy of the consent form. Informants were given the options of anonymity, partial anonymity, or full disclosure. Many consented to full disclosure, while some chose pseudonyms and preferred publication of their words but not their identities. Informants came from a variety of socioeconomic backgrounds. They were domestics, mechanics, poets, ministers, factory workers, business owners, housewives, community activists, funeral directors, taxi drivers, and teachers, among a host of other occupations. Their ages ran from 12 to 85.

In the beginning, I took the perfect liaison, Lindi, to Alexandra. She was a Sowetan and a Sesotho tutor, and quite versed in isiZulu, making her fluent in two different language families. Lindi and I first met through an NGO called Transfer of African Language Knowledge (TALK), which provides tutors and immersion experiences. Because we had established a rapport, I asked Lindi to accompany me to Alexandra. Our first journey began on a warm December day. When we arrived in the township, Lindi stated, "This is your Alex." I was not prepared for what I witnessed. The streets teemed with people, too many people for this semi-introvert, but like everyone else, I waded through the crowds and did my best to blend in as a "Coloured."

Initially, I thought that my 20–20 vision had deceived me. The poverty was so stark that Alexandra's confines showed a great disparity between the haves and the have-nots. Some homes, standing from the township's earlier years (going as far back as the 1910s), symbolized the wealth of yesteryear. Corrugated shanties, by contrast, emphasized twentieth-century squalor ushered in by three major demographic changes: the 1980s "ungovernability" campaign, the 1990s Zulu-Xhosa ethnic wars, and in the same decade, President Mandela's pro-immigration policies.[76]

During and after Mandela's presidency, Africans flooded South Africa, and Alexandra, in particular, where the same inducements that attracted the original settlers in 1912,[77] such as close proximity to Johannesburg and cheap accommodations,[78] lure these foreigners now. Many migrated from Mozambique, Zimbabwe, and other neighboring African countries, all wanting to attain a better life in Johannesburg. Their stories await serious research and interrogation. The question is, how to interview them? I faced this dilemma when I conducted my field-work. Add my nationality, gender, as well as perceived race and age to the equation, and I potentially faced an uphill battle. I learned that even South Africans encountered similar challenges in their quest to preserve their historic past.[79]

Acceptance into the Alexandran community came with my acquired knowledge. Whenever I talked about something other than the infamous Msomi and Spoiler gangs, the response was overwhelming: "Wow! You know our history," or "You're from *pesheya* (overseas) and you know us!" I didn't just give them dates, I also offered names: Schreiner Baduza, Florence Moposho, Alfred Nzo, Topsie Piliso, E. P. Mart Zulu, Vincent Tshabalala, Reverend Sam Buti, Brian Baloyi. The list goes on and on. I even provided a brief historical background of Alexandra, acknowledging how it started as a Whites-only area in 1905, and following dismal sales, Alexandra's original owner, attorney and land speculator Herbert Papenfus, converted the township into a freehold in 1912. In one of the rare places in Johannesburg where Africans and Coloureds could legally own freehold titled land,[80] people from all over the country flocked to populate it. Prominent families included the Twalas, the Moposhos, the Noges, and the Pilisos among other early settlers of Venda, Tswana, Shangaan, Pedi, Sotho, Xhosa, and Zulu origins. Larger stands, proximity to Johannesburg, and affordable homes[81] lured these inhabitants. Alexandra was allowed to flourish even after the enactment of the 1913 Natives Land Act,[82] which set aside land for African occupation and also outlawed squatting by Africans on White owned farms. Government officials wanted Africans to no longer subsist and live independent lives, but instead to become migrant laborers and work for Whites for extremely low pay. That Act also set aside land, with the most arable spots and largest percentage going to Whites. African land remained far removed from urban South Africa, and this made Alexandra more desirable because of its close proximity to Johannesburg's bustling metropolis. Even Alexandra's hilly and rocky terrain [a topographical feature that turned off White inhabitants] failed to thwart settlement among Africans and Coloureds. Originally, forty families settled in Alexandra. As years passed, however, the population swelled to its present size of 350,000.[83] In addition to Africans and their ethno-linguistic diversity, "Alex," [as it is popularly called]was also home to a small but budding populace of Indians and Chinese, who occupied the township illegally because freehold status excluded them. Asians lived mostly near Wynberg, [the White area separating Alexandra from other neighboring suburbs], and on Alexandra's First Avenue, where they sold wares of all kinds in buildings that doubled as shops and homes. Some Asians, however, lived sprinkled among Africans. Alexandra was a cultural mecca; where many languages flooded the streets, people donned traditional regalia, and dancing and singing performances occurred on the Pan African Square. Through the testimonies of my interviewees, I learned that some of the country's most well-known singers had darkened Alexandra's musical doorstep. When she was a part of the Manhattan Brothers, the legendary Miriam Makeba had wowed Alexandran audiences and set their musical taste buds on fire. Not only was Alexandra instrumental in providing the venues for artists outside of the township, its residents also welcomed and supported their own homegrown vocalists and musicians. With their "groaner," The Dark City Sisters had enthralled audiences with their unique vocal abilities and their fashion style, as they dressed in traditional Swati clothing. Later on, the likes of Condry Zigubu, Jika Twala, and others would win over Alexandrans' musical pallets.

Through my informants, who filled in the blanks that I left out, I learned that Alexandra was more than a story about the two rival gangsters, or a crime infested haven, instead it was a home to the many that lived there and made its vibrant history special, noteworthy and iconic. As the dialogue continued, I listened intently to the different anectdotes that my informants rendered. Some, drew me in, by whispering for effect, and with the drama heightened, these chroniclers of Alexandra's past, had me under their mesmerizing spell. As each person spoke about their past, I not only learned their individual histories but also the collective one of the township.

I obtained my first interview by walking along Rooseveld, near the Madala Men's Hostel. That road was the site of killings during the 1990s, when, allegedly, hostel dwellers fired at unsuspecting targets. As we took in the sites, punctuated by the mammoth hostel that towered in the sky, Lindi and I both saw this middle-aged man, whom we thought looked good, not because we wanted to date him or admired him physically, but because we believed that he possessed substantial knowledge about Alexandra. It turned out that our perceptions had been correct. Not only did John "Boykie" Mhlontlo know about the township's history, he also helped to document it by taking photographs that chronicled weddings, funerals, baptisms, and other important events. (Unfortunately, he destroyed his collection for fear of arrest under apartheid.) Once I explained my project, this former ballroom dancer agreed to an interview at his sister's place the following week. His sister ran a local *shebeen* (beer hall) in Beirut, an area dubbed a no-go zone in the 1990s because of the ethnic violence that broke out there. Mhlontlo, whose animation showed throughout the interview process, answered questions ranging from the personal to local politics.

Some of the stories were so riveting and heart wrenching that they caused me to sit in darkness. I struggled with how to capture the pain, the sorrow, and the joy of these Alexandrans, who stopped doing their chores, walked or chauffeured me around, and spent endless hours conversing with me. When I finally found peace, I saw the various connections that my informants had made. They spoke about gender, activism, death, women's groups, professionalization, transportation, entertainment, culture (singing competitions, poetry, and sports), and resettlement among other topics. Informants picked topics that were relational and familiar.[84] This tactic works for both the researcher and the narrator, and it was one I readily adopted as an oral and social historian.

In their own unique ways, these narrators reconstructed the past using different symbols and topics. One woman in particular, Sarah Mthembu, who was an adjudicator for the 1980s People's Courts established to hear cases on domestic abuse, theft, larceny, and other crimes, ended her narrative by discussing a tree. Not as symbolic as Africa's iconic baobab tree, Mthembu's natural wonder shielded her from a police raid when she lived in a makeshift shack in the front yard of her Seventh Avenue home.[85] With her story, I became more aware of how trees and other features of the landscape functioned in the analysis of resistance. For example, Alexandra's only river, the Jukskei, played a pivotal role in the underground movement. Traditionally its banks served as places where women laundered their employers' or their own clothes or socialized; however, during the liberation struggle, operatives altered and expanded the river's everyday function. With the river bank's canopy cloaking insurgents in secrecy, trees provided the perfect way to conduct subterfuge, to initiate prospects, and to serve as a firing range.

Former factory worker Caroline Nkosi introduced me to Alexandra by outlining the streets that defined the township. These same streets, once named for Europeans, but now honoring African heroes and heroines,[86] also revealed clues about the landscape, particularly in its understanding of death. Had she not introduced me to Alexandra by discussing its spatial arrangement, I might not have understood the full effect of the gridiron pattern that defined an Alexandra heavily monitored by apartheid authorities. What started as a basic lesson turned into a new exploration, especially when Nkosi began talking about her late brother, renowned saxophonist Isaac "Zacks" Nkosi. "Zacks" popularized Mbaqanga (meaning steamed maize bread in Zulu) a musical genre that fused elements of Kwela, marabi, and American jazz.[87] He produced three albums, which included his most well-known work, "Our Kind of Jazz."

After Nkosi told me about this talented musician who fronted the City Nine Jazz Band, and who was also the family breadwinner, I immediately wanted to hear his sound, so she obliged and played a relic of the near past, a cassette tape. When I heard the first beat and the horn's bellow, I was immediately transported into a world where "Zacks" offered "his" Kind of Jazz. I could imagine listening to him at his Tenth Avenue home during his annual New Year's Eve celebration or at concert halls or in attendance at wedding ceremonies, festivals, parties, and other small- and large-scale venues where he performed.[88] He left such an indelible impression on South African culture that the township and the country were bereft when he passed away in 1981. Nkosi discussed his death by giving me a memorial brochure that featured a smiling "Zacks" dressed in traditional Swati regalia with his trusty sax draping his neck. The program also featured a list of speakers and vocalists slated to celebrate and to interpret her brother's life.

With this document, this treasured keepsake that Nkosi gave me, I began to question how survivors honor (ed) the deceased unofficially when no pageantry, program, or obituary existed. Instead of (and in addition to) rendering speeches, reading poetry, or singing, Alexandrans redefined the concept and the production of an obituary when they recalled how people died before the TRC and when they spoke to me. Many times, as the testimonies in *Apartheid on a Black Isle* reveal, the state turned Alexandra's streets into killing fields, teeming with tanks, police officers, and bedlam. These scenes were not only etched in the memory of Alexandrans, they also testified about witnessing loved ones dying from gunshots, beatings, stabbings, and other forms of violence. These accounts or "*reconciliations*" with a trying emotional time allowed the bereaved to heal, to gain solace, and to reflect on how the apartheid regime consumed their everyday lives and even their periods of mourning. Women also healed by writing letters. In "I Scream a Nightmare," Helena Pohlandt-McCormick analyzes the letters that Sowetan mothers wrote to their children before skipping the country and leaving them with loved ones. These letters discussed their remorse, acknowledged their personal failures, and asked for forgiveness.[89] Not only did these letters convey grief, they also explained how mothers spiritually died. The women's families, the "survivors," were left to cope with their "passing." In Alexandra, loved ones interpreted "passing" through the testimonies they rendered. Instead of love letters, they created obituaries. Titus Mathebidi and Ben Mhlongo's testimonies further convinced me that I was onto something.

At the time of his interview, Mathebidi worked in the taxi industry, and was one of the students involved in the 1976 uprising. He attended high school in Soweto because only one existed in Alexandra. Mathebidi recounts, "You know we used to be called 'Stone throwers' and hey we nearly messed up the whole system but then not killing as such. A few of the people were killed."[90] His statement, "a few people were killed," led me to investigate that matter further, in particularly finding out who had lost their lives. Several informants suggested that I contact the Reverend Sam Buti because he allegedly had a list of decedents' names, but when that exploration proved futile, I consulted an official document. According to the Cillie Report 39 Alexandrans had died during the year-long protest. Eight of them were women. When asked about whether or not women participated in the student uprising, poet, township activist, and San Kopano Resource Centre employee Ben Mhlongo responded with this:

Females are not really mentioned on June 16. But there is the one who is close to Hector [one of the first children to die in Soweto]. Not so much is known about females . . . , that's why I am saying some of those things are not being written, anybody who clipped the newspapers or watched the television it is only the men who [are] mentioned.[91]

Mhlongo referenced Hector Petersen's sister Antoinette, who is pictured running alongside Mbuyisa Makhubu, who straddles the young boy in his arms. This made me think and question how females could enter the conversation on the student uprising. The Cillie Report had laid out a possible approach through death, yet this became more and more apparent after consulting the TRC online archive and talking to Mrs. M. L. Mbatha. Mrs. M. L. Mbatha, like Irene Tukie March and other mothers featured here, lost children in violence. Mbatha's son died in her arms, and Irene Tukie March's son died two days after the uprising began in Alexandra. Through the prism of death, I unearthed how women mourned,[92] how the government regulated funerals, and how women and men traveled to the gravesites, even if it meant leaving the country, to honor the deceased. When they crossed international boundaries, survivors repatriated and interred the corpses on South African soil.

While Mhlongo opened the floodgates on history's silences, he also taught me what it meant to be a researcher of Alexandra's past. I had to be an activist. That meant not only learning all things Alexandran but also participating in the community and experiencing township life. I did this by visiting a *shebeen*, by worshipping at St. Hubert's Catholic Church, and, at Mhlongo's behest, by attending a poetry reading. As I sat in one of these *shebeens*, local taverns that illegally sold alcohol during apartheid, I tried to imagine the pre-apartheid days. In these spaces *shebeen* goers had fun and socialized, but they were also dangerous places. As one *shebeen* owner, Tente Mngoma, pointed out, during apartheid, the police often used the *shebeens* to set people up. Police officials often brushed up against people to make it appear that they knew each other and thus when others witnessed this they labeled the unsuspecting targets as spies.[93]

Suspicion was also aroused when *shebeen* owners refused to allow political meetings to occur in their establishments. As this informant further recalls, "I know a lot business people that died from all of this; some of them were burnt alive . . . becausethey suspected them of working with the government."[94] I listened to this story and reflected on those days when even a cough had the potential of putting you in danger.[95] I also enjoyed the music as it changed from a popular struggle song—"Shosholoza"—made famous by Zimbabwean mine workers[96] to a contemporary ditty—"Amaqwati"—sung by jazz great Gloria Bosman.

Anti-pass campaign veteran Morwesi Dorothy Pitso further introduced me to Alexandran culture by taking me to a singing competition. Local talents battled for fame, similar to the American TV shows *The Voice* and *American Idol,* for bragging rights as the best solo or group vocalists. I also performed community service. That was a rewarding experience and brought me even closer to the township that gave and continues to give me so much. I not only inserted myself as a researcher into this community, I also became part of it, so much so that when I took a South African around the township, people greeted me as if I was the indigenous person and she, the foreigner. They exclaimed, "Hey Dawne, how are you?" I had become part of Alex, as it was already part of me. Bravo to a mission accomplished! And although *Apartheid on a Black Isle* is a production of several years of research, my love affair with Alexandra will continue long after its publication because "once Alex gets into your soul, it stays there." My soul is forever nourished by the bounty of Alexandra's history and the humanity of its people. A brief tour, beginning with the famous Pan African Square, will illustrate why I love Alex.

A Brief Tour of Alexandra

In 2002, I met Dorothy Morwesi Pitso, who not only served as an interviewee, but also helped me secure 30 additional interviews. Together, we walked all over Alexandra. Our last walk together was in 2007, the same year she died from complications from diabetes. I did not know at the time that that would be my last time seeing her. If, however, I had been perceptive, I would have picked up on the clue when she asked with regard to working with me in the upcoming year, "Will we be here?"—to which another one of my informants, Susan Piliso, responded, "Where are we going?" Pitso then smiled as if to reassure us, but I think her inner wisdom knew better. I will always cherish my education of Alexandra's streets and its history through her gaze. A quick stroll along Reverend Sam Buti Street (formerly Selbourne) and back to Pan African Square will capture some of what we witnessed during those walks.

Upon entering the township, from Louis Botha Avenue and passing Vale Garage and then across the bridge to enter Wynberg and Watts Street, visitors there notice the informal sector with hawkers selling goods and wares of all kind. People, wearing an array of colors and styles, flood the area, and speak many African dialects as they interact on the Pan African Square. On that same square PUTCO buses, which once parked before being driven out by the taxi industry in the 1980s, have been replaced by kombis that line up to carry passengers to Johannesburg and beyond. Official business also occurred there. The Alexandra Land and Property Association (ALPOA) once heard the testimony of people who, having lost property during the removal days, registered their claims. This same site also held cultural events. Simon Noge, known affectionately as "Slow Motion" on the soccer pitch, recalled watching many of Alexandra's ethnic groups excite audiences with song and dance in the days of his youth.[97] Today, the square houses a mini mall where people can eat, shop, and conduct finance at Kentucky Fried Chicken (KFC), McDonald's, Pick n Pay, and Ned Bank among other businesses. As a major hub of activity, the Pan African Square sits diagonally across from St. Hubert's Catholic Church, which appears on First and Second Avenues and on the Reverend Sam Buti Street.

Founded in 1918, St. Hubert's boasts one of the township's largest numbers of congregants. This historic landmark sits on the township's Number 1 Square, which lies between First and Third Avenues.[98] The other two squares extend from the Twelfth and Fifteenth Avenues, with the Number 2 Square bordering the Number 3 Square, which faces the township's southern portion near Twelfth and Thirteenth Avenues. Public squares officially served as sites for conducting political meetings, church gatherings, and sporting events. Residents needed no permission to stage public events, however, admission fees applied for spectator sports, such as football, tennis, baseball, basketball, and boxing, which included pugilists like Philemon "Hurricane Hawk Tshabalala," Jaos "Kangaroo" Moato among other athletes.

On the squares' pitches and courts, Isaac "Chain Puller" Chocho[99] and Stanley "City Council" Mashinini dazzled audiences with their dribbling, and seven-time tennis champion Richard Mogai[100] perfected his volleying and positioning. Football was another major attraction among residents, and newspaper reporters flocked to the township to provide extensive coverage. Besides the play by play action, reporters noted nicknames such as "Fish and Chips," "Indian woman," and "Buya Msuthu Buya Ndoda" without explaining their derivation to clarify the sports culture that had developed among athletes in Alexandra.[101] Instead, what appeared were snippets such as this: "Joseph 'Buick' Morapedi was in terrific form on Saturday. He pioneered his side to victory."[102]

When protests and political meetings occurred on the squares, they often highlighted subsistence issues. In the late 1940s, business owner Schreiner Baduza set up a city of tents to bring attention to the nationwide housing shortage. Gangs like the Spoilers and the Msomis ruled their own turfs, and like Baduza created a territory within a territory. Both the ANC and the PAC held meetings on these squares: the former around a "large pickle stone on Twenty-Second Avenue,"[103] and the latter on the Number 2 Square itself. Saturday markets, where organizations like the Daughters of Africa (DOA) sold goods to raise funds to support their political initiatives, were a featured tradition dating back to the early 1900s.[104]

Buses shuttled passengers from Fifteenth Avenue along the Number 2 Square, where Lilian Tshabalala labored as a queue marshal and as a protester when she led the Women's Brigade. At the King's Theatre on Second Avenue or the Entokozweni Youth Centre on Ninth Avenue, dwellers held singing competitions and beauty pageants. Streets also teemed with talent as Aaron "Big Voice Jack," Lerole or Lemmy "Special" Mabaso displayed their skills on the penny whistle, a plastic instrument adapted from the rural areas. Famed cornet and trumpet player Hugh Masekela also had his origins in Alexandra. With streets numbering from one to twenty-three and seven perpendicular avenues, now assuming the name of famous Alexandrans, the township rests on a steep gradient.

Going further along this gradient on Reverend Sam Buti Street, passing the Msimang Centre on Second Avenue, and sloping downward on its natural staircase, lies the Unitarian Church, formerly the DRC, on Fourth Avenue. There, the pastor who bears this street name ministers. Three streets down on Seventh Avenue, now a heritage site is Number 52, former president Nelson Mandela's Alexandran home, which visitors can reach by turning left on the Reverend Sam Buti Street when going in a southern direction. Besides these landmarks, the street teems with people walking up and down, with their body language indicating they have somewhere to go, have heavy burdens that weigh them down or they stroll carefree and speak to friends. They even hail the many taxis that invade and inundate the street to take passengers from Old Alexandra to its newest subdivisions or back to Johannesburg. Like the vuvuzelas in the 2010 Fifa World Cup, the incessant blowing of the kombi horns in cacophony or euphony— however one perceives the "sound"—is a dead giveaway to others when speaking by phone that one is in Alexandra or any township for that matter. Another giveaway occurs when one is there and witnesses the occasional animal vying along with cars, and walkers, for space along Alexandra's busy streets.

Even though this township flirts with tradition and modernity, it is unmistakably an urban jungle mired in all the woes that poverty breeds. According to longtime resident Caroline Nkosi, "The United States is the First World, Johannesburg is the second world, but Alexandra is the Third World."[105] Just as Alfred Nzo Street or Vincent Tshabalala Road some streets over, Reverend Sam Buti Street highlights economic disparities of all kinds, with corrugated shanties appearing alongside mud brick homes. Near the end of the street and before reaching the fork in the road where the Meshack Kunene Stadium, which held the largest funeral service for 150 people killed during the 1986 Six Days' War, and the San Kopano Resource Centre stand, the former Msomi headquarters lies on the left and deceased former Spoiler gang member Johannes "Bam" Thabete's house lies on the right.

Going right from this fork leads to Twelfth Avenue, which eventually crosses Alfred Nzo Street, where a row of pastel-colored flats stand. At the crossways, a left leads to the new subdivisions and a right pass continues onto Rooseveld Avenue and back by the Madala men's hostel, which leads to First Avenue. During the 1970s, Indian shops dominated the trade there. Today, informal squawkers line the street, which forms a curve where one witnesses the old Alexandra Health Committee offices on Second Avenue near an open field. Also, on that street taxis park. Across the street from these vehicles lies the Pan African Square, where we began our tour. This ends the excursion but the not the exploration into this vibrant community whose story appears on the following pages.

C HAPTER 1

"W E A RE T OO O LD TO M OVE,
W HERE A RE W E TO G O?": F ORCED
R EMOVALS IN A LEXANDRA

In 1971, 65-year-old shoemaker and barber Jackson Banyeni received a notice to vacate his property from Alexandra's governing and policing authority, Peri-Urban Areas Health Board (Peri-Urban). Peri-Urban gained control in 1958, when it replaced the Health Committee[1] that had managed the township's affairs since 1916. Charged with the responsibility of ending gang rule,[2] and conducting pass[3] raids, Peri-Urban consisted of African and White police officers who enforced law and order throughout the township.[4] Peri-Urban was also empowered with banishment orders, which longtime activists Reverend A. A. Tanci and *Azikwelwa* (We Will Not Ride!) bus boycott leader Dan Mokonyane received in 1960.

Two years before their departure from Alexandra, the duo founded the United Anti-Peri-Urban Areas Action Committee (UAPUAAC). That body created an undated flyer entitled "Alexandra in Danger: Unite against Peri-Urban," which describes the township's condition and status as "one of the sore spots of white rule."[5] Alexandra languished far behind other residential areas that possessed indoor plumbing, paved roads, and electricity. Its primitive sewage system infested water supplies, and litter inundated its grounds; its *dongas* (ravines) carved its landscape into separate pieces. Even after the government's appraisal of Alexandra, Peri-Urban did little to develop the township. According to the UAPUAAC, Peri-Urban:

. . . made extravagant promises of great benefit to the people and over a half a million pounds was offered as so-called free gifts for lights, water, roads, sanitation, etc. [that resulted in] . . . the marvelous deeds [of providing] . . . two little ambulances and some shiny dusty bins.[6]

Even today residents share this sentiment, as a chorus chimed in with this: "Peri-Urban did nothing except imprison the Msomi gang,[7] fixed one road and harassed us for pass law violations."[8]

While Peri-Urban possibly faltered in enhancing the township's environs, the body compensated for its negligence when it policed Alexandra and honored its primary responsibility of reducing the township's population from 120,000 to 30,000[9] inhabitants. That meant sending eviction notices, placing numbers on selected homes, canceling residential permits, and issuing a summons for illegal occupation. After completing those tasks, Peri-Urban provided trucks to carry families and their belongings to homes that were often far away from resources and lacked indoor plumbing, roofs, tiles, or ceilings.[10] According to Todd Lethatha, whose family left Alexandra involuntarily when he was four years old to live in Soweto's Diepkloof Zone 4, "people didn't know their destiny, the place where they were going to be dumped. They didn't know how it looked, you know. They were also worried about transport."[11] Even though no railway line connected Alexandra to Johannesburg, residents had the luxury of walking to their places of employment. This convenience was not lost on Lethatha, who zeroed in on the challenges that moving presented. In Alexandra, ". . . People could walk to surrounding industries. Now all of a sudden they have to be pushed to a place which is far away from their resources."[12] Not only was proximity an issue so were the townships' sizes. Soweto was a sprawling complex of townships whereas Alexandra was densely packed into one square mile. Soweto's distance from Alexandra's iconic smoky skyline was also a disadvantage for those people still running businesses or wanting to maintain social ties in Alexandra and who had to rely on public transport. Even those with private cars felt the gravity of the distance. For some time after the family's removal in 1962, Lethatha's father committed himself to making the forty-mile roundtrip commute to Alexandra daily to manage his businesses. After working as a driver for several companies during the Second World War, Lethatha's father exploited the transportation industry by owning several taxis that ferried Alexandrans to Johannesburg and beyond. He also owned a grocery store on Eighteenth Avenue and wanted to continue to support his ever-growing clientele. Eventually, however, the financial, physical and social costs began to add up, as the commute and other obligations, caused this entrepreneur to run out of steam and sell his enterprises.

When the government removed the Lethathas from Alexandra, they not only left behind friends, they also bid farewell to the same racial inclusiveness that their previous home in the cultural mecca of Sophiatown had offered until its destruction in 1955. Soweto, which was not as racially diversed, [13] also offered segregated living conditions even among Africans who were grouped ethnically, with the Basothos living in one section, the AmaZulu in another and so on. Although they lived in Alexandra for only seven years from 1955 to 1962, the township's spirit touched their hearts, as family members still visit on Sundays when Alexandra brims with people, and the streets teem with activity. This, Todd Lethatha exclaimed was one of the things that the family missed most about Alexandra's humanity and spirituality. Alexandra's close-knit environment fostered community identity, a sense of familiarity, informal networks, property rights, religious affiliation, social ties, the convenience of centrally located shops, and Johannesburg's proximity.[14] Alexandra also offered an interracial environment with Coloureds and Asians living alongside Africans. When Banyeni finally moved to Soweto, he left all these comforts, opportunities, and offerings behind.

This self-employed man, who had begun living in Alexandra in 1933, refused to leave and used the media to argue his position. Banyeni stated, "I am prepared to go to jail if it comes to a push. I am no longer prepared to move out of Alexandra."[15] He thought about moving to Mozambique, the land of his forefathers, "[but] not without authorities giving [him] R10, 000...for [his] expropriated property."[16] Banyeni's stance earned him a three-month prison sentence without an option for a fine since he had failed to comply with a previous ruling.[17] The magistrate told Banyeni: "You are an old man who could have been my father. I pity you, but there's nothing I can do for you."[18] He also lost his trading rights and faced the economic downturn with Edith, his wife of 33 years, his four children, and several grandchildren. While Banyeni completed his sentence, Edith moved to Pimville-Klipspruit and continued to labor, albeit with some interruptions because of her health, as a domestic in a suburban Norwood home.

Banyeni's story encapsulates the varied experiences of many Alexandrans who were forcibly removed from their homes or rooms or who remained in the township and learned to "resettle" in a community that had changed demographically and physically. Years after the 1952 Mentz Commission recommendation, government officials finally changed Alexandra's status from a family dwelling area to a place for single sex hostel dwellers in 1963.[19] An excerpt appearing in the *Johannesburg Star* in the late 1960s encapsulates what apartheid proponents wanted Alexandra to become, " . . . a fatherless, motherless, childless city of 20,000 single men and 10,000 single women [forming] a labor pool for northern Johannesburg."[20] To ferret out and incorporate residents who worked in Randburg, Edenvale, Kempton Park, Benoni, Germiston, Boksburg, and Bedford View among other places, Peri-Urban developed a system of classification. To reside in Alexandra, applicants had to produce documents detailing their proof of employment, marital status, birthplace, and tenure in Alexandra. Table 1.1 further explains who qualified to live in Alexandra: [21]

Table 1.1   Qualifications for Alexandran living

Section 10.1 (a) persons born in Alex and lived there all their lives qualified for Section 10.1 (a). Pupils who attended school outside of Alexandra still had residential rights as long as they returned during the holidays.

Section 10.1 (b) allowed persons who did not qualify for an (a) right, but had lived in Alexandra legally with a permit for 15 years or had worked for one employer for ten consecutive years, or with different employers for 15 years, to have a (b) right. One year contractual labor and frequent visits to a rural home did not preclude persons from this (b) right. This right entitled the grantee to live in Alexandra, to rent or buy a home, and to work in the approved White area.

Under the last category of qualification, Section 10.1 (c), were persons who did not qualify for an (a) or a (b) right, and met these criteria: had a husband with an (a) or a (b) right; an underage man living with his parents who had an (a) or a (b) right, then a person qualified for (c) right. Applicants attaining this right could work in the White area, but they could not buy a house or rent one; however, they could seek accommodation in a single hostel. To qualify for rights under this section, applicants had to prove that a husband or parent had Section 10.1 (a) or (b) privileges.

Applicants provided stamped reference books or employer letters and housing permits for verification to first Peri-Urban and then the West Rand Administration Board (WRAB). When it took over in 1973, the WRAB continued its predecessor's mandate, expelling non-permit holders and accelerating its campaign to expropriate property owners.[22] In its first year of operation, the WRAB relocated 56,574 people, equating to more than 10,000 families.[23] Evicted parties moved to Tembisa, Katlehong, Diepkloof, Pimville, and Meadowlands among other places on the East and West Rand. The move was so pronounced that a daily African newspaper, the *World*, reported that a heavy stream of refugees left Alexandra voluntarily and for the first time rooms were reported as vacant.[24] One of the volunteers was W. D. Nkhahle, who relinquished a backyard room to live in a four-roomed house with front and back gardens.[25] Former Protection and Vigilance Association (PVA) chairman Andries Malaka, who grew tired of Peri-Urban's pre-dawn raids, also opted to leave Alexandra.[26] As a property owner, Malaka paid 75c for his Alexandran stand, while other dwellers, such as shopkeepers and tenants, paid R2 and R1 a month, respectively. Although he paid less rent, Malaka wanted solace and preferred leaving his home than continuing living in a township where he lacked yard space and possibly feared for his life. Gun fights between the rivaling Spoilers and Msomi gangs broke out repeatedly so much so that the township earned the colorful nicknames of "Little Chicago," and "Hell's Kitchen." Rather than face their wraths, many Alexandrans left to escape their treacherous and deadly hold.[27]

Some Alexandrans faced the removal process head on and refused to leave. *Kaffir Boy* author Mark Mathabane's family moved from a designated removal site to another street. Reverend Joseph Malinga of the Zion Apostolic Swaziland Church created a makeshift home within an abandoned car.[28] In another tale, resoundingly familiar, Bishop Mokone's family of eight rented a room for five years. Mokone's problems started in 1974 when his African landlord agreed to sell his stand. Within three weeks, the WRAB demolished five rooms and told the Mokones to remove their belongings and seek accommodation elsewhere. With no other housing alternative and no income save for the R6 his wife earned from pulling weeds at a golf course, Mokone resorted to collecting pieces of corrugated iron. With that material he built a shanty for his family.[29] Mokone kept his family intact, while others failed to grasp his fortune, and became separated. No one, whether married or single, infirm or healthy, or young or old, received preferential treatment in Alexandra. Johannes Moloadi, 111 years old, faced eviction. His 59-year-old granddaughter, Sarah Noge, whom I will discuss later, refused along with him to move, citing, "we are too old . . . where are we to go?"[30]

By using the stories of everyday Alexandrans, this chapter provides an insider's view of the removal process, recovers lesser known voices, explores the significance of property, and explains how people used their bodies to memorialize their pain. To address these issues, the chapter deconstructs the term "resettlement." Resettlement and its synonyms, relocation, immigration, passage, exodus, movement, journey, and voyage, all convey movement from one place to another. Such a definition negates emotional responses and assumes that people simply change their physical environments. Yet, people undergo rehabilitation and reorganization whether they move or not. When this occurs, affected parties reestablish community ties, deal with the trauma, and transition to a new political economy.[31] They also, as the Alexandran case study reveals, "resettle" corporeally, emotionally, and physically as their minds, bodies, and souls adjusted to changes within their personal lives and the community at large. Their personal stories reflect how Alexandra's inhabitants stood their ground, how they lost income, how the state compensated property owners at rates far below market value, how dwellers lost evidence of their labor and industry, and lastly, how residents coped when loved ones left. As their stories reveal and as the authorities proved, property was after all a moveable commodity.

STORIES OF THE DISPOSSESSED

When discussing their battles with Peri-Urban, and the WRAB, respondents frequently provided a road map for how they conceptualized themselves, and their environment.[32] These narratives reflect identity, and aid in understanding the social world, and also reveal information about intimacy, authority, and responsibility.[33] Alexandran narrators discuss compensation, paying rent, maintaining the family unit, resisting the government, staying and moving away from Alexandra, and defining property ownership and the rights accompanying it. Headlines such as "I Won't Go Said 42-yr Resident," "Jail for a Man Who Will Not Quit His Site," "16 Will Lose Stands," "We'll Fight Say Alex Landowners," or "Churchman Thrown Out on Street" convey the types of stories covered and produced.

In one featured story and photograph, a wide-eyed Noge and her grandfather show their unity by nestling together on the stoop. They, as most Alexandrans, look worried, and—if at all possible given the circumstances—dignified, as they pondered their fates. Along with Noge, Jackson and Edith Banyeni also became household names. Not only did readers become involved with their stories, they also cheered on this couple who became media sensations. The Banyenis epitomized ordinary Alexandrans: hardworking, god fearing, family oriented, and poor. Despite the fact that the Banyenis lacked money and financial security, they recognized the media's importance. With it, they gained free exposure and reached hundreds similarly affected. They also were complicit in the media's production of their image and how the written and photographic record immortalized them. They "resettled" in front of the White controlled media. Doreen Mashonte did this under less than ceremonial circumstances and amid the deaths of her mother and brother.

As the daughter of Alexandra's first Coloured school teacher[34] and a Zimbabwean auto mechanic, Mashonte led her own personal crusade against the forced removal process. Mashonte's story began in 1924, when her parents first purchased a double stand from Mrs. Lulius Campbell. There, Mashonte recalled, her family grew vegetables, plums, grapes, and other produce in their backyard. Every day after school, Mashonte tended the garden. She even ploughed. Life seemed serene until that fateful fourth day of June in 1972. Then, Peri-Urban with its infamous history of violence, and unlawful pass arrests, made its presence felt firsthand. In one fell swoop, the local authority desecrated the Mashonte home by breaking family heirlooms.

Another standowner, Matilda Modiselle, also described the police's professional demeanor: "I'm gravely concerned about the manner in which these policemen damage our property."[35] This rudeness, coupled with the disdain for family history, highlights their lack of professionalism, and in Modiselle's case, their racism, as one White policeman used a derogatory term and called her a 'bloody kaffir.' The police also removed the doors of Modiselle's home. Neither woman cowered. Modiselle proclaimed, "We are prepared to die for our property."[36] For her defiance, Modiselle faced arrest along with eight others, including a pregnant woman. Mashonte also refused to move. She recounted, "I wasn't going anywhere; you see I'm still here."[37] Mashonte was among the 700 Coloureds[38] slated for removal.

As a group, Coloureds fought their dismissal by forming their own organization, called the Save Alexandra Coloured Party (SACP). On the day that the SACP members met at the King's Cinema,[39] the site where many American westerns appeared on the silver screen, they sang the national anthem, "Nkosi Sikelel' iAfrika." Afterward they discussed their opposition to moving to Eldorado Park, Newclare, Western Coloured Township, and Klipspruit West among other places.[40] One of the meeting's organizers, Percy Williams, proclaimed, "We do not wish to practice discrimination by being separated from Africans" while another woman, Gladys Coglin, stated, "Coloureds had been living happily with blacks in the township. There was inter-marriage between them and the families were happy."[41] Not all shared this view, as Tshediso Buti proclaimed that after the removal process, Coloureds distanced themselves from Africans or moved out.[42] Mashonte stated as much when she described a life in Alexandra without her siblings, who came back to the township as visitors.

Life for widow Sarah Noge was also challenging. Noge was a bona fide Alexandran, born there in 1915. As a mother of five children, she also took care of her grandfather Johannes Moloadi, whom

I introduced in the opening paragraphs. Noge depended on her tenants' rents to survive. Along with 14 other standholders, Noge registered her grievances with the WRAB, where she learned that not only would she face eviction, but also pay a permit fee. About this imposition, Noge commented, "I don't know what it's all about. When he gave me a document I refused to sign it and told him I would not do that until I had been paid fully for the value of my property."[43] Noge echoed the same theme that Banyeni had expressed previously and that had impacted Health Committee employee Thomas Sipho Pilliso's family: inadequate compensation.[44]

In 1917, Piliso's family moved to Alexandra, when the township was just emerging as one of the few places in Johannesburg where Coloureds and Africans could own property in the city center as freeholders.[45] Well aware of this unique opportunity, Piliso's father and uncles, who migrated from King Williams' Town in search of employment and a better life, purchased two double plots on Third Avenue. His father, Samuel Piliso, worked for the Native Affairs Department, while his mother, Topsy Piliso, was a housewife. She was also politically active as a member/officer in the female empowerment group Daughters of Africa (DOA) and as a card-carrying ANC member as she often held meetings in her home.[46] His mother also ran the household alone after his father passed away in 1944.[47] In 1972 and 1975 Peri-Urban sent the Pilisos notices, informing them of the impending expropriation.

When Peri-Urban notified the family, authorities offered the Pilisos R6000 for the larger plot and R4000 for the smaller one.[48] The same board offered Noge R3000 for a double stand with a five-roomed house, worth at least R8500. This trend of undervaluing property was so prevalent that a *Sunday Times* headline read, 'Half-Value Property Scandal,' and featured Noge and others similarly affected. The list, which included Titus Tshipala, who inherited his Eighteenth Avenue property nine years after his father died, was endless. For his property valued at R21, 000, the state offered him R11, 000, several thousand shy of its original market price.[49]

When local authorities assumed control over Noge's and Piliso's properties, they negated their right to use the land as they saw fit,[50] and to regulate the resources that it produced.[51] Noge experienced this aspect personally when she surrendered her right to earn revenue from a second cottage on her former property.[52] The Pilisos and the Mashontes also faced changes. Piliso's properties often held ANC meetings, where the likes of Nelson Mandela and deceased former minister of foreign affairs Alfred Nzo[53] often assembled. Mashonte's mother used her home as a classroom. She helped people calculate birth dates by recalling specific events in history.

Whether used for political, economic, or social purposes, these Alexandrans' homes served as spaces to conduct any business that they so desired. However, when Peri-Urban and the WRAB intruded into their sanctums, they polluted their homes with their cavalier disregard for family life, for memories, for personal belongings, and for privacy. Titus Tshipala's story best encapsulates this. When four Whites and six Africans representing the WRAB came to Titus Tshipala's house in the wee hours of the morning, they told him that the Board owned the property. Following this pronouncement, the men combed every room, at first ransacking each one, until Tshipala objected. Then they informed Tshipala that he needed to visit the Board to find out how much he owed in rent. Tshipala stated, "I wanted to know how I could pay rent for my own property?"[54] Noge also seemed befuddled. As one of the people on Third Avenue who refused to move in 1975, this Alexandran won a partial victory when she saved her birthplace from destruction, but lost her property rights and became a tenant.

Renting came with its own stipulations. Men, at least 21 years of age, who were South African citizens and qualified to live in a pre-scribed area, and had wives who lawfully worked in the area with no dependents, enjoyed rental privileges.[55] Couples qualified for family accommodation provided that each spouse met certain stipulations, such as an extensive length of time in Alexandra and a record of 15-year employment in Johannesburg. Sometimes these regulations tore many couples apart. This happened to Florence Malema. Born in Johannesburg in 1934, she married a bona fide Alexandran. They held their marriage ceremony in Alexandra, and it was duly noted in their certificate. Even though she lived in Alexandra with her husband and children for years, she failed to qualify for family accommodation because she occupied the township illegally. As a result, the govern-ment told her and her husband to separate and live respectively in the women's and men's hostels. Her children's fate also lay in abeyance because if she and her husband lived in the hostels, the children could not stay with them.

Also compounding problems was the fact that Malema had no ties with a homeland. In 1970, as a continuation of Separate Develop-ment, the South African government enacted the Bantu Homelands Citizenship Act. That Act introduced the Bantustans, ten homelands[56] divided by ethno-linguistic differences that skirted South Africa's fringes. Recognized only by the South African government as separate countries, these homelands became reservoirs for the extra people that flooded the cities. Africans possessed rights within these Bantustans; however, they continued to labor in South Africa, but under stringent impositions such as the Natives Urban Areas Acts, imposed in 1923, 1936, and 1945. Those laws regulated the influx of Africans into the cities, created enclaves based on race, enforced the carrying of identity and employment passes, and further entrenched the separation of races in public spaces such as theatres, beaches, and restaurants.[57] Not only were these homelands a continuation of existing racial policies, they were also ways in which the government used the landscape to determine the interactions between and among Africans by delegating how they could live.

Malema's "sentencing" to a South African homeland would preclude her from legally returning to Johannesburg and living there as an Alexandran resident because the state would have already endorsed her out of the city and the township. The only legal way that Malema could return to Johannesburg, was if she worked, and then upon completing her employment, she had to return to her respective homeland where she could live "happily" with her family. Malema also faced another consideration, life in Soweto, where the government also suggested she relocate. Malema refused and faced arrest several times for illegally occupying Alexandra. She questioned, " . . . twice I've been told to get out of Alex. But I came back to Alex, to my husband and children. What else can I do?"[58] Malema was part of a very vicious cycle that unapologetically dismantled family life for the opportunity to have a sustained, pliant, and cheap labor force working for a white minority.

Not only did apartheid laws affect employment, and habitation, they also curtailed sexual relations. Laws such as the 1949 Prohibition of Marriages Act and the 1950 Immorality Act had already existed in the books and established guidelines for prohibiting interracial sexual intercourse. With the creation of hostels in Alexandra, the government went further in prohibiting sexual relations by declaring it illegal for Africans to procreate within these dormitory-like buildings whereby each section contained its own security gate in case riots broke out.[59] While the regulation applied to Africans only, it was still a racialized piece of legislation that dictated how Africans could use public and private space. This legislation also extended beyond Alexandra's square mile because as a *Rand Daily Mail* headline read, "Africans 'may be told to go home for sex.'" The article goes on to explain that if Africans desired sex, they had to return to their respective homelands, especially if they lived in Alexandra's imposing single sex hostels. Johannesburg City Council's Non-European

Affairs Committee chairman Sam Moss declared, "In terms of man-made law—not natural law—Africans could live in White areas only as single people."[60] He further stated, "According to Government policy the Africans are here to sell their labour and have no assurance of permanency."[61] Moss makes an interesting point about permanence. Temporary status meant that Africans possessed no rights, other than what their labor guaranteed, and that was not much.

It seems that authorities wanted two conflicting outcomes: they wanted to undermine African reproduction within certain areas of White settlement but still wanted to encourage enough reproduction for their labor needs. Lack of transportation and money also monkey-wrenched any potential sexual unions had the parties opted to return to their respective or assigned homelands. Just as the government stripped property owners of the right to earn money, conduct business, and foster family relations, it also deprived laborers of a natural necessity. Treating Africans as if they were nonhuman fitted apartheid's proponents overall objective: to humiliate and divide Africans. With every aspect of their lives policed, Africans underwent emotional, corporeal, physical, and financial resettlement.

Not only did some Alexandran dwellers lose homes, they also received compensation far below market value.[62] They understood the difference between an investment and depreciation. The former, of course, accrued interest while the latter devaluated. Resettlement also entailed losing the status and identity that property ownership created. Gender, class, and race determined how people maintained or lost societal positions.[63] Having the title "Standowners" (property owners) connoted a lot in Alexandra. It granted the parties certain inalienable rights: to earn money, to entertain, to expand, to procreate, to have visitors, to landscape their yards, to control the water supply, to establish the rent, and to sell and expect a profit. Noge, Piliso, Mashonte, Modiselle, and others lost these rights and this affected them emotionally. In some cases, the reactions were corporeal, when their bodies also assumed the pain.

The Bodily Impaired and the Dearly Departed

Apartheid's effect on the susceptible Black body remains immeasurable. Not only did Africans exhibit their inner turmoil through heart ailments, insomnia, and other maladies, their bodies also became new sites where politics played out on a more personal level.[64] Women internalized their pain rather than dealing with emotional issues outright. This was nothing to be taken lightly as many females featured in

Apartheid on a Black Isle acknowledged their health problems[65] and attributed their declining states to what the government did during the forced removal process, the student uprising, or other historical events in which Alexandrans participated or by which they were adversely affected. For some Alexandrans the pain was so unbearable that they died grief-stricken. Others, like Edith Banyeni, who discussed her health in the media, were among the bodily impaired.

When Banyeni faced the forced removal process, she underwent her own form of mourning. At the age of 74, Banyeni attributed her rise in pain to her sudden dismissal from Alexandra. She stated, "I am slowly dying. The pains all over my body are just unbearable. I cannot tell what is eating me so much . . . I think the cause is the forced removal process . . ."[66]

Banyeni attributes her maladies to the destruction of her Alexandran home and the relocation to another township. In an article and photograph featured in the *Rand Daily Mail*, Banyeni peers out of a window, looking very dejected. She appears with one hand on her cheek, as if in a thinking position, and the other arm to her side. With her facial expression capturing all the woes that besieged her family, she represented many Alexandrans whose bodies manifested their inner turmoil. In an attempt to explain why she failed to move out on Peri-Urban's requested date, Banyeni stated to the reporter, "I have explained to them I am all by myself and don't have any strength left to enable me to move out my belongings. Nor can I do that with the help of my grandchildren who are just minors."[67] Both reasons for not being able to comply refer to the body, as her grandchildren were too young to help and she too lacked the physical strength.

When she returned from work on the day of her eviction, Banyeni found her house in shambles. Peri-Urban had removed all the furniture and other belongings, and then to insure that the family moved, authorities demolished the inside, a tactic they frequently used to enforce compliance. Banyeni had enough strength to use the media, in much the same fashion as her husband. She asked, "Can't your newspaper ask the authorities to allow us to stay on until Jackson is released from jail?"[68] Her pleas fell upon deaf ears, as she and her family remained in their partly demolished home. She commented, "Right now we are living in constant fear of our lives. The rooms have been demolished. And for a sickly person like [me] this is very unfair. At night cold winds blow in."[69]

Initially recalcitrant, Banyeni eventually gave in and faced the Christmas holiday for the first time in 33 years without her husband, in her new Sowetan house, which she declared, was not a home.[70]

Even though her new four-roomed semi-detached house appeared better than what she previously owned in Alexandra, Banyeni still criticized it:

I hate the gaps between the top of the walls and the roof. I can't sleep well at night. The wind keeps blowing in. One will need lots of newspaper to stuff the holes.[71]

These conditions impacted her health adversely. And without her husband, Banyeni's isolation trebled.

Doreen Mashonte's and Thomas Sipho Piliso's mothers were among the dearly departed. Following Peri-Urban's visit to the Mashonte home, her mother was so upset and heartbroken that "she took grief and died in three days time."[72] Peri-Urban's violatile manner of conducting business weighed heavily on Mashonte's heart. "How could she go on,"[73] questioned the inherited household head, knowing that she faced losing her property?"[74] Her family had occupied their double stand for over 48 years, where they had created lots of family memories. Mashonte's father operated his mechanic business in the backyard where informal settlers staked a claim to the land. Her mother was also a music teacher. "She could even teach the Indian children; you could hear them, how they could sing. My mother was a great friend of the Indians and the Chinese."[75] This woman, who gave so much to the community, died suddenly, following Peri-Urban's decision to expropriate her property. "She died on a Wednesday and we buried her within a week."[76] Mashonte suffered a second related loss when a heart attack killed her brother.

Although she left Alexandra rather than remain without her property, Topsy Piliso "was so bereft that," according to her son Thomas Sipho Piliso, "she left [Alexandra] to live with [his] sister in King Williams' Town [along the Buffalo River] in the Eastern Cape."[77] Topsy Piliso chose to migrate, an action usually taken by men to provide financial support to their families living in the rural areas or an option that ANC and PAC activists chose when wanting to join their respective underground movements. As an elderly woman, Piliso gravitated toward her birthplace. There, she received some solace," but not much as she died heartbroken in 1976 at the age of 85. Thomas Sipho Piliso's mother passed away in February of that year, and the family upon her request, buried her in Alexandra. It was only fitting that this "Daughter of Africa" returned to the home she had made with her husband, who had also been interned there. Her "return" also signified a form of reconciliation with the soil, with her family, and with the government that had forced her into self-imposed exile. Piliso's mother reclaimed her deed to Alexandra, where for 55 years she had raised a family, and had served as a housewife, and an activist.

While self-imposed exile served as one option, others remained in their homes and died of natural causes. These different forms of death, from the metaphorical one that exile or removal bred, to the actual physical passing, explained how respondents grieved. Each of them yearned: Mashonte for a parent and siblings; Piliso for a mother and family property; and Banyeni for a spouse and an Alexandran home. Their corporeal experience revealed how much Peri-Urban and the WRAB had impacted them or their loved ones. With the system's endless rules, dwellers claimed the one area where they felt empowered: their bodies. Many people internalized their inner pains, and as a result their bodies became new sites where apartheid played out on a more personal level.[78] Some people, such as Mashonte's and Piliso's mothers' bodies simply gave out on them, causing them to succumb from heartache, homesickness, and yearning for what could have been. They were homeowners who had attained property rights and assets that they could pass on to their children to further the family's lineages. Not being able to withstand the stress of losing their homes, these Alexandran women surrendered physically rather than renouncing themselves spiritually. And. with their burials on Alexandran soil, these women "resettled" into the community. Their new "homes" presented a different form of ownership. On those plots and sanctuaries where the decedents rested, survivors reflected and staked claim to new family land, where they not only honored, observed, and remembered the township's geneaologies but also their families' histories.

CONCLUSION

All of the stories provide some insight into how Alexandrans coped with the forced removal process. They also reveal ways in which gender and age frame the vignettes presented. Noge exhibits a traditional and nontraditional gender construction because she served as her grandfather's primary caretaker. She was also the breadwinner for five children. Noge entered the public domain exclusively reserved for men, and therefore assumed a masculine role as head of household. For Noge, the forced removal process disrupted the realm in which she practiced domesticity, and motherhood. This one event, which shook all of Alexandra, also turned Noge's private role into a public one. She used it and her age to question the government's decision and the options that awaited them. Noge, Mashonte, and for a while Banyeni managed homes without the presence of able-bodied men. All of these women experienced division and alienation of some kind. Mashonte's sisters went to live in Coloured only townships and visited whenever possible. Noge lost her income, thus facing the separation between supply and demand. Banyeni missed her husband and wifely duties. Florence Malema apparently lost the right to live with her family as the state consigned her and her husband to single sex hostels, and forbade them to procreate in Johannesburg.

An emasculated Jackson Banyeni had worked for decades as an entrepreneur so that he could provide a house for his family. His house not only represented evidence of his industry, but also his legacy. Bishop Mokone, on the other hand, also had his masculinity challenged. Mokone regained some semblance of masculinity when he gathered enough corrugated iron to build a shack for his family. While his identity was not as a property owner as was the case with Banyeni, Mokone knew the importance of having one's own space. His family needed it, as did his self-esteem. Johannes Moloadi depended on his granddaughter Sarah Noge to care for him. Well into his hundreds, the state refused to acknowledge his seniority, choosing instead to evict him. When the South African government restructured urban space at the inordinate expense of ordinary Alexandrans, it dehumanized them. With their personhood challenged, these Alexandrans and other affected parties had to adjust to their new found lives. This meant reinforcing family ties in the spaces they created as homes, even if it meant occupying shanties, as Mokone did.

Because the government challenged their identities as Alexandran homeowners, Banyeni, Noge, Piliso, Mashonte, and other affected parties learned to adjust to their new found lives. Their "resettlement" entailed learning to live without loved ones, experiencing the "new Alexandra" with its razed homes and hostels looming over the township's skyline, and enduring changes within their bodies. Some people chose to "resettle" in front of the media, while others did so quietly in their homes. When they used the media, Banyeni and his wife pleaded their case for all to see in black and white. Even with the press's support, the couple was unable to prevent their inevitable fate of moving to Soweto. People who remained in Alexandra long after the era of forced removals attained political tenure with some concessions. Dwellers lost property rights, adhered to 99-year leaseholds, and occupied spaces within the township as tenants or as migrant laborers. These actions stripped dwellers of independent living, and the right to define the use of their land.

While people and some land changed hands, the disruption in Alexandra allowed for the development of a sophisticated underground network. Chapter 2, "Oiling the Machinery," highlights Alexandra's extensive role in the underground.

"Oiling the Machinery": Recruitment and Conversion in Alexandra's Underground Movement

During a routine and highly secretive recruiting trip in South Africa's Northwestern Province activists Simon "Bafana" Mohlanyaneng[1] and David Ramusi approached 15-year-old Solomon Baloyi, who was on his way back from attending a soccer match in rural Jonathan. The operatives planned to extend Alexandra's theatre of operation by gauging the interest of this fertile ground. Their chances were optimized by the schools being closed. The student uprising had swept the nation into an orgy of violence and protests. Pupils had taken to the streets, as they had no classes to attend, so Bafana seized this opportunity to impress upon Baloyi that he should join the armed struggle as many of his own colleagues had done.

Operatives used their creativy to advance the liberation struggle because Alexandra resides within the bosom of White suburbia and was constantly under its gaze. Insurgents often left Alexandra's insulated location to conduct recruitment drives and establish cells in the urban and rural areas in Soweto, Pietersburg, Sekhukhuneland, and other townships and regions throughout the nation. During the two days that Bafana engaged in instruction and recruitment, he captured the initiate's imagination in three ways: he discussed South African history, explained how to burn down buildings, and provided a weapons' exhibition. Bafana's zeal was so evident that he encouraged Baloyi to find three people to teach them "how to shoot to get their country back."[2] His revolutionary rhetoric did not end there. He not only explained the cell system, but also provided a detailed sketch of what he described.[3]

This chapter introduces Alexandra's underground movement by exploring the ways in which operatives used not only the streets, but also utilized the Jukskei River and even safe houses to carry out the aforementioned tasks. The Jukskei River provided the space for initiates to undergo a "political" baptism, where they emerged reborn as many Protestant adherents did when ministers immersed them in water to affirm their relationship with God.[4] Many channeled the ancestors or viewed the "baptismal" experience as a passage to manhood. This cleansing and rejuvenation served as an opportunity for activists to bless the safe houses that they used to hide out, conceal weapons, devise strategies, and fraternize. Through using both the urban landscape and Alexandra's natural features, operatives not only provided political education and weapons exhibitions, they also created cells that expanded the terrain in which they functioned.

CELLS AND THEIR STRUCTURE

Using Alexandra as a base, Bafana, Naledi "Chris" Tsiki, Martin Mafefo Ramokgadi, Mosima Gabriel "Tokyo" Sexwale, Jacob "Curry" Seathlolo, and others known as "the Pretoria 12" implemented and executed the Mandela Plan (M-Plan).[5] Concerned that the government would ban the ANC, Nelson Mandela drew up a blueprint for launching urban warfare that relied heavily on the formation and secrecy of cells.[6] In his autobiography, *Long Walk to Freedom*, Mandela describes the plan that he developed in the 1950s:

The smallest unit was the cell which in the urban township consisted of roughly ten houses on a street. A cell steward would be in charge of each of these units. If a street had more than ten houses, a street steward would take charge and the cell stewards would report to him. A group of streets formed a zone directed by a chief steward, who was in turn responsible to the secretariat of the local branch of the ANC. The secretariat was a subcommittee of the branch executive, which reported to the provincial secretary. My notion was that every cell and street steward should know every person and family in his area, so that he could be entrusted by the people and would know whom to trust. The cell steward arranged meetings, organized political classes, and collected dues. He was the linchpin of the plan. Although the strategy was primarily created for urban areas, it could be adapted to the rural ones.[7]

Dividing up the urban landscape was easy as the acquisition of blueprints obtained from city councils allowed the ANC to use the state's form of surveillance, control, and sequestration to divide townships into highly tuned, evolved, and mechanized sites of resistance.[8] Not only did Mandela provide the blueprint, he also institutionalized the structure by establishing a chain of command with power flowing from the provincial secretary to the cells and vice versa. Cells crucially impacted the ANC as they were the clandestine engines for social change and opposition to the suffocating clasp of the apartheid regime.

Cells sprouted up organically all over the continent. They popped up in Kenya, Morocco, and Algeria among other places before or around the time that the ANC developed the M-Plan in the 1950s.[9] Buoyed by newly released political prisoners who trained cadres who had infiltrated South Africa in the 1960s, the development of internal networks within the country grew by leaps and bounds by the next decade.[10] Sowetan Naledi Tsiki was one of the country's most daring operatives. Joining the underground in his early twenties, Tsiki received military training in Lesotho and Moscow, and after touring different regions, he forayed into Alexandra where he served as that township's supreme commander before being replaced by Tokyo Sexwale. Not only was Tsiki a skilled marksman, he was also adept at forming cells as this quotation reveals:

We link[ed] up with another chap who was working with Mange. This is Bafana Mhlananeng [*sic*] you know, Bafana Sithole. We work[ed] with this guy. We beg[a]n to look out. I meet up with [Martin] Ramokgadi. I discuss with him that, look, we need some transport in the initial stages—he already knows what we are, who we are . . . Bafana is already recruited. We recruited another fellow called Roger, who was good. He recruited another fellow who was a trade unionist, and we showed them basic training. We recruited another fellow. Three people, basically, who were able to assist us with establishing bases, places to stay, you know. We also beg[a]n to work with another person who was working with [Martin] Ramokgadi, Mr. Jacob Seathlolo, the uncle of this body, Khotso Seathlolo. Now we begin to have a fairly secure place in Alexandra.[11]

On a mission to expand the underground, recruiters thoroughly canvassed townships for potential prospects. Their mandate was to gauge the recruits' interest, and their trustworthiness. No matter how much recruiters screened new cell members, danger and betrayal always lurked. Longtime activist Freddy Lekiso Kumalo, who was a cell operative for 32 years,[12] explains the peril involved with the selection process. He states, "You see my job now it was a very difficult one to send people out for military training . . . because you recruit and some of them [may be] police . . . you don't know."[13] In spite of this possibility the gains toward liberation outweighed the risks even if, as Kumalo shares, it meant death. According to Kumalo, "You know total liberation is a very painful process because in that fight there is going to be a lot of causalities and even death. Now who wants to die first? Everybody wants to because independence was needed."[14] Although Kumalo speaks of the hazards involved in the underground, he successfully recruited dozens of people who helped him "oil the machinery" by carrying out missions, engaging in recruitment, and establishing new cells.[15]

As forthcoming as he was, Kumalo politely refused to answer certain questions, stating, "I will take certain information to the grave,"[16] reinforcing Raymond Suttner's contention that even when researchers locate informants, they withhold or embellish information.[17] Kumalo was correct to be concerned about safety. Insurgents went to great lengths to prevent betrayal by reinforcing the code of secrecy, but this was not always guaranteed. During a routine visit to one of Alexandra's external bases in neighboring Swaziland, Bafana learned the shattering news of an operative's alleged duplicity. And immediately upon returning to Alexandra, he went directly to the main safe house on Sixth Avenue and warned his comrades who found new places of refuge. Even with this added security, the provocateur, could still garner the attention of a welcoming police officer, who would use any nuggets of intelligence to silence the country's most wanted dissidents. In this case, the turncoat knew knew the insurgents' physical identities and code names. Also in jeopardy were the cells' most intimate plans, such as potential targets, the routes taken, the cells' structure, and the sources of funding. Although police informants existed, authorities also gathered their own incriminating evidence.

Compiling files on suspected "terrorists," as the state often referred to freedom fighters, was systematic and routine. The police amassed an impressive dossier of intelligence by taking photographs at funerals, meetings, and other public gatherings. They also harassed and bullied parents, friends, and other loved ones. Sometimes the police paid operatives visits, but they often came up empty handed as freedom fighters eluded arrest by hiding in another safe house or by going into exile in neighboring countries or even abroad.[18] Those not fortunate enough to skip the country often faced stiff prison sentences or detention.[19] Under the 1963 General Law Amendment Act No. 37 the police could hold anyone suspected of committing political crimes for 90 days and further deny them rights by refusing legal counsel. Sometimes imprisonment lasted longer, because as soon as the police released suspects, they detained them again for another three months.[20] To avoid these occurrences and to alert others of impending arrests, activists used the underground's highly successful grapevine where information spread like wildfire.[21] Sometimes the police tipped off freedom fighters, as this quote reveals: "Tell Mike [Michael Dingake, who was an antiapartheid activist], we are coming to raid this place tonight. He must take precautions.... The Special Branch knows he stays here. It is useless in denying it. Please warn him." [22]

With the ubiquity of the apartheid regime, Kumalo and other operatives were under immense pressure to maintain their code of secrecy, as it enabled the movement to thrive, to evolve, and to soar to even greater heights. Secrecy governed all relations, determined the forms of resistance that developed, the routes taken, and the codes created.[23] It also provided a lens into the liberationists' inner world.

Secrecy and Its Relationship to the Underground

Aided by the Mandela Plan operatives relied on secrecy to engage and destabilize the apartheid regime. Secrecy was so paramount that "If I say cell leader you can know me," stated Kumalo, "but she [as he pointed to a research assistant] is not supposed to know me."[24] Cell leaders' identities remained a secret, except to liaisons, persons carrying information and instructions to pass along to foot soldiers. Even though their activities took place on a public stage, Sexwale defendants were invisible actors because they carried out work not easily recognized as political or relating to the liberation struggle.[25]

In order to perform camouflaged or concealed activity, Sexwale defendants and other cell members attended meetings and then "disappeared." According to former physician Thabo Mnisi, who spent years on Fidel Castro's isle, insurgents carried out duties by delegating certain tasks because "they didn't want to be seen in...public...and [they] only surfaced when [funeral activities or meetings occurred]...then [they] would come in, make a speech, and disappear. That's how it worked." [26] Kumalo's identity remained intact for 32 years because "[he] adhered to not going to restaurants, cinemas, or [places] where people [were] gather[ed],...[because] somebody would be there to report, so that is how [he] survived."[27]

Operatives held clandestine meetings at different locations throughout Alexandra, which included the cemetery, the stadium, and the Thusong Cultural Center.[28] They also maintained safe houses. Safe houses served as weapons repositories, and as places for operatives to don disguises and to seek refuge.[29] According to former activist and financier Sipho Zungu, "a safe house is a place where a small group of people come together and plan, not only plan, [but also] compare literature . . . [and] conscientize the people. Where you could get together without fear you know without being arrested."[30] When operatives used private residences they picked elderly people because they served less jail time, knew Alexandra's history and understood the ANC's goals.[31] One of the more creative safe houses was a sewer situated between Eleventh and Twelfth Avenues. Zungu, who participated in these subterranean meetings, described the environment as warm and cozy, especially with the sun beating down on the concrete during the late afternoon. While safe houses provided the space for discussion, recruitment, weapons demonstrations, and accommodations, they also ran the risk of disclosure by the numbers occupying them. In Swaziland, the police often worked in concert with South African officials so occupants at KwaMagogo (Number 43) and the White House had to keep up the appearance of normality for neighbors and the police who noted activity within these households.[32] In his autobiography, *My Fight against Apartheid*, former activist Michael Dingake explains why this would cause a problem:

How do you keep 11 complete strangers from the prying eyes of the neighbours you cannot vouch for? What made the undertaking untenable was that the toilet, like all Soweto toilets, was detached from the house. Eleven bladders activated by numerous cups of tea brewed out of the sheer boredom would not help to reduce unwanted ups and downs in the yard and the equally undesirable exhibition.[33]

Dingake's concern about excessive trips to the toilet was warranted, given the close surveillance the police paid to certain township dwellers. Sometimes to reduce risks, as Elias Masilela shows in *Number 43 Trelawney Park*, they posted sentries. The police knew about KwaMagogo, but the house never experienced any raids. This differed from Rivonia, where the police swooped in and arrested 19 antiapartheid activists, which included Nelson Mandela, Walter Sisulu, and Ahmed Kathrada, on July 11, 1963.

Because this mass arrest occurred, informants existed among their ranks, and the state monitored African movement daily, cell members feared dissention and disseminated knowledge on a need-to-know basis.[34] Their interaction, and the secretive nature under which it occurred, bred intimacy. In most close relationships people give and conceal knowledge because they require distance and nearness.[35] As a result, they report little about their inner lives or in the operatives' case, the movement's interiority.[36] With secrecy, cell operatives implemented a code of conduct that enabled them to experience a strong "we feeling"[37] among those who knew the privileged information.[38] For instance, the river "baptism" came with its own set of rules. The principal one was secrecy. Johannes Baloyi recalls, "upon the advice of the tall man I did not discuss [the conversion] with anybody because I parted with the tall person...[and] he told me it was a secret [I] must not tell anybody."[39]

In fact, secrecy was so important that "[the operatives'] lives depended on the knowledge that they retained, or used, especially with the apartheid regime collecting information on a daily basis."[40] Africans turned the politics of secrecy to their own advantage. When meeting new people, insurgents used prearranged passwords, described their clothing beforehand, and met at bus stops and other crowded, less conspicuous places.[41] Having aliases also helped. People assumed code names such as "Nighttime," "B," "Pete, My Baby," or "Hot Stuff," among others, to identify the newly anointed or the seasoned operative. If the police ever arrested insurgents, they would reveal their aliases rather than their real names. When a half-clad Sexwale faced arrest in December 1976 during a predawn raid in Alexandra, he refused to identify himself and instead offered his alias, Newcastle butcher Solomon Khumalo.[42]

While cell members exercised every precaution possible, they enhanced their chances when they also communicated secretly. Sometimes messages appeared in unsuspecting sources. After receiving a suitcase containing a secret compartment filled with money (R500), one of Alexandra's diehard activists, Martin Mafefo Ramokgadi, handed Peter Mohlala a pack of 20 Consulate cigarettes.[43] Inside the inner flap of this seemingly harmless item was an undisclosed directive to Thabo (allegedly Mbeki, the future South African president). Cigarette boxes were perfect for transmitting information, as Victor Sithole, who served as a courier, explained, "If police stops me on the road, I can take a cigarette, put back the box and...start smoking. I can even give that policemen a cigarette to smoke and yet inside is the letter."[44] Sithole further elaborated on how this worked: "There were two layers of paper, and the message was written on the white layer, inside at the bottom of the two layers of cigarettes."[45]

Insurgents also conveyed messages using starch water, black tea, orange juice, and milk, which appeared on the backs of letters that they decoded with hot irons.[46] Operatives also created their own language, which they used in their correspondence. Seemingly innocuous words like seed, spade, or garden forks referred to ammunition, scorpions, and grenades, respectively.[47] Postcards also contained insiders' information, with scenes revealing clues for the intended receiver. A car meant "leave the country" and a river meant "mission accomplished." Envelopes of varying sizes contained their own hidden transcripts. Normal pink sized ones spelled danger and warned the recipient,[48] while others provided information such as where to meet or where to find arms caches.

Another popular method included tearing out pages and inserting messages in the Bible.[49] Authorities often overlooked the Bible, and viewed it as less incendiary compared with works such as Antonio Gramsci's *Prison Notes*,[50] Frantz Fanon's *Wretched of the Earth*,[51] or Karl Marx's *Das Kapital*,[52] and even works by South African notables such as Andre Brink and Nadine Gordimer, which the government also listed as banned material. Sometimes:

Two people located in different places would agree on the book to be used and construct a message by indicating a page, a line, and then a letter in the line, all by a number. With the word guest for example, a person counted the number of letters in the line on a page of the book where the "g" appeared and then did the same for "u" and so on. This took a great deal of time and in some cases became an emergency method only, used where the preferred method might have been intercepted and either the operative or the handler wanted to check whether there had been interception of chemically treated paper, or "invisible ink", or more sophisticated ways of coding learnt by those who had received intelligence training in the Soviet Union.[53]

For dissemination to a wider audience, bucket bombs allowed operatives to communicate without revealing their identity or location.[54] One pamphlet entitled "The Voice of the ANC—the War is On" called for all Africans to unite and commit on a specified date to an armed revolution. Appearing two months after the famous 1976 student uprising began, this pamphlet called for the destruction of trains, other vehicles, and buildings. With its large font in the first two sentences, the excerpt below captures the original text, which reads as follows:

The War is On so lets take it to the Whites right into town. Kill them if you can. Burn their buildings. Let the trains and their vehicles go up in flames. Let us show them that there is nothing will ever go right with us and please don't fight your children . . . . . We will die but there will be survivors. If they detain our brothers and sisters let them detain us all, let them detain all of us. To hell with our oppressors. Brothers and sisters, the war is on. As from Monday the 23rd of August 1976 onwards let us make them listen to us together with their arms, and they are gonna lose this war. Uhuru is here. Come on, brothers and sisters, power. When you have finished give it to the next brother or sister. Let the enemy not see this.[55]

In the last sentence, the document encourages brothers and sisters, a symbol of Black unity, to spread the word. Authors even called for imprisonment when they declared, "Let them detain us all." They wanted to fill the jail cells, in much the same way as their American counterparts did, during the Civil Rights Movement. With its audience as parents and children, the flyer appeals to the parents' sensibilities in allowing the latter to participate in the struggle without reservation. The future, as the document implies, belonged to the youth, and their involvement in dismantling apartheid insured that they experienced one. And with the rallying call of "Uhuru," a Swahili term meaning freedom, evoking pan African solidarity, the authors united Alexandra with other places on the continent, particularly Kenya, which gained its independence from Great Britain in 1963. With the "War is on," a new vocabulary, invisible writing, the Bible, and other books where passages concealed messages, activists invented unique ways to communicate. This insiders' knowledge awaited prospects, who in order to enter the world of espionage and subterfuge, had to be vetted and inducted.

RECRUITMENT AND CONVERSION

Political Education and Military Training

To become a member of a South African cell, prospective recruits followed certain protocols. All insurgents underwent a conversion experience. Sometimes these events took place in people's homes (safe houses) or along Alexandra's Jukskei River. Military and political training also took place in Tanzania, England, Mozambique, the Ukraine, Zambia, Egypt, Russia, China, Swaziland, Cuba, and Lesotho among other places in Europe, Africa, and the Americas. This military training within and outside Alexandra was like the conveyor belt ... that [pumped]food to the [the politically hungry] masses,"whose insatiable appetite fed off [56] the education that they received on the underground.[57] According to former exiled activist Thabo Mnisi, who experienced forays in Botswana, Angola, Zambia, and Cuba before returning to South Africa in the early 1990s, "Some people joined the struggle not necessarily because they were recruited by us, but because they identified with the issues that we raised."[58] Issues covered an array of topics including the ANC's history, southern African resistance movements, South Africa's image abroad, Marxism-Leninism, and a weekly current events analysis all highlighted by monthly political discussions.[59]

To supplement the educational instruction, recruits also had military training that consisted of six subjects: conspiracy, fire training, sabotage, topography, reconnaissance, and political lectures.[60] During this process, prospects met seasoned operatives and learned about the ANC's history and South Africa's political situation, followed by a display of artillery demonstrations. The story of Naledi Tsiki and Samson Ndaba's induction illustrates a typical recruiting meeting.

On a couple of occasions in January 1976 Ndaba opened his home to seasoned activist Naledi Tsiki, [whom I introduced in an earlier section]. In the initial meeting, Tsiki, who also assumed the pseudonyms Patrick Mandla Tumeni Magagula, and Chris, disclosed his double identity and, provided the initiate with much needed intelligence. Ndaba soaked up this information like a sponge and took down notes with reckless abandon.[61] The meeting went so well that a follow-up conversation ensued, with Tsiki showering Ndaba with information about fire training. Fire training involved the use, maintenance, and dismantling of weapons such as the TT firearm and Scorpion submachine gun, which served as part of Tsiki's exhibition.[62]

While the freedom fighter explained how the TT firearm contained eight or ten bullets, a knock at the door interrupted the process, forcing him to conceal the paper bag underneath the table. When Ndaba opened the door, a man named Victor, whom Tsiki had awaited, entered. Ndaba, following the interruption, relocked the door and the weapon instruction resumed with Tsiki repeating information as well as beginning the discussion on submachine guns. Hand grenades came next. Tsiki explained that although he only possessed one model, hand grenades came in defensive and offensive models, and unscrewed one to expose its deadly powder. These weapons enabled insurgents to hit targets within enclosed areas, to elicit blasting, or to practice combat maneuvers. Six consecutive lessons soon followed with Tsiki promising firearms to future prospects once they completed recruitment. A few days elapsed, with Tsiki showing up at Ndaba's place again; however, this time, he had Bafana, who initiated the property owner. Following a grueling exhibition, the three men shared a hearty meal.[63]

For the moment, their work was done, and the process of conversion had begun as initiates had entered the first phase of political indoctrination and full-fledge recruitment. Not only did operatives have to harness the prospects' interest, they also had to persuade them to declare their allegiance. In many cases throughout Africa, freedom fighters recited oaths, offered their blood or sacrificed animals to symbolize their unity and adherence to the laws governing the cells under which they operated. For instance, when Kenya's freedom fighter and Mau Mau activist Karari Njama took the oath, he went to a dimly lit hut, decorated with an arch composed of bananas, maize stalks and sugar cane stems tied by a plant. In that space, he pricked the middle finger of his right hand with a needle until it bled.[64] Then, Njama:

... took a Kikuyu gourd containing blood and with it made a cross on our foreheads and on all important joints saying, 'May this blood mark the faithful and brave members of the Gikuyu and Mumbi unity; may this same blood warn you that if you betray our secrets or violate the oath, our members will come and cut you into pieces at the joints marked by this blood. We were then asked to lick each others blood from our middle fingers and vowed after the administrator: 'If I reveal this secret of Gikuyu and Mumbi to a person not a member, may this blood kill me. If I violate any of the rules of the oath, may this blood kill me. If I lie, may this blood kill me.'[65]

In South Africa, operatives also took oaths, however, a reticent Freddy Lekiso Kumalo refused to convey the particulars, resigning only to admit that the process required dedication and substantial time.[66] Presumably, oath taking allowed South Africa's freedom fighters to assess the commitment of recruits who treaded new and dangerous terrains. In their deadly world of subterfuge, loyalty, confidentiality, and unity were needed in carrying out missions that sought to overthrow a well-entrenched South African government. Apartheid officials not only controlled the political sphere, and the economy, they also had the power to decimate the entire African populace with their heavily stocked armory. With their unity cemented by handshakes, initiations, and oaths, operatives pledged to fight to the bitter end.

Cell members also underwent a spiritual rejuvenation when they became politicized. According to one former operative: "When we joined the underground, we united with the whole African continent, Ghana, Mozambique, Zimbabwe and other newly independent African states. The Jukskei provided the setting for this symbolic solidarity."[67] Fabled for its gushing waters that according to folklore once swallowed up children because of a mysterious snake that lurked there,[68] the Jukskei River flows from Alexandra to the west of Pretoria where it joins the Crocodile River and eventually merges with the Hartebeesport Dam.[69] Several hundred squatters lived in makeshift shanties along its banks until a cholera epidemic broke out in 2001, forcing them to seek accommodations elsewhere. Now the once inundated river bank boasts lust green pastures and its dribble is a mere fraction of its once powerful current.

Back in the 1960s and the 1970s, however, those same banks served as a site for secret meetings and conversions. One of these highly clandestine encounters involved veteran activist Bafana, who divided his time between the underground and everyday life by perfecting his artistry as one of the township's "up and coming" bugle players. At 2 P.M. on an unspecified date, Bafana met three males, whom he followed along with a very tall man only known as Moyaha. After walking several blocks along the banks of the Jukskei River, they eventually found a spot among the trees and, still within eyesight of neighboring houses. Once seated, a woman poured Bafana some beer, and then she and the tall man seemingly disappeared among the canopy of trees.

Following their departure, Bafana, who demonstrated his multilingualism when he alternated between Sesotho and isiZulu, began the conversation by discussing South Africa's colonial history.[70] Bafana's trip down memory lane, however, was not for nostalgic purposes; rather it was done to provide contextualization, to stir up passion, and to show operatives how they could play a role in changing the political climate that imprisoned them. He began with the well-documented arrival of the Dutch along South Africa's Cape of Good Hope in 1652,[71] then segued into the apartheid era. Following their earth-shattering election in 1948, the Afrikaner-led Nationalist Party assumed control of South African politics. With their victory, the party began entrenching racial segregation under its inhumane policy of apartheid. Laws regulating residential living, restaurants, sexuality, and employment among other prohibitions further entrenched Africans' inferiority. Even in Alexandra, where Bafana functioned as an operative, the government curtailed the freedom of its inhabitants when it empowered Peri-Urban as the township's governing authority. Peri-Urban colonized Alexandra, and put in place its own administrative structure, enforced territorial segregation and changed the township's landscape. The local authority also enforced the pass laws, and with this checks and balance system, Peri-Urban like the European colonial powers who created identity documents in Kenya (*Kipande*), and Rwanda to classify ethnicity, and Zimbabwe to separate insurgents from the general population, monitored the daily movements of its inhabitants. Choosing instead to paint a broader intellectual canvas, Bafana failed to "globalize" the struggle. He also missed the opportunity to personalize the liberation movement by making connections to everyday politics in Alexandra. For Alexandra was the poster child for apartheid's brutality and inhumanity. Its forced removal process attested to that. In spite of these criticisms, Bafana successfully swelled the ANC's ranks.

Things went so well that he scheduled a meeting with Moyaha for the following day but something unexpected occurred that alarmed him and his colleague immensely. According to a major South African newspaper, three African males, allegedly detonated a grenade that, injured several people in their deadly wake. Concerned about his safety, Moyaha chose to remain underground rather than appearing in public, so the meeting was postponed until a few days later when he issued the summons for this much-anticipated reunion.

On that occasion when Jackson Ngubane, "Nighttime," Bheki R., and others received training and walked to the Jukskei river, the sun shone brightly, and Alexandra's skyline basked in its brilliance. It was by business owner Jackson Ngubane's estimations a great day in this storied township. That day he joined the ANC. Lured by the fact that he had lost several friends to apartheid's brutality, Ngubane professed allegiance to the country's oldest nationwide black protest organization, unequivocally. Even today he possesses no remorse for his decision years ago. If anything, Ngubane relishes the moment he joined. In speaking about "the walk" to the Jukskei River, Ngubane states, "Maybe not as orderly but we formed a processional to the river. It was as if the walk took on a divine purpose."[72] Bheki R. explains, "We knew that spies existed but because we walked 'normally,' we didn't arouse suspicion."[73] Also aiding the amblers were a man and woman, who walked ahead of them, and scanned the terrain, and later appeared at the river.[74]

During "the walk," recruits and operatives sauntered along Alexandra's steep gradient, which sloped downward and upward like a staircase, passing along the way, a maze of avenues, double-ups and a landscape littered with mud brick homes, churches, and businesses. Upon their arrival at the river bank, the tall man continued the conversion process, by demonstrating an air rifle.[75] This gathering represented more than just an informational or exhibition-filled meeting. Initiates also practiced shooting at three tins and a cardboard box. On each side of the cardboard box the tall man drew a head and a chest. He then hung his rough sketch to a tree, and instructed his trainees to half cock the weapons, and release, and shoot at the highlighted areas.

"The tall man started shooting while standing and showed us shooting, lying down on the stomach...whilst squatting and...also walking."[76] Tsiki further elaborates about this exercise, "You had to deal with methods of shooting from a moving vehicle, in the dark, in the light. . . . [There was also] night shooting, day shooting, shooting from water . . . all kinds."[77] The weapons of choice were Tokarev, a Soviet semi-automatic pistol, which used eight rounds of magazine, another semi-automatic pistol called the Mokarev, a mini-submachine gun known as the Scorpion, and an AK47, which acted as an automatic assault rifle. Tsiki confessed about his skills, "I would class myself a poor pistol shot and a good Scorpion and AK shot. This part of our training we enjoyed the most."[78]

After target practice, the tall man handed Raphael a gun and told him to conceal the instructional tools, three tins, and the cardboard cutout behind the bushes. The practicum was over, and although the tall man refrained from sprinkling water on initiates as in a real baptism, they did undergo a conversion-like induction through political education and military training. This combination of military training and spirituality represented the norm. Each man who underwent the river conversion experienced something similar and different. Bheki R., for example, explores masculinity and ritual when he revealed that "the river was a place where I entered into manhood."[79] Traditionally in the rural areas, young men entered into manhood by exhibiting their prowess while stick fighting.[80] While Bheki R. did not fight as traditionally done; he did, however, undergo a performance by demonstrating the ability to fire a weapon, and by showing his mostly senior trainers that he could excel as an underground liberationist. He recalled:

I was twenty when I underwent this experience and after that day, I viewed South African politics in a different way. That's when I became a man because I understood the whole complexity of what apartheid meant. No longer did I view things as simply black and white, but I understood how we as a people had the strength and resilience to fight and win our liberation.[81]

Another informant, only granting his codename "Nighttime"—a name he earned because he canvassed Alexandra and other townships at night—explains, "For us during umzabalazo (the struggle), the ANC was like a religion. The Jukskei River was life altering because the ancestors were among us."[82] Nighttime fails to cite any one particular spirit, although his frequent reference to his grandparents, who migrated to Alexandra from the rural areas in the early twenties, when Alexandra was a fleeting township, illumines his ancestral connection.[83] Ngubane also channeled a love one. He explained,

"I saw my grandmother. She was a powerful woman who never backed down from a fight. She entered and touched my soul. Even in my elation, I wept uncontrollably."[84] Nighttime's and Ngubane's conversion experiences echo sentiments shared by former Zimbabwean insurgents who invoked the spirit of nineteenth-century resistance leader, strategist, and mystic Nehanda Mbuya during that country's Second Chimurenga from 1972 to 1980.[85] Zimbabwean freedom fighters believed so much in ancestral worship that they declared, "We are going to liberate the country [for Mbuya Nehanda]."[86] Like the Zimbabwean combatants, Ngubane and Nighttime conjured up people who **not only played important roles in their** lives, but who also led by example, instilled pride, and bequeathed legacies that deserved reverence.

Besides experiencing the ancestral love that showered upon them along the banks of the Jukskei River, initiates also sang.

As a large part of the struggle, singing allowed operatives to enhance their morale. According to Nighttime, "songs nourished the soul and provided us with the strength to fight apartheid. Black people have always expressed their fears, and triumphs through song. It was our earliest form of reconciliation."[87] Initiates turned the Jukskei River into an outdoor stage when they sang "Senzeni Na," with its repetitive indigenous lyrics asking this poignant question, what have we done?[88] Similar to the ANC's underground station, Radio Freedom, which opened and ended with a song,[89] operatives incorporated music into their political education and military training.

With song, Africans conveyed messages without arousing the government's suspicion in much the same manner that American slaves used old spirituals like "The Gospel Train Is Coming" to refer to the Underground Railroad or the "Drinking Gourd" to indicate the Big Dipper that led to the North Star and their guide through the woods, and pathways to freedom.[90] While the Jukskei River provided a place to recruit, it also symbolized a different type of liberation than that previously described. Instead of directing people where to go, its calming waters allowed prospects and seasoned operatives to liberate their spiritual and emotional beings. By doing this, they became "free" in spite of the ubiquity and brutality of apartheid. Nature played another important role. For meetings along the river, the bushes and trees that concealed weaponry served as targets, and shields to the outside world.

Not only did cell members transform one part of the river bank into a firing range and arms cache, they also experienced epiphanies. Bheki R. crossed the threshold of manhood, Nighttime reconnected with long lost relatives, and Ngubane atoned. According to Ngubane, "I didn't always live life faithfully, but allowing my soul to experience what the river represented and to be recruited along its banks, I knew I had been saved."[91] Bheki R. also appreciated the river, as this quote reiterates: "after experiencing this dramatic change in my spiritual well-being, I also decided to recruit others to join the ANC. I made sure that they had the river experience. It was one of our best kept secrets."[92] Based on their testimonies, we may conclude that the river did more than just serve as a secret place; it also resurrected people's lives and provided an opportune place to educate, to spiritually awaken the semi-comatose, and to enlist them in the underground.

CONCLUSION

Not only did cells provide the opportunity to become an ANC member, they were also instrumental in fashioning camaraderie. Each cell member's safety depended upon the other. Secrecy was not only a mode of operation to conceal information from family and the police, it was also enforced to protect the identities and lives of underground participants. Oftentimes prospects and insurgents met in someone's home or safe houses where they received political education and military training. Initiates learned about ANC history, they also read works on political theory, participated in military drills, and as another part of their orientation to the underground, were exposed to all different types of weapons and settings.

For example, at the Jukskei River, prospects engaged in firing drills. Shielded by a canopy of trees, and women who often laundered their clothes, and with a sizeable female presence, they could use them as decoys to cover up the fact that they turned the river bank into an arms cache, training ground, and recruitment center. The river provided the perfect place to conduct underground work. And with the river's calming waters, recruits also underwent a conversion experience where many entered their spiritual realm and conjured up visions of ancestors. Not only did these experiences enhance morale, they also showed the ways in which the ANC turned the tables on the apartheid regime and operated above ground and in broad daylight. Alexandrans used the township's natural features to protect them from authorities, to practice marksmanship, to create the appearance of normality, to operate legally, and to recruit. The Jukskei River not only carved Alexandra's landscape, it also harbored one of the township's most well-kept secrets as prime training ground. Alexandra had other places that operatives could have used to recruit: between the alleyways known as "double-ups," in the no-go zones, and on the athletic fields, however, the Jukskei River provided something that the other places did not have in abundance: trees. For Alexandrans, nature and subterfuge went hand in hand.

In Chapter 3, "Mobility and Camouflage in Alexandra's Underground Movement," I discuss how operatives moved around and created cells in other South African regions.

"MOBILITY AND CAMOUFLAGE IN ALEXANDRA'S UNDERGROUND MOVEMENT"

On November 30, 1976, Mosima Gabriel "Tokyo" Sexwale[1] and three others[2] waited alongside the road at Bordergate, an area sandwiched between Mozambique and South Africa, and lying approximately 280 miles from Johannesburg. They carried suitcases (presumably booby traps). One police unit observed the wanderers and radioed in to headquarters, prompting another armed unit to head out into a northerly direction to respond to the call. Upon arriving, the police officers questioned the foursome about their luggage and requested to open the totes. The men declined. Not believing their story of not having keys, the police motioned the men to board the truck. They obliged and squatted together on the floor board. Suddenly, this unity ended when Sexwale moved forward into a crouching position and took a seat upon the radio box. It was then that the driver smelled an odor and applied the brakes, but it was too late as Sexwale had already hurled a hand grenade onto the truck's front seat. Fire from the burning Land Rover lit up the sky and shrapnel blew everywhere, with some fragments landing and lodging into one police officer's body. While the police officers writhed in agony, Sexwale and the others escaped in a kombi that raced to the scene.[3]

Injured passengers left bloodstains all over the kombi, which Ramokgadi later designated his brother to clean. That was not the only evidence of what transpired. At the crime scene, the police found a defensive Russian hand grenade called a "pineapple." Another discovery occurred a month later when officers found a bag near a tree some distance from where the explosion had occurred. The bag contained a scorpion gun, 4 magazines of ammunition, and other items, and in addition to this evidence, the authorities had the shrapnel that they removed from Constable Brits' body.[4] When the men returned to Alexandra that night, they feared exposure of their identities. Sexwale stood out because he had a huge Adam's apple and cleft in his lip. The kombi also stood out, with its mustard color, so the driver parked the vehicle in a discrete place. And after an eventful day, the men went "underground" by sleeping in different safe houses.

By identifying where, when, and how Sexwale and other insurgents crossed local, regional, and international boundaries we can help piece together the function of cells, their mechanics, and their development. To discuss these activities, I use the term *political mobility* to denote movement carried out by comrades or parents to support activities related to the struggle, that is, providing transport, arms, chemicals, food, political education, and parental love.[5] Travelers went to neighboring countries, townships, and other South African regions to visit imprisoned children, to carry out subterfuge, to exchange information, to find safe houses, and to establish cells. These activities are considered political and oppositional because they often occurred secretly [sometimes with the state's approval as with prison visitations], within apartheid's strict and repressive regulation, and under the cover of darkness and light.

While attention to mobility explains how people moved around by car or foot, it also shows how operatives engaged in camouflage and concealment to defy authorities. Not only did camouflage play a role in helping to fashion clandestine activity, it also revealed the ways in which mobility gained importance. Mobility enhanced secrecy as operatives used their bodies, their farms, homes, gardens, and even their cars to hide, store, or bury weapons and/or intelligence. Because they hid these items, Sexwale, Ngculu, and others were able to transport much needed weaponry to cells within and outside of Alexandra. By using mobility as an analytical category, I will explain how operatives carried out missions, analyze how Martin Mafefo Ramokgadi supervised Alexandra's transport system, and lastly, show how the underground was another way that Alexandra was part of a national struggle to topple apartheid.

MOBILITY

The importance of mobility became evident in the Sexwale trial proceedings as prosecutors attempted to prove culpability by asking questions that established known associations, insurgents' meeting places, frequency of gatherings, and methods of communication. Like the property issue that features in Chapter 1, mobility was far from a leisurely exercise[6] in South Africa. On many occasions, the state controlled movement even within the African-designated residential areas. When former steel worker Jabu James Malinga refused to give authorities information in 1986, the police brutalized him at the Jukskei River before continuing their abuse in the neighboring White suburb of Kelvin.[7] Traveling gave Malinga a respite to recuperate and to suddenly "remember" what he had conveniently "forgotten."[8] Because the state dictated where he served his "light sentence," Malinga underwent political mobility in two different ways: by moving involuntarily from Black Alexandra to White Kelvin, and by adhering to secrecy. Malinga's resolve was so strong that he refused to give in even when the authorities had successfully loosened his teeth and subjected his body to other abuse.[9] In this case, the police "allowed" Malinga's movement because it satisfied the state's sadistic and brutal retaliation against Africans and its affirmation and entrenchment of White authority. From its election victory in 1948, the Nationalist Party had sought to inhibit African movement by further removing them to the outskirts of urban centers and ultimately to ten ethno-linguistic homelands. As a result, the government monitored African mobility to work, to visit incarcerated and exiled loved ones, to cross borders, and even to do something as routine as going shopping.

Despite these attempts to control their movements, Alexandrans went to great lengths to travel as they saw fit. Many times taxi drivers linked cities, towns, and nations.[10] In 1974, Victor Mogale entered the transport industry, first as a taxi driver before acquiring his own van and becoming part of the Alexandra Taxi Association (ATA). When asked about his activities during the struggle, he stated, "I played an important role by transporting kids from point A to point B. You see at that time it was a bad situation . . . people were killed by the police."[11] Mogale ferried students from Soweto, Sharpeville, and Alexandra and other places to designated pickup and dispatch points. During his interview, Mogale discussed the time when the police almost arrested him and his occupants, whom he believed wanted to skip the country. "I had about ten kids in my car. I said I was hijacked by those kids, they didn't have any identification so I took them as ordinary people."[12] Mogale bestowed upon them the adjectival term "ordinary" because they dressed casually and did not as many had done before, wear wigs, cleric collars, or use face paint to disguise their true identities.

Youth were not the only ones leaving South Africa. Sometimes parents traveled to express and affirm love. In 1985, Hilda Phahle, along with two other mothers, traveled to Botswana, the site where her son George, a self-employed businessman and his wife, Lindi, a social worker for the Botswana government had died violently. George was an activist and even before his departure to Botswana in the late seventies, the police had constantly harassed the Phahle family by tapping their phones and monitoring their movement. When those actions failed to intimidate the family, the police stepped up their harassment. During two visits prior to her son's and daughter-in-law's deaths, Phahle faced the following: a thorough search of her car at the South African border and questioning by a lieutenant for two hours, which resulted in an admonition, "If George refuses to come back he is going to die a very *'gevaarlike dood'* (a very terrible death)."[13] In another example, Sowetan mother Nomkhita Mashinini underwent two separate excursions to see imprisoned sons Dee and Tsietsi Mashinini in Swaziland and Botswana.[14] Their trips, not only showcased mobility, it also illustrated how people affirmed parental love, chose to mourn, or celebrate loved ones. The very fact that Phahle and others had crossed international boundaries to see the sites of death, a subject in Chapter 5, or visit prisons was in itself an act of resistance.

Sexwale defendants noted other excursions in their testimonies. Their local, regional and international travels were all forms of political mobility. Alexandra, like Soweto, was not only a dispatch point; it was also a receiving area, where operatives sought refuge or transport by calling on Ramokgadi's services. Back in the early sixties, Ramokgadi, who served as the ANC's chief internal organizer at the time,[15] began recruiting deportees who had 48 hours to leave Alexandra, by arranging their transport out of the country.[16] Even after spending time on Robben Island, the prison notorious for its discriminatory racial practices, and its hard labor,[17] Ramokgadi's commitment never faltered. He stated:

We came off Robben Island from 1974 through 1977 and we worked with the youth. We organized the uprising. We were strong underground and didn't want anyone to know . . . . We would just call in two youths at a time and teach them and they would spread out. It was like pouring petrol on fire.[18]

Ramokgadi tested the apartheid waters yet again by allowing his Eleventh Avenue residence to serve as a safe house. At any one given time, Ramokgadi harbored at least two or three insurgents if not more at his place. Two of his guests assumed the code name of a fictitious baked good. On the day that a courier visited the safe house, he brought along two sealed envelopes. Inscribed with the names John and Martin, one of the envelopes issued a directive, "I have come to collect the wedding cakes."[19] As aliases for Alois Manci and Pat Mayisela, ANC leaders summoned them to neighboring Swaziland where operatives received orders, trained and launched offensives.[20] The "wedding cakes" formed part of the ANC's larger network that Ramokgadi supervised.

A lot of responsibility rested on Ramokgadi's shoulders as he also funneled the organization's money. On some occasions, he personally went on fundraising missions. That was the case in April 1976, when he used another person's passport to cross the Swaziland border. There were three major pickup points along the Swaziland/South Africa/Mozambican border: the "Luthuli Highway" located near the town of Lomahasha on the Swaziland side; Morogoro in Namaacha on the Mozambican side, and "eS'kolweni" near the Lomahasha School.[21] Operatives also "crossed" when they entered countries using official border posts at Swaziland's Oshoek/Ngwenya, Mozambique's Nerston, and Bordergate and Lesotho's Pongola. Sometimes at these posts, travelers bribed officials not to document their passports so that fewer stamps appeared in them. Alternatively just prior to reaching the border, some insurgents jumped the fence and went into the bush.[22] Ramokgadi chose to enter Swaziland "legally" and used his time there to appeal for greater financial support. His pleas did not fall upon deaf ears, as throughout that year, Ramokgadi accumulated R7500, which he used to purchase additional kombis, transport operatives, and provide safe houses, food, fake passports and bail. The breakdown of his accumulations over a six month period appears below in Table 3.1:[23]

Table 3.1   Financial breakdown

R500–00	January 1976
R2000–00	May 1976
R2000–00	July 1976
R1000–00	August/September 1976
R1000–00	November 1976
R1000–00	December 1976

At the time of his arrest in 1976, 68-year-old Ramokgadi, along with his partner Joseph Tseto, supervised the ANC's transport system that consisted of at least two kombis, a Ford Fairmont, and a Valiant station wagon. As the main organizer of Alexandra's secret ferrying system, his modern day Underground Railroad[24] had many stops that connected Alexandra to Dube, Diepkloof, Nelspruit, Pietersburg, and Sekhukuniland among many other places. Ramokgadi kept the keys and lent the vehicles out upon request. Drivers often conveyed passengers to Mpumalanga in the northeast, to Swaziland in the south, the Mozambican border in the east or Sekhukhuneland in the northwest. Passengers met at Ramokgadi's home under the pretense of going to meetings, funerals or weddings. Even for excursions within Alexandra, Ramokgadi orchestrated transport. On December 30, 1976, for example, Ramokgadi asked Tseto to fetch the two seasoned activists Sexwale and Bafana from Seventh Avenue to Onica Mashigo's Tenth Avenue home.[25] Sometimes these meetings turned into recruitment opportunities as was the case with Carl Stephen Rabotho, who drove Sexwale from First Avenue to Sixth Avenue. Because Sexwale and another longtime activist had vetted Rabotho, and deemed him trustworthy, he was able to receive instructions in weaponry at the Sixth Avenue location.[26]

Mobile connections with other townships were also apparent. In another example of local movement, Tseto conveyed the aforementioned comrades and Tsiki to Sixth Avenue where Jacob "Curry" Seathlolo lived. Then, they headed to Dube, Soweto. From Dube, they went back to Seventh Avenue. The Dube residence served as a safe house where Sexwale often slept and where they exchanged information. Another frequently visited Sowetan site, Diepkloof, served as a recruitment area. Following a meeting in Alexandra with Peter Mohlala and Victor Sithole about scholarships abroad, Ramokgadi arranged for the latter to meet him at Diepkloof's bus rank. When Sithole arrived, Ramokgadi was already there waiting. The two exchanged pleasantries until they arrived at a house where an older lady greeted them.

At this same location, Sithole met John Nkadimeng. Nkadimeng was a senior operative who often worked at the safe house KwaMagogo (Number 43) in Swaziland.[27] After greeting, Nkadimeng began interviewing Sithole. Only when Sithole revealed his skills as an accountant, did Nkadimeng's face light up and he immediately stated, "Ramokgadi, this is the man for our bursary scheme, did he speak to anybody in particular then?"[28] With the bursary scheme, the ANC set aside money for families who had loved ones or friends detained or sentenced on political offenses. Insurgents often recruited prospects by offering scholarships where they could study abroad in Africa, Europe and the Americas. After Nkadimeng explained what he meant by bursary scheme, Sithole left and went home to another part of Soweto.[29]

Weeks later, and on separate occasions, Nkadimeng and Ramokgadi engaged in mobility yet again when they paid Sithole a visit at his place of employment. After expressing regret that the scholarship had not materialized, Ramokgadi asked the banker if he planned on going to Swaziland. When Sithole responded affirmatively, Ramokgadi gave him a pack of Consulate cigarettes to deliver to a home in Manzini, where he insisted that the recipient read the message immediately. When he delivered the item, Sithole was told that the intended receiver was in Botswana.[30] Although Sithole never received the scholarship, he participated in the underground in a co-opted manner since he waited on the unfilled promise of a bursary. His involvement allowed Ramokgadi to keep up appearances and transmit information, as his frequent Swaziland trips to visit his wife did not arouse the state's suspicion. Sithole's participation also cemented established relations in Swaziland, which was a major base for Alexandran operatives. Nkadimeng's participation also revealed this interconnectivity.

Ramokgadi also knew the importance of connecting the townships, and establishing safe houses in other places especially since the Special Branch (SB) had his home under surveillance daily as this quote illustrates, "Please don't come this time to my home because the S. B.'s check on me these times of the morning."[31] Functioning under pressure made what Ramokgadi accomplished even more daring, and showed his dexterity in devising ways to advance the resistance struggle. Mobility between and among townships further shows how dwellers connected not only in terms of their sequestration by the apartheid regime, but also by the cells that they formed and developed. This need to enlarge Alexandra's role also extended to places throughout the country.

Making sure that operatives arrived at predetermined sites, performed necessary reconnaissance, and gathered the needed intelligence, influenced how cells functioned and grew. They flourished because of secrecy, timing, and the careful preparation of activists like Ramokgadi, who was a mastermind at engaging in camouflage and mobility. On at least two occasions, he instructed his brother Alpheus (A. R.), who doubled as a driver and an herbalist, to drive people to Nelspruit. Nestled along the Crocodile River, Nelspruit lays 205 miles east of Johannesburg. A. R.'s first stop, with Alois Manci, one half of the "wedding cakes," was at the corner of Louis Botha and Corlett Drive. Those thoroughfares where Norman Shabalala awaited with four others existed roughly less than five miles from

Alexandra and lay near the crossroads of the M1, a major highway connecting the southern suburbs to the central business district (CBD). To get to Nelspruit, all seven passengers took the road heading to Modderfontein where they found Ramokgadi's kombi in Witbank not far from the former Jans Smuts Airport Road. The car and the kombi crossed the railway line, which headed to Pretoria and then turned right. A. R. continued to follow the kombi; an instruction issued by Shabalala at Witbank. When they reached a certain point in Nelspruit, Manci and Shabalala left the vehicle and boarded the kombi and went into a nearby farming village in Malelane.[32] Meanwhile, A. R. returned to Alexandra with Bafana where Ramokgadi greeted him with these words, "It was good that you traveled well."[33] A. R.'s experience sheds light on how operatives moved around. His story also illustrates the caution that members took. Initially, they traveled in separate vehicles and when the insurgents neared their destination, they headed for the kombi. A curtain hid passengers from view, preventing A. R. from knowing the vehicle's exact count or the occupants' identities. This trip signified something else. It showed a pattern of operation for insurgents and indications of an established base or one they sought to create between the urban and rural areas. Ngculu offers an explanation as to what possibly transpired:

When we met in the rural areas we headed to the induna's place to state our purpose and explain why we wanted to create a network within their lands. We wanted the ancestors' blessing, and after receiving it we went on with our political work. We established safe houses, cells, and provided political and military education.[34]

Kumalo's testimony expands the conversation further by explaining how they decided to initiate missions:

If the commander is going to . . . talk to the leadership, let's say we come to the terrain, . . . you first come to the villagers you sit with them, you greet them, you become friendly to them and you get all of their grievances between them and the farm owner . . . If [the commander says] explode the place into pieces . . . Then we will start our skirmishing say like roads leading to a farm way, we dug a little hole there and put a T double S. I want to be very clear with the leadership. We were not allowed to place landmines in the crèche[day care centers] or any place because they have whites there no. Our struggle ha[d] . . . nothing to do with . . . color. That landmine had the potential of blowing up targets as far as 500 meters away from where the insurgents stood. That was a nice thing because we were not blood thirsty terrorists as we were labeled, but we were fighting for total independence.[35]

"Between October 1976 and March 1978, the ANC staged 112 attacks; [with] an average of one small bomb explode[ing] each week for the five months after November 1977."[36] Before detonating railway lines, pylons, bridges, sewage systems, water pipes and telephone poles, and other soft targets, operatives performed reconnaissance. During their fact-finding missions, the men examined the proximity of the police stations to civilians' homes to calculate length × breadth × constant.[37] Tsiki, Bafana and other insurgents used this intelligence to determine how many explosives; they needed to derail a train track or to detonate other targets.[38] Operatives used amatol, dynamite and other plastic and military explosives which they connected to safety fuses before cutting them and preparing the bombs for detonation. They also used compasses, took photographs, and read and highlighted maps, noting specific topographic features, and landmarks such as the police station.[39]

For the plot to blow up Pietersburg's railway line (present-day Polokwane, which lay approximately 206 miles from Johannesburg in the Limpopo Province), they left Alexandra and visited the site, where the men observed the train traffic. Because no passenger lines ran between the hours from midnight to 4 A. M., they decided to blow up the railway track during those times. The following morning, the men left very early and retraced their steps by going back to the small farming town of Kaapmuiden that had previously connected Delagoa Bay to Pretoria by rail.[40] When they arrived just before 6 P.M., Bafana and two other people awaited them. After convening, they decided to take refuge in Alexandra before carrying out their mission. Tsiki explains what happened next:

we went over to Alexandra township and then settled there for a few days, looked for transport ourselves, got the transport, and then got into our transport to that place, Pietersburg area, and then from there laid the charges, and then we drove back. And then we were of course, armed all along, you know. We were armed because I mean, we had all kinds of things which, if there is any problem, we had to be ready. We were armed with Scorpion pistols.[41]

Tsiki's experience shows how an Alexandran cell operated and expanded beyond the township's confines to demobilize or restrain the mobility of the South African government. While Tsiki failed to reveal why they sought to detonate this particular railway line, certain hypotheses can be drawn. A brief historical account of Pietersburg will shed some light on their decision. During the apartheid era, Pietersburg had an overwhelmingly White majority with Africans living on the outskirts of its periphery.[42] As a result of residential seg-regation, Pietersburg acted like any other South African city, hosted Africans as laborers by day and sojourners by night. The town's name also instilled Afrikaner pride as it celebrated the political career of famous Voortrekker and past South African President Petrus Jacobus Joubert. Pietersburg had something else going for it. It was also one of the largest urban centers north of Johannesburg.[43]

Paralyzing commercial and civilian transport had the potential of putting White South Africa on high alert and making a defining political statement.[44] The Bordergate explosion which introduced this chapter also fell into this category, as it garnered the attention of the South African Police. Not only did its officers sustain injuries, the police also lost a vehicle, as the Land Rover was completely destroyed with only its frame remaining. Sabotage was not only a means to resist apartheid but was also a way for the ANC to continue its policy that existed before the Rivonia arrests, whereby insurgents engaged in similar activities to derail the government or at least make a rip-ple in the tide of inhumanity and repression that besieged Africans.[45] These attacks also bolstered the ANC's reputation, as its resurgence as a defining political organization impressed Africans who looked to the body for leadership and to lead them to the proverbial Promised Land.[46]

In the final analysis, these activities also convey what operatives did above ground, and reveal another story of them evading the law or working within its confines. Camouflage or the art of concealment also played a role in this liminal space. Richard Ngculu put it best when he stated, "secrets were those things that we wanted confidential, but we took the unspoken word and added a new dimension when we used camouflage to transport and smuggle weaponry."[47]

CAMOUFLAGE

One of the most popular and well-known cases of camouflage involved the Greeks and the fabled Trojan horse, which they presented as a gift to their opponents during the Bronze Age. The horse served as a hiding place for Greek soldiers, who upon nightfall flooded Troy and conquered the city. That move ended the ten year war, but not the practice which replicated itself in various forms throughout the world. Much later during the seventeenth century when slavery existed in Jamaica, maroons there hid among a canopy of trees to ambush a highly visible British army who stood out because of their trademark redcoats. In this practice known as "bushing up," only the maroons' abengs, conch shells used to pass along messages and to signal danger, remained somewhat visible.[48] Like the vegetation that shielded the maroons from view, earthen colored clothing allowed armed units to blend in with the natural environment, similar to flounders, decorator crabs or other sea creatures that avoid predation by using rocks or algae to shield them on earthen sea floors.

In *Culture in Camouflage*, Patrick Deer analyzes how painters, sculptors and other artists played a role in concealing patrol gunboats and battalions using different styles of art such as expressionism, cubism, and avant-garde among other options. Deer writes, "Across no man's land the German expressionist painter Franz Marc...was...to paint nine huge tarpaulins 'to hide the artillery emplacements from the airborne spotters and photography."[49] In another example, an unidentified Zimbabwe female combatant engaged in camouflage when she feigned her death, by hiding among a pile of dead bodies. She recounts this horrific event:

I slept amongst the dead bodies where blood was flowing. I put my hands in the blood and put it on other parts of my body. When they came, they kicked some of the dead bodies and I was one of the people who was kicked with those heavy boots. I pretended to be dead.[50]

Camouflage not only involved trickery, deceit and manipulation, it also enhanced mobility. In apartheid South Africa, former Communist states, and Latin American and other societies where dictatorships ruled, people engaged in ingenuity to change the political climate under which they lived. That meant bending the rules, transforming their immediate environments, using segregated living conditions to their advantage or their gender to hide their identities or their political purpose. During apartheid's height in the mid 1970s and 1980s, activists used camouflage to tread the permeable boundaries of legality. As Tsiki explains "camouflage was a method of concealing material or oneself."[51] Operatives engaged in body camouflage when they changed their physical appearance by growing beards, donning longer hair, wearing glasses, and hats and by changing their gaits.[52]

Cell operatives received special instructions if stopped by police at roadblocks. Instead of resisting arrest, underground members allowed the police to search their vehicles but not their bodies, which often concealed grenades, and chemicals. The day that Tsiki and others carried out a sabotage plan in Pietersburg, he recalled, "We carried the scorpions on our body and the tins of explosives in the large handbags Moses left us."[53] Deemed subversive by the South African government, persons carrying these contraband items faced stiff penalties if caught and convicted. However, not even the imminent threat of police arrest, in a South Africa blemished worldwide by government repression, police brutality and unexplained deaths deterred these men and women, and the people they ferried or recruited into the underground movement.

Sometimes the police ignored women altogether and enforced traditional patriarchal interpretations of femininity to consign and relegate women to domestic roles rather than those involving espionage and artillery.[54] Thus, activists saw the value of using women as operatives to escape, to elude and to defy the police. Some men even dressed as women as a means of camouflage. Following the student uprising, Tsietsi Mashinini, who went into hiding before going into exile, where he ultimately ended up in Guinea and died there in 1990, dressed up in women's clothing in order to visit his parents in Soweto.[55] Mashinini feminized what originally represented a masculine space. His "new found" identity allowed him to oppose apartheid and its surveillance to see loved ones.

While Mashinini feminized his body, Richard Ngculu transformed the kitchen, a traditional space for women, into a weapons' arsenal. Ngculu employed domesticity in the movement and therefore continued his everyday functions as the family's chef. He specialized in "culinary delights" as he often called his chemistry experiments. Ngculu succeeded based on trial and error. One time Ngculu's initial foray proved disastrous as he almost set his home on fire, the only time he aroused suspicion. Then, his family questioned why he put a hand towel near the stove rather than inquiring about what he had "cooked." By upholding the veneer of normality, Ngculu maintained this secret until he finally disclosed the information to this [(author)], years after his involvement and several months before his death. Ngculu shares:

My wife suspected my duplicity but she never knew that I worked with chemicals. I did the cooking so I knew how to hide the chemicals, the weapons, and the explosives. I saw the kitchen as my lab, practicing and perfecting my craft, so to speak. One of the things that came out of my experiments besides the weapons that I created was how I was able to alter things that lay around the house that we used in the struggle. I hid "my ingredients" and concocted ways to mix them together.[56]

Inside canned fruit, Nestle Cacao, milk, Milo and other items, Tsiki, Ngculu and other operatives concealed hand grenades and other explosives. With their labels and contents removed, insurgents further defaced the cans by cutting holes into their sides which they later sealed with insulation or cell tape. To avoid detection, they filled the tins with cotton wool or sawdust to match the items' original weight. As soon as someone took off the labels, the objects exploded.[57] Operatives hid TNT within bars of soap and drilled holes to insert wires and a detonator.[58] A package of Consulate cigarettes proved to be another viable tool of camouflage:

...in the cigarettes there was some aluminum cylindrical objects which were inserted...You see the diameter was slightly smaller than the diameter of the cigarettes. And their length was...about half the length of a cigarette. The other half of the cigarette had the tobacco...these cylindrical aluminum objects were detonators...[that operatives] smuggled in from Swaziland...It was easy to smuggle these explosives into the country because of the manner of the wrapping.[59]

Chemicals also looked seemingly innocuous. Potassium chlorate, a substance used in making explosives, resembled ENO, the white powdery anti-acid medicine that reduces bloating. As a deadly explosive, potassium chlorate produced a spectacular blast, and with its appearance inside metal pipes, made for a highly mobile substance. Mortaring charcoal, sulfur and potassium nitrate in wooden bowls into a fine powder and placing the contents inside metal pipes also ignited when using a detonator.[60] Empty bottles and medicine capsules turned into explosives when mixed with a combination of petrol, sulfuric acid, grease or tartar. Sometimes insurgents took ballpoint pens and poured mixtures of glycerin, polish and magazine which they then placed inside a cigarette box or they mixed pills with the above mentioned ingredients to cause a fire.[61] Another concoction called for mixing together potassium chlorate and sugar in a capsule containing glycerin, and sulfuric acid.[62] When operatives mixed spirit, glycerin and magazine, the objects turned colors when dissolved in water and when left in jackets in shops, like Checkers and O. K. Bazaars, and other soft targets, combusted.[63]

Ngculu stored all of these "ingredients," in his kitchen, hidden beneath canisters, behind canned goods, and in plastic underneath the flour. Like Shana Penn's Polish women, who used their kitchens, to hide illegal material underneath the refrigerator, in the pickle jars, flower pots, cosmetic containers or underneath the baby's diapers,[64] Ngculu also politicized family space. He routinely cooked, a skill and interest that his mother nurtured when he was young, and that he used to seduce his wife. Even before he had joined the movement, the Ngculus' kitchen was already a masculine area that only changed when others entered to eat, and to have family time.

With many of the "ingredients" looking like basic sugar or flour, Ngculu pulled off a terrific feat. This transformation not only connoted a reversal of gender obligations, it also set Ngculu apart from other operatives. His camouflage built upon an identity he already nurtured. By making and distributing firearms and other weaponry, Ngculu contributed to the liberation struggle in a manly way, even though his "cuisine" and his chef skills challenged prevailing constructions of masculinity.

Jacob "Curry" Seathlolo's customary wife, Emily "Bushy" Seane did the converse when she entered her husband's garage.

Typically in garages, men stored items, bonded, recruited, drank or parked their cars. Seathlolo, who was a former Spoiler gang member turned activist, and a Sexwale defendant, carefully hid important items at several sites at his disposal: his brother's home, his farm, and his own residence, the latter place he shared with Seane. One day while doing routine chores, Seane went to the garage to obtain a tin of paraffin. When she reached inside the container, a surprised Seane discovered paper inside this 20 liter drum, she took the container inside the house for further inspection and summoned Seathlolo's mechanic and friend Freddie "One-Night" Motaung, to inspect the package. After taking out five scorpion pistols, and a hand grenade, Motaung placed them into a cardboard box and carried the objects home. Once there, Motaung dug up a tree and put the parcel inside that hole.[65] Motaung used the garden, an area traditionally reserved for women who enjoyed planting trees or who in the South African context buried illicit alcohol to avoid police raids.

These gendered spaces allowed for fluidity as men and women traversed traditional socially constructed boundaries to complete tasks pertaining to the underground or simply everyday living. The need to further use camouflage is also evident as Motaung took the packages to his yard where he performed a "burial," which he only "exhumed" upon the police's behest. He also renders Seane invisible save for the exchange. Motaung assumes a manly position by protecting Seane by disposing of the "evidence" that not only compromised her feminine virtue and erases her alleged complicity even though she found the items accidentally, but also his friend and employer Seathlolo's dissemblance. This need to form a shield around his employer and his live-in girlfriend shows how fraternity worked in the underground.

Another account featuring Seathlolo and Motaung further illustrates how Alexandrans used camouflage. On one occasion, Seathlolo needed his Ford Fairmount serviced, so he and Motaung took his vehicle to the local garage. Upon arrival, Seathlolo lifted up the hood and took out the oil pan and a newspaper wrapped revolver hidden underneath the engine. Motaung questioned his boss about the weapon, wanting to know how he had acquired it. Instead of answering, Seathlolo demonstrated the weapon's functional ability; however problems developed when the barrel lay on the butt, making it very difficult for him to return the gun to its original position. Seathlolo feared a fatality and cautioned Motaung with these words, "let's leave this alone otherwise we will kill ourselves."[66] Seathlolo then rewrapped the weapon, and using the garage as a dead letter box (DLB), he left the gun there for an unidentified person to collect. With dead letter boxes, persons dropped off and distributed information or weaponry without seeing the intended receivers.[67] This added to the insurgents' compliance with secrecy and reinforced the liberation's movement structure.

While secrecy governed all relations, it also determined how people functioned in a professional manner.[68] Etiquette and a code of conduct existed among the operatives. When they established cells in the rural areas, operatives held meetings with the village leaders. By doing this, activists obtained the elders' permission to start cells in their respective village. Ramokgadi and others who participated in the cell in which he supervised, functioned within and outside Alexandra, and as a result, they established a base before venturing to other parts of the country. Operatives also hosted prospects and veterans in Alexandra by offering them accommodations in safe houses sprinkled throughout the township. These were the "monuments" on the landscape that the freedom fighters altered to continue and sustain the nationwide fight against apartheid.

Conclusion

By using international and national roads to support the liberation struggle, operatives created a major artery to safe houses, money, recruits, and activists. They also protected their cell members' identities, maintained secrets, and allowed the police to search their cars rather than their bodies. Like the women in Chapter 1, their bodies defied apartheid officials. As places to store weapons, insurgents' bodies politicized the private, and concealed their public personas.

When operatives crossed boundaries, whether international borders, regional lands, or townships, they nationalized the struggle even further by establishing networks in some of the most remote and populated places. Their terrain of operation mostly existed within a 300 mile radius, a far cry from Alexandra's hemmed-in square mile. In spite of Alexandra's captive location, operatives like Ngculu and others used its double-ups (shortcuts) to pass along information, weapons, and chemicals. Sometimes, they used avenue to avenue movement to reach the safe houses sprinkled throughout the township on Fourth, Fifth, Sixth, Seventh, Tenth, and Fifteenth Avenues.[69] In those places, operatives strategized and brainstormed ways to build additional cells outside Alexandra. With Ramokgadi's direction, his Alexandran cell developed networks in Pietersburg, Sekhukuniland, Soweto, and Swaziland.

Besides showing how operatives moved around and left weaponry, the testimonies and the trial proceedings also show how men bonded. In Seathlolo's case, he used the drive to the garage to recruit Motaung. In much the same way as other recruiting demonstrations occurred, Seathlolo explained how to operate a gun and promised Motaung one if he so desired. Seathlolo also provided entrée into the underground in another way. Seathlolo gave Motaung chemicals and other parcels to take to his farm, thereby entrusting him with further knowledge of his double identity. While these two men interacted in the car, it represented a homosocial space (where one sex interacts). Ngculu's kitchen by contrast was a heterosocial and multigenerational space because men, women, and children entered his "chemistry lab." Ngculu's forays into the kitchen revealed two things: how he made the space masculine with his body and feminized it with his skills. Seane's entrance into the garage also shows how she muddied the traditional masculine space, but feminized it by getting oil needed for cooking and heating. Men and women also feminized the movement by using household objects to disguise explosives. Taking everyday items, defacing and removing their contents, helped operatives to create the illusion of normalcy.

As a result of their ingenuity, dwellers acted publicly without being noticed,[70] until they disclosed their double identity or engaged in a mission that captured the nation's attention. Mobility played a large role in fashioning how insurgents created cells, transported weaponry, funneled money, and performed reconnaissance and carried out missions. Operatives wanted to engage in subterfuge to paralyze the state and its organs. The same thing happened during the student uprising.

Chapter 4, "They Shouted Power: During the Student Uprising," analyzes how Alexandrans used destruction to register their dissent against the government's decision to impose Afrikaans as a medium of instruction for all subjects that African pupils took. Dissenters took to the streets, where they mounted an extensive campaign to raze schools, and other institutions that contributed to their inferior status.

C HAPTER 4

"T HEY S HOUTED P OWER": D URING THE S TUDENT U PRISING

On June 18, 1976, two days after Sowetans opposed the imposition of Afrikaans as a medium of instruction for all classes, Alexandra erupted and joined in solidarity. Around 8 A. M., Alexandrans began attacking Indian owned shops and the WRAB offices. When the upheaval gained momentum two hours later at 10 A. M., marchers had enlarged their following. At least 150 participants, situated between the intersection of Selbourne and Second Avenue, stormed the streets. With their hippos and casspirs, and tear gas canisters and assault rifles, the police made an impressive stand, but not an impregnable one as they faced a crowd armed with bricks, stones, and dustbin lids.[1] The police sounded the loudhailers, and when this proved futile, they met the throng with brute force. Four people died. Six people were wounded. Ten faced arrest.[2] By four o'clock that day, eight skirmishes had taken place and more onlookers and protesters had flooded the streets. Whenever people saw each other, they clenched their fists and shouted "power" and demanded that it be repeated. Bottle shop Supervisor Mr. T. Maboela recalls:

…Whenever they said "power" they uplifted their hands and said "power," and I remember some of their cars when they got in to Alexandra, they were stopped and had to put their hands through the window and say "power" and then they will let him pass. And there was one stubborn man who, when they stopped him to say "power," he would not and his car was stoned.[3]

One mother of the township's victims, Irene Tukie March, also discussed the importance of raising a clenched fist. She states, "We were told to make a salute, a fist and if we salute then you get a sjambok behind by the police, you are aimed at. So it was a chaos.... Are you lifting up your fist or are you prepared to be shot at."[4] March's, and Maboela's testimonies reveal the inner pressure that Alexandrans faced: show their unity and face repercussions by the police or refrain and endure the community's wrath. Many chose the former option. One observer stated, "I know that the police would have shot me if I had saluted, but I didn't want to let my community down, so I clenched my fist."[5]

In protest, Alexandrans remade the political and physical environment that they inhabited. They set government-run beer halls and schools on fire, hurled Molotov cocktails at the police, created traps, erected barricades and hijacked, overturned and stoned PUTCO buses. The police's decision to cordon off the township, and prevent PUTCO buses from entering and following their normal course of slumbering along Selbourne to the Fifteenth Avenue rank, failed to thwart the revolt; if anything, these actions heightened it. Even though Alexandra was in close proximity to Johannesburg, its working populace also had to commute to faraway places. Buses and their lack of affordability aroused Alexandran ire. Tariffs cost R5 ($.10) each way and did not distinguish between stages traveled. Besides their costs, bus drivers provided irregular service and in the process reduced family time, made laborers tardy, absorbed hard-earned wages, and with overcrowding,[6] offered hazardous riding conditions. For these reasons, Alexandrans targeted and used them as weapons.

While protest participants did not put forth a millenarian vision or divide the township into yard, street, and block committees as they did in the 1986 Alexandra Rebellion,[7] they did use space to register their discontent. Because the protest assumed a spatial form,[8] I argue that the 1976 student uprising served as a prototype for the later revolt in the following ways: how they used their bodies as spatial entities (Chapter 5), how dwellers converted government-monitored space into a site of resistance, how they deployed traps, how they established bases of operation using the homes of ordinary residents, and how they commemorated death. Alexandrans' operating theatre included the highly commuted Selbourne Avenue, a major interior artery housing an array of shops that linked equally commercialized First Avenue to the rest of this densely packed township. With its appearance near Alexandra's entrance and within earshot of the multicultural site of the Pan African Square, Selbourne was uniquely positioned to draw attention to residential disquiet. The response was so visible and overwhelming that Alexandra's streets became sites of violence and fear. They also became morgues. A senior police officer, who contributed to the death toll, captures the struggle's temper and tenor: "We ran forward into a crowd of 800 Bantus who were shouting and giving the Black Power sign . . . I ordered them to disperse and one charged me with a brick. He was just about to throw it when I fired at him with an R 1 (automatic rifle) and he fell."[9] Irene Tukie March also describes the state of war: "Since I was born I never saw a battle-field . . . but when I reached First Avenue I saw camouflaged clothing there and . . . it was really burning. Gunshots were fired; people were going up and down."[10]

As spirals of smoke clouded the sky, other parts of Alexandra looked so war torn that many people feared going outside. Domestic laborer Miriam Sekele, who left work early to make sure her children were safe, recalls Alexandra's embattled state:

. . . it was terrible on that day, what, there were a lot of hippos a lot of shooting you know just went like this when you hear a shot, you just duck, you duck and duck, and duck. When the kids start[ed] shooting there was one cop lying there, and then you know a lot of bullets. So, we just pray to our God, oh God let us just reach home. There was a bottle store here at 7th Avenue up there, so the hippo went there and one of the gangsters pinched a PUTCO bus from where I don't know if he took it from the line, rammed into that bottle store, broke down and then you should see people rushing, others going to get beers, hot stuff, I am telling you, I wouldn't go near it, I was just shivering in the house.[11]

Another mother and property owner who asked for confidentiality discussed her daughter's participation by asking a rhetorical question. "How can you go to work when your child is in jail for three months?" Mrs. M. reinforced the gravity of the situation by sitting motionless. Tears streamed down her face, and a somber mood flooded the half-lit room. When Mrs. M. finally "awakened" from her semi-induced comatose state, she lamented, "Promises, promises, what did we get? They don't remember us. It hurts, man. I always want my mind to go blank."[12]

This woman's remarks support the need for Alexandra's reclamation for posterity and for personal dignity because, until recently, few scholars had analyzed Alexandra's contribution to the student uprising.[13] This previous silence had more to do with the coverage allowed during the revolt. Sometimes, few reports appeared because riot squads had warned journalists to leave Alexandra for fear of their lives.[14] Other reasons had more to do with damage control. Unlike Soweto, Alexandra resided near White suburbs, so authorities wanted to create the illusion of safety and containment for their benefit. Had they known that 24 people had died in one day[15] or that Alexandra was more intense than Soweto during the first two days,[16] this would have heightened unrest and perhaps further accelerated White flight. It also could have garnered moral support from liberal Whites, something the government also sought to prevent. More than anything, the state wanted to continue its appearance as an impressive and united monolith.

In keeping with their bureaucratic system of compiling files on Africans, authorities allowed for an official inquiry into the student uprising. Headed by Justice Petrus Malan Cillie, the report, which begins with Soweto, itemizes the actions taken by South Africans across Gauteng, the Eastern and Western Cape, and KwaZulu/Natal among other regions. The report also provides a timeline of events that took place from 1976 to 1977. Its major contribution was charting how protests began and developed over a span of time. Participants, punishments, and deaths recorded, an official total of 39, round out the other categories of analysis.

While highlighting forms of resistance and police reprisals, the Cillie Report omits African, Asian, and Coloured voices. The only time the subjects' speak is when describing acts of violence or when opposing the state with clenched fists, hijacked buses, stones, and Molotov cocktails. Not only is this problematic, it paints Africans, Coloureds, and Asians as perpetrators and not as victims. During the student uprising, Irene Tukie March lost two sons, and other mothers like her also grieved for prematurely deceased children. Instead of providing some discussion on how the revolt impacted Alexandrans on a more personal level, the report's scientific analysis negates the human side and leaves out important narratives like that of Irene Tukie March. That is not the document's only flaw.

Instead of understanding how the acquisition of food and other household items constituted a form of resistance, the Cillie Report as well as a recent work by Noor Nieftagodien and Mark Mathabane's classic work label all activity as either looting or rioting. While Nieftagodien writes, "some of the marchers turned their attention to looting shops on First Avenue as Radebe testifies,"[17] the Cillie Commission describes, "a group of about 150 looters, who were giving the black power salute, taunted the police on Selbourne Avenue,"[18] and Mathabane initially writes, before changing his opinion a few pages later, "one morning I followed a mob that was going about the ghetto burning and looting stores and butcher shops belonging to Indians and Chinese."[19] With their voices silenced save for acts against the state, Africans appear to have responded haphazardly to the revolt without any plan, direction, or goal. Oral testimonies and ANC documents not only present the converse but they also show how they acted with a purpose.

In contrast to other protests such as the bus boycotts, Alexandrans, during the student uprising, developed unique methods of resistance, such as using their bodies to commemorate death, turning Alexandra into a battlefield, commandeering private property,—and using leaflets to encourage further resistance. With their clenched fists, stones, and rifles, protestors—whom the Cillie Commission Report labeled as thugs, looters, children, scholars, and parents—used arson, "borrowed" buses, demolished schools, shops, and other buildings, confiscated property, sang freedom songs, and to further express their disquiet, refused to write exams.[20] Alexandrans also took to the streets carrying placards with bold eye-catching statements, "Vorster and Kruger are rubbish multiply by nonsense, away with Afrikaans" or "Notice, Ladies and Gentleman no work tomorrow."[21] Using an array of tactics, Alexandrans attacked the apartheid regime head on and with full steam.

In response, the police engaged in a policy of containment by cordoning off Alexandra's entrances. With both the state and the residents jockeying for position, Alexandrans, who no longer had to deal with property expropriations because the government had halted evictions, hunkered down and used defensive and offensive maneuvers to gain the upper hand, if only for a short time. In the end, the state's muscle won and far outmatched an opponent armed only with dustbin lids, stones and hijacked buses. When the revolt ended a year later in 1977, hundreds of people had lost their lives throughout the country.

Turning Alexandra into a Battlefield

Shops

South Africa's landscape explains a lot about the country's history, cultures and traditions. It also tells how the nation constructed its multiple identities through the erection of statues, mosques, and other monuments and architecture. Apartheid proponents built the Language (Taal Monument) and Voortrekker monuments to entrench and celebrate Afrikaner power and authority. When it created townships, the regime established separate residential areas for Whites, Coloureds, Asians and Africans to entrench its racial policies. That meant that factories buffeted places such as Alexandra from its White neighbors. Alexandra's interior space also reflected policy decisions based on race. Officials allowed the erection of government-run beer halls where Africans drank legally unlike the shebeens, where its kings and queens brewed and served beer illicitly. With their standardized curriculum highlighting Afrikaner history, the schools also reflected apartheid policy. By tearing down, burning or attacking these establishments, Alexandrans dramatically altered their physical worlds.

For nearly a month and sporadically thereafter, the drama unfolded in spectacular fashion. Alexandrans blazed a trail of destruction. Two outbreaks occurred on London Road near the western end of the township, where participants tore down entrance barriers at the Hi-Ho Lawnmower Factory and the Mimosa Café. The former location lost additional revenue when protesters threw typewriters, calculators and other equipment from the building's first floor while protesters set the latter place on fire.[22] They also targeted Jewish shop owner Green, who sold Fish and Chips, meat and other produce in his First Avenue shop. Even within this African and Coloured Township, apartheid reared its ugly head, as Green divided and distributed food by race, reserving the good meat for White butchers and selling cattle heads, entrails, hooves and heavy bones and other scraps to Africans.[23] For this injustice, residents nearly burned Green's shop to the ground.[24]

The revolt also exposed long-simmering tensions between Africans and Asians. Historically, the relationships between Africans and Asians were tenuous at best. As far back as 1949, tensions had mounted when the African Traders Association (ATA) launched a campaign to remove Indians because they competed with Black-run businesses.[25] Indians, first came to South Africa to work the sugar plantations in Natal around 1860,[26] and slowly migrated from the country's eastern coast to Johannesburg, where about a hundred or so landed in Alexandra. They lived on First Avenue in quarters behind their shops. With their "...sell everything stores and produce stalls,"[27] Indians owned the main shopping center on First Avenue, where one of its stores, Seedat attracted an ever growing African clientele who purchased school supplies and other items from its heavily-stocked shelves.

Similar to their Chinese counterparts, Indians earned the community's wrath because even though they occupied Alexandra illegally, they reinforced strictures of apartheid. Mark Mathabane's mother knew this intimately when she tried countless times to seek employment in the Indian stores. He wrote, "She began crying...[and] told me that going without a job was nerve-wrecking, that she was tired of being turned away from jobs at the Indian place because she could not read or write, [or] because she did not have a permit...."[28] With all of these things stacked against her, his pregnant mother also suckled an infant[29] and had to devise other ways besides seeking employment, to provide food, clothing and shelter for her ever growing family. His mother had thought that the "Indian place,"[30] would have provided the salary that she and her family desperately needed, but it too was a part of apartheid's bureaucracy. Possessing an invalid pass or none at all, doors closed even in an integrated Alexandra. When the Indian shop owners denied her employment, they curtailed the social mobility of Mathabane's mother and reminded her just as the apartheid regime did, that she was an African, a second-class citizen. This rejection was something that other Africans had shared at one time or another. For that reason, many revolted and targeted Indian businesses, because like the schools and the beer halls, they were some of the "monuments" that littered Alexandra and reinforced state power and African inferiority. They were also the same places that fell during the uprising.

Approximately 200 Africans and Coloureds aimed at least two shops belonging to Indians on the northern side of Vasco da Gama near Louis Botha Avenue, bordering the veldt that separated Alexandra from Marlborough and other White suburbs.[31] Shops were "...-small, with corrugated iron roofs [that] stretch[ed] to cover a wide concrete veranda. Their stock [consisted of] clothing, basic provisions, bicycle spares and bolts of cotton. They all smell[ed] musty."[32] One shop was gutted completely and burned, while the other one, participants tore down the barricade and stormed it. They also threatened the family who lived behind the store in "...houses surrounded by a dusty courtyard;"[33] however, the police arrived before they could harm them. The Indian family, which remained hidden until the Riot Squad entered the building, dragging people out, appeared visibly shaken.

As the Indian couple cried, they credited the police, who rounded up the protesters, with saving them.[34] In this same altercation, three people lost their lives. One African woman, who was shot dead, fell face down, while the two African men, who tried to enter through the shop's back window, lost their lives in the process.[35] Until Colonel Slabbert issued a call to cease fire, the police shot a barrage of bullets, and then resorted to chasing individuals with batons before making arrests.[36] Protesters targeted Indian shops because they desired their goods. "We also targeted these shops because an Indian man killed an African during the protest."[37] This killing further heightened tensions between the two groups, so much so that people joined the struggle and fought like there was no tomorrow.[38]

Africans also distrusted the other Asian group occupying Alexandra, the Chinese, who not only owned shops but had also introduced a local lottery game called Fah-fee,[39] often running around the township in their American made cars to collect and pay out debts. Africans believed that one Chinese family, who ran a shop on Twelfth Avenue, earned their riches by overcharging and cheating them, and therefore prospered at their expense.[40] When Asian and White flight occurred as a result of the uprising, Chinese owners like this unidentified man's employers left Alexandra, leaving the stores barricaded and dogs to guard them. Distracting the animals with poisoned meat, he and others then cut through the barricade, entered the store and "went shopping" while the dogs grasped and groan, only later to die at the hands of a machete.[41] People needed food and household supplies as these quotations illustrate:

"this bag of mealie meal will last forever," "this paraffin drum will keep the family going for months," "I have enough candles to light up the whole [of] Alexandra," and "the rats will wish they never invaded our house. This bag of Rotex will wipe them off the surface of the earth."[42]

Many participants attacked places where store operators devalued Africans' consumer purchasing power and their self worth.[43] Mark Mathabane recounted, "I became aware of the senselessness of what we were doing. But those misgivings gave way to euphoria as I saw black peasants making off with plundered goods. I joined in."[44] In this modern-day version of Robin Hood, Mathabane picks a loaded term to describe and relate the poverty he witnessed within his home and Alexandra. The term peasant typically refers to small-scale farmers scattered throughout Africa, Asia, Europe and Latin America and those severely economically deprived and who occupy the lowest social rung. It also points to a feudal system whereby fiefs lord over the peasants as the apartheid government did over Africans. In apartheid South Africa, Africans, like peasants, possessed no civil or political rights. For Mathabane to use that term over other words such as thieves, bandits or robbers suggests that he grasped the totality of the political situation and the unequal relations that existed between the store owners and the patronage.

As these examples show moral retribution guided these protestors. Their actions were political as marchers attacked places where store operators devalued Africans' consumer purchasing power and their self worth. Further exacerbating the long simmering tensions was an apartheid government that did nothing to remove Asians, who occupied Alexandra illegally and even violated the ideology behind Separate Development, and the Freehold status under which Alexandra's original owner Herbert Papenfus had created the township. This indifference also represented a possibility that the government wanted these interactions to occur because they could still divide and rule. Another possibility that community activist and philanthropist Linda Twala raises is that by this time the government viewed all township residents as Black, including the Indians and Chinese, and therefore refrained from bothering the Asian residents.[45] Whatever the reason, Alexandra's multiracial community existed with all its tensions and diversity.

Homes and Traps

Conflicts not only erupted between ethnic groups, but also between the generations of Africans living in Alexandra. Land, an issue featured in Chapter 1, became part of the struggle's terrain and youth "confiscated" private property whenever possible. Susan Piliso found this out first hand. After spending years in Soweto because of her health, Piliso returned to Alexandra in 1951, at a time when the Msomi and Spoiler gangs rivaled each other for turf, and for their victims' hard earned wages, which they garnished by brandishing tomahawks, knives and guns. Before moving to her present location on Third Avenue and marrying her husband of many years, Thomas Sipho Piliso, whose story appears in Chapter 1, Piliso lived two streets over on Fifth Avenue near the highly active Selbourne Avenue (present-day Reverend Sam Buti Street). After reminiscing about local sports figures such as boxer Jaos "Kangaroo" Moato and musicians such as penny whistler Aaron "Big Voice Jack" Lerole,[46] Piliso's testimony continues with her niece's involvement in politics in Orlando West and then eases into Alexandra where she provides an example of how the youth disrespected the elders during the student protest.

One day a group of uprising participants came to her house with a large tank which they placed on her front stoop. The tank contained benzene, methodine, spirit, petrol, paraffin and other explosive material. Using a pipe, they funneled the contents into bottles that they later hurled at police. Initially, Piliso refused to let the tank stay there but the protesters won out. They even warned her to stay inside with the doors locked and not to talk to the police. If the police came, they cautioned, avoid telling the truth. Piliso cowered not because of fear, but because she remembered what happened to a friend. Initially, her friend had refused to accommodate the uprising participants, so they came back with a van full of people, forcing her to provide shelter and blankets.[47] With no men in the house, these women appeared vulnerable and with their seniority challenged, they temporarily lost the right to govern their properties. This sort of takeover was reminiscent of Peri-Urban's (Chapter 1) intrusion to the many houses it expropriated. Piliso and her friend's home became public spaces and also disputed properties, as each group, the owner and the protesters, vied for control, not only of the stoop but also the entire house.

Male protesters dictated how females within the group acted. Piliso comments, "Jah it was always the men's [exercising control] always. Females would come in do funny things and act like chickens."[48] Piliso's testimony also underscores rules of engagement. In times of war, as was the case with the student uprising, activists commandeered private homes to enlarge their fields of operation. These homes, as Piliso's testimony further conveys, served as bases where they stockpiled weapons or created them. With a "join or else"[49] ultimatum dictating participation, Piliso and other women like her, had no choice but to surrender their properties, their personal space and their time to the struggle.

Even on the streets, the youth dictated how the elderly contributed to the uprising. With their goal of not accepting "no" as an answer, many older people felt obliged to participate. Former ballroom dancer and novice photographer John "Boykie" Mhlontlo explains, "These youngsters on the road, they do their things and they are not going to beg you and if they find you, you've got to join them."[50] Piliso corroborates Mhlontlo's story. She stated:

They dug holes in the roads around Fifth Avenue, and whether you liked it or not, you start digging, put your bag there, especially men, they would dig and then go home. As long as you put your hands in you have helped them.[51]

Filled with zinc and topped off with soil, these holes trapped oncoming police casspirs and other state vehicles, sinking them into the earth, sometimes enflaming them. As a youth Godfrey "Ginger" Tshabalala freely participated in this activity, which mostly occurred during the afternoons because Peri-Urban often arrested people at night for pass law infractions. He recalled, "Yeah, when they came, we were hiding ourselves. We started throwing petrol bombs...It was risky by then."[52]

Initially, protesters thought the police were firing blank shots until people started falling one by one.[53] Instead of leaving the bodies, others picked up the wounded, took them to the clinic and left them. Even the Cillie Report points this out when it revealed that 12-year-old Shadrack Kekane's body arrived at the police station by an unknown person.[54] According to the Cillie Report, Kekane was the youngest casualty of the student uprising, however Abi Mo.'s testimony revealed an even younger victim. A "bus driver" ran over a toddler, crushing the infant, and leaving the tires' indelible prints on his mauled body. According to this bystander. "when I witnessed this death, I began to question why the apartheid regime existed, and how it made Africans part of a vicious cycle that they could not control."[55] Other Africans also looked within. Their alternative entertainment centers, the shebeens, not only provided the space for socializing, but also served as the sites where families lost their fathers, and wives lost their husbands to the potent potables that altered their minds and consumed their hard-earned wages.

Shebeens, the WRAB, Bottle Stores, and Beer Halls

Shebeens were illicit places in African homes that offered home-made and distilled brews. Their mostly male patrons became wedded to alcohol that they provided. Mathabane even commented on this aspect when he discusses how his father came home intoxicated on a number of occasions, forcing the family to endure his drunken state minus the week's wages.[56] People elected to drink to self medicate apartheid's woes: finding money for bribes, navigating illegal city living, putting food on the table and paying rent. Shebeens' impact on family survival and the struggle was not lost on the ANC, which issued its own leaflet on the matter. The flyer highlights the parties' faces, looks, general demeanor and lack of self-esteem and motivation. Entitled "The Voice of the ANC," the flyer indicts alcohol users and suppliers when it calls for the destruction of shebeens and offers these reasons for their demise: "look at what liquor has caused our people: red eyes, lazyness (sic) their families have broken down, rotten smell out of their mouths, jelly paunches and muscles, colour of their skin has changed, death, became hoboes.[57]"

According to this bold, militant document, Africans did all kinds of unhealthy things while under alcohol's influence: showed their private parts to children, engaged in murder, sought divorces, used profane languages, and lived in a manner not suitable for Africans.[58] This was especially crucial at a time when during the 1970s people adopted Black Consciousness. Espoused by activist and martyr Steve Biko, Black Consciousness called for African self-determination, psychological freedom, and economic independence.[59] Not only was

Black Consciousness an antidote to years of inferiority, reinforced by laws, geographies, landscapes, pay and social status, the ideology was also a way for people to embrace their African identities. Many Alexandrans had Afros, and donned dashikis, and caftans.[60] They also celebrated their beauty, all shades of it, even when newspaper ads carried photographs advocating for lighter, whiter Africans.[61]

This was not a side issue. Even the strongly provocative document such as "The War is On," fumed against such practices; its authors exclaim, "you see boards advertising so-called complexion, only to try and brainwash us, to hell with white skin, black is beautyfull [sic]." Not only did Africans have to counteract commercial advertisements, they also faced, as was the case throughout South Africa, signs and nomenclature which further denigrated them. Terms such as Coolies, Bantu, Bushman, and Kaffir, appeared on signs used to label race designated areas. Apartheid policy and its manifestation on the ground bothered Africans so much that they questioned their beauty and their societal value, which made Biko's teachings all the more appealing, and inviting.

Drinking alcohol interrupted this process of self awareness and self love and made its drinkers self-loathe. The "Voice of the ANC" continues with this stern warning:

My brother and you my sister, if you are a shebeen king or queen, as from Monday onwards (23 August 1976 onwards) you don't sell any liquor that contains alcohol because anybody who is found selling liquor his or her house gonna be burnt down to ashes. Burn them down. Let us take this message to all the shebeens. You have been warned and this is the last warning. Stop selling liquor it destroys our nation.[62]

In an attempt to rebuild the "nation," "rioters set fire to a bottle store in[sic] First Avenue[63][while] about 50 Black men ransacked a bottle store in [sic] 17th Avenue." [64] Maboela recounts what he witnessed on the uprising's first day at the bottle store he supervised:

I went straight to work and opened and locked myself in the bottle store because there was some work to be prepared there. Once I was in the bottle store I heard they were throwing stones on top of the building.[65]

He continues his story by discussing what happened next:

When I looked...the street was full of school children and they had all kinds of dangerous weapons and they were shouting: "Power, power, power, power!" Whilst I was there, still surprised, there came an old man and took me by my hands: "Look just go away from this gate because this [sic] people will soon injure you and some of them know that you are a supervisor here and will demand the keys in order to go and open the safe."[66]

Within moments after he crossed the street, Maboela saw a bus full of school children ram into the building. When satisfied that an opening had been made, the "driver" along with others went "shopping" and confiscated beer, brandy, whisky and other kinds of alcoholic beverages. Not even the police interrupted this drinking and pillaging frenzy, as some stragglers who remained behind chopped down a tree and set the bus on fire.[67]

Alexandrans attacked bottle stores and beer halls because the West Rand Administration Board used their profits to finance its administration, to build more homes,[68] and to support the 1970s homeland policy.[69] No money was earmarked to benefit the Alexandran community which supported these establishments with their meager incomes and contributed to at least 21 percent of the WRAB's increasingly growing revenue.[70] This not only represented a way in which authorities continued to devalue African life, it also showed how they continued to exploit the very existence of African culture. Well aware of the WRAB's negative impact upon Alexandran society, youth:

...bent on smashing the bureaucratic system that stifled their lives, tore through the place, smashing windows and overturning filing cabinets that contained records on individuals, their application for homes, and legalities governing their rights to seek work.[71]

The WRAB represented everything that apartheid stood for: curtailment on the physical and social mobility of Africans; second-class citizenship; and the depiction of Africans as numbers or subjects in files. The state went out of its way to control and manipulate African life, and as a result of years of subjugation, Alexandrans and other Africans throughout the country seized the opportunity that the student uprising presented to fight back.

Just as the schools, shebeens, beer halls and Asian-owned businesses reinforced racial segregation and hierarchical structures, so did the buses. As weapons of the weak,[72] these vehicles allowed uprising participants to destroy shops, the WRAB offices, beer halls and other buildings in order to redefine what the landscape looked like and represented. When Alexandrans took to the streets, they openly registered their grievances against an apartheid regime that had for decades stifled their political mobility, their daily living and their education.

Interracial Cooperation, Afrikaans and Schools

Generally schools are institutions meant to advance students' opportunities, but in apartheid South Africa they were far from motivational; if anything they inhibited pupils' aspirations. With their inadequate facilities,[73] schools represented a microcosm of wider societal problems. These institutions enforced racial and ethno-linguistic exclusion. Zulus attended their own school as did other ethnic groups. Poet and community activist Ben Mhlongo confirmed this separation when he states, "[we] [could] mix where we stay[ed] but when it came into school that's when we started seeing the divisions."[74] For instance, even though Mark Mathabane spoke five different languages, he attended a school that focused to the dismay of his Venda father, on his mother's language, Shangaan.

These segregated schools also offered Africans substandard education. According to Mhlongo, he wanted to be a lawyer. "But that didn't happen . . . because of politics . . . Politics did a lot of damage in deterring . . . young people from [being] what they wanted to be in terms of their occupation." [75] They were trained to serve in menial capacities for the benefits of Whites. Slain apartheid architect and Minister of Native Affairs Hendrik Verwoerd proclaimed as much when he quipped:

There is no place for [the Bantu] in the European community above the level of certain forms of labour . . . What is the use of teaching the Bantu child mathematics when it cannot use it in practice? That is quite absurd.[76]

Africans rejected their inferior education as this militant leaflet entitled, "Bantu of Alexandra," which called for a work stayaway and provided a brief history of education for Africans declares, "We also know that with the introduction of Bantu Education the standard of education for the Black man was lowered."[77] Alexandrans also deplored the conditions under which they received education. Besides overcrowding, these institutions lacked desks and seats, and there were an insufficient number of toilets.[78] Students left school and some failed " . . . not because they could not keep up with the lessons; rather because . . . they hated . . . Afrikaans . . . , it was the oppressor's language."[79] People also rejected Afrikaans because they did not want to mimic the White man and privilege his language over their own.[80] Not only did Africans refuse to renounce their cultures, "the whole of Alexandra . . . didn't write exams in 1977 to avoid humiliation."[81] Even though they enjoyed greater privileges than Africans and spoke Afrikaans, Coloureds also participated in the struggle.

Historically, Coloureds and Africans had less than amicable relations not only in Alexandra but also throughout South Africa. Alexandra's early beginnings trace back to a Coloured entrepreneur, Lulius Campbell, who in 1913 purchased the township from attorney Herbert Papenfus and served as secretary for the Alexandra Health Committee, which had representation from all sectors of the community.[82] Coloureds, like Africans who had the ANC Alexandra Branch, established their own political institution, the Alexandra Coloured Associated Associations (ACAA). That body fought for better transport, the hiring of a Coloured road inspector, and fought against Johannesburg incorporating Alexandra into the municipality arguing that, "the Coloured people of the township...should have special representatives to represent the Coloured interest."[83] In this same undated memorandum, the ACAA wanted to create a special Coloured cemetery, though that never happened.[84]

Earlier Coloured settlers, as it appeared, bought into the segregationist ideology even though many lived with Africans in the same yards.[85] Most Coloureds lived from Second to Seventh Avenues, with a few sprinkled in the remaining 16 avenues that Africans mostly inhabited. They even attended separate churches. The African Methodist Episcopal (AME) Church mostly welcomed Coloured followers.[86] Education also reinforced segregation. Bussed out of Alexandra, Coloureds learned their subjects all the way in western Johannesburg in places like Coronationville where they received secondary and high school education. Some schools however did exist in the township such as the Alexandra Coloured School on Second Avenue.

Coloureds were drawn into the protest by force or commitment to the ideals that the uprising supported. Homemaker Carol Britz offers insight into African/Coloured relations, while also further illustrating the peer pressure that existed during the student uprising. Born in Alexandra in 1953, Britz received her education at the Alexandra Coloured School, and later attended high school in Coronationville outside of Johannesburg. Every morning at half past four, she woke up, and started doing household chores before commuting by bus. When the student uprising hit, Britz was at Standard 6. She explains how things transpired, "So when they (Africans) came, they just took us out of the classroom, threw us out and said jah, we must join them because they said that don't want to ban Afrikaans they don't want to do Afrikaans anymore."[87] Britz and her colleagues failed to understand why Africans opposed Afrikaans since it was their mother tongue. Even with this lingering question, Coloureds joined in unity as Britz revealed, "Well you know we weren't like bloody national or anything but we had some privileges (free stationary and waived school fees) that they didn't have so we walked out so that they may also get."[88]

In a move deemed treasonous to both the government and Black Consciousness proponents, African and White women also joined in unity to protest the imposition of Afrikaans. Founded in Soweto in 1976, the multiracial Women for Peace (WP) campaigned for women's rights, apartheid's abolition, and female empowerment.[89] It was standard government policy to prevent Africans from presenting their grievances before Parliament however, because White women supported Women for Peace[90] doors opened for property owner, former nurse and mother of renowned novelist and poet Mongane Wally Serote, Alinah Serote. Serote first became politically aware when the police detained her son without charging him in 1969. She stated, "I was told the reason they detained him was because of the type of books that he was writing. You know he wrote books about Alexander, but I couldn't understand why he got arrested when he was telling the truth."[91]

It was not until she heard and began participating in the Soweto branch of Women for Peace and established an Alexandran one that she had her consciousness raised. Although her ideological beliefs differed from her Black Consciousness proponent son, who argued, "…there [was] no time for talking to a white person at [that] moment,"[92] she went ahead and forged relations with White women. "Because we had the whites, [such as mining magnate Harry Oppenheimer's wife Bridget Oppenheimer] Serote recalls, and their daughters, we could go forward. We knew that alone we would be fodder for their guns. They would kill us."[93] Before Parliament, Serote implored the government to listen to children and not kill them. Then, she explained why the students opposed Afrikaans.[94] By exhibiting her bravery before Parliament, Serote personalized the story by putting faces on the masses of people affected by apartheid legislation. Her dialogue with high government officials not only enabled her to enter mainstream white society and plead on behalf of the youth, it also allowed her to fulfill and politicize her maternal role.

Although they did not know each other, Serote and Philip March similarly attacked the Afrikaans issue. While on his death bed, March, whose mother tongue was Afrikaans, and who also attended a Coloured school and nightly "soccer" meetings which turned out to be political gatherings, explained to his mother why he participated in the student uprising. He offered a hypothetical scenario of him having to learn Zulu at the Standard 9 or Standard 10 level.[95] Learning a language at a later stage of education impeded progress and growth. Plus, it placed more of an economic burden on parents and students. Former activist and financier Sipho Zungu explains,

if you were about to write a thesis, and planned and timed it well, and this would be your last year of studies, you wouldn't have resources to repeat. . . . Groups of people . . . were forced to study in a language that is not theirs. Some were in their final year, and when they failed because you had to translate everything into Afrikaans, [problems developed when] . . . parents didn't have money to send you back to school and the system says that you are now [too old] to be in the same class with these kids. You found yourself in the streets, angry and frustrated and unable to find a job. . . .[96]

In defiance of this entrenchment of inferiority, 13 schools in Alexandra faced destruction and defacement. Africans gutted two classrooms at the Bovet School on Sixteenth Avenue.[97] Other damage occurred when unidentified persons tore up books and wrote "Black Power" on the blackboard at the Coloured School on Second Avenue.[98] Protesters broke window panes, intimidated students and disrupted normal proceedings at several other schools throughout the township. They also set buildings on fire. Incendiarism has a long history in South Africa and throughout the world for that matter. People use fire in agriculture to clear land and to fertilize the soil, and as a weapon of the weak, to redress grievances. According to James C. Scott "relatively powerless groups utilize [fire] against those who seek to extract labor, food, taxes, rents and interests from them."[99] The threat of arson was so apparent in Alexandra that authorities prevented a café located less than a mile from the township from selling paraffin.[100]

Despite this precaution, Alexandra went up in flames several times. Table 4.1 charts how fires occurred throughout Alexandra in the protest's earliest months. Events appear in chronological order, beginning on June 18, and concluding on September 27. After September 27 sporadic activities occurred.[101]

Residents set Ithute, Alexandra High, Kaddie School (completely destroyed by fire) and Alexandra Secondary School among other institutions on fire.[102] Alexandrans used fire because as Tshabalala maintains "we wanted to destroy what apartheid represented. Besides, anybody could create a fire."[103] In his explanation of fire, Tshabalala raises several issues: the ability to create fires, the commonplace and accessibility of matches, and the democratization of arson. As long as residents had matches they could attempt to destroy any target.

Table 4.1 Paths of Resistance

Friday, June 18
14h00: Several buildings were in flames. Most of the buildings belonged to Indians and Chinese.
19h44d: Rioters set fire to a bottle store on First Avenue.

Saturday, June 19th
07h25: Unknown persons set fire to Green's Fresh Meat Supplies. The Sandton fire brigade put out the fire.

Tuesday, August 3rd
20h00: Slight fire damage was caused at the Alexandra Coloured School in Second Avenue. The occupants of nearby houses put out the fire.

Thursday, August 5th
20h30 to 21h00: There were two attempts at arson, one at the Pholosho School and the other at the Gordon School.

Monday, August 9th
14h00: The Alexandra High School was set on fire.
20h50: The Kaddie School in Twelfth Avenue was completely destroyed by fire.

Tuesday, September 16th
06h00: A cupboard with books was set on fire by a group of youths at the Pholosho School.

Monday, September 27th
20h00: An attempt was made to burn down the Zenzeleni School in 19th Avenue

---

Matches were commonplace and readily available in Alexandra because the township lacked electricity so residents had them on hand to light candles. Not only were matches accessible, they were also easy to transport and hide thereby making mobility with this "weapon" even more feasible.

With fire, Mrs. M. L. Mbatha explained, "we could create a spectacular show and destroy intended targets. We could also force the government to use its arsenal to put out the fires that we started."[104] By having the police's manpower diverted, Alexandrans could continue to wage war and gain a momentary advantage. They could also expose the state's vulnerability. Seen miles away, smoke could signal that all was not well in Alexandra. Because they were bent on obliterating apartheid's symbols, Alexandrans used the landscape to execute and sustain their battle against the state. Morally, they won, and for a minute those who shouted "power' remade the political and physical environment that they inhabited by destroying symbols that added to their inferiority. Photographs below highlight some of the damage done to schools, homes and buildings.[105]

Conclusion

Repetitive destruction or the attempt at it had alarmed the state. Although the Cillie Report and some other accounts have made it seem as if Africans rioted in an irrational, unplanned fashion, my research shows that protesters carefully targeted the very buildings and institutions that apartheid proponents had erected and used to instill inferiority. They destroyed the sites where shop owners cheated them, acted discourteously, or infringed upon their ability to make a living in the township. Alexandra, like other places in South Africa, existed in a competitive market for goods that sometimes remained out of the dwellers' economic reach. As a result, tensions and resentment mounted for years and erupted during the student uprising as residents took advantage of the abandoned White and Asian owned stores to go "shopping." Those shops represented another form of hierarchy and clearly put Africans on the lower rung. This was too much to take, especially for a citizenry who had nominal government authority and who lived in one of the few places in the country where Africans could own land in the urban center. As much as the student uprising was a visible protest with all the fires erupting and smoldering, it was also a psychological boost to the people involved.

When Alexandrans destroyed property, they overturned the dominant power structure. They used fire, stones, bricks and hijacked buses to erase semblances of apartheid history. Alexandrans wanted to do away with alien cultures[106] that permeated their society and entrenched inferiority. Most importantly, protesters used the limitations of the township's geography to register their disquiet in ways that reverberated throughout South African society. In a movement that began in Soweto and picked up frenetic pace in other urban and rural areas, Alexandra's contribution bears witness to the resolve and complexity of what the student uprising meant and became. Not only did the most serious conflicts occur in this township, it also has the dubious distinction of losing a large number of its residents in the uprising's very first days.

As pervasive as the destruction was during the student uprising, so was death. Death not only defined ways in which the state further entrenched its authority, it also explained how people chose to mourn, which I take up in Chapter 5.

Aerial View of Destruction, June 1976, NAR: Photograph, SAB K345

A Building on Fire, June 1976 NAR: Photograph, SAB K345

Children of Alexandra, June 1976, NAR: Photograph, SAB K345

"We Want Vorster," June 1976, NAR: Photograph, SAB K345

"A Kombi Destroyed by Fire," June 1976 NAR: Photograph, SAB K345

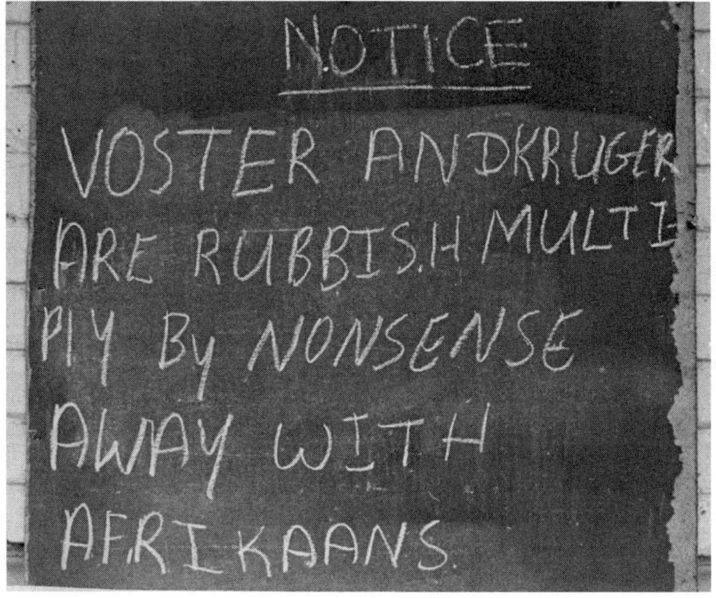

"Away with Afrikaans," June 1976 NAR: Photograph, SAB K345

C H A P T E R   5

"They Died Horribly": Celebrating the Lives Lost During the Student Uprising and Beyond

Sitting back in her worn leather chair, retired domestic laborer Mrs. M. L. Mbatha proclaimed, "when apartheid interfered with funerals, we...found...other ways to grieve, [because] we couldn't always express our sorrow at funerals or...nourish our spirit with songs."[1] This mother of four had lost her youngest son when he was just 13. Suffering from gunshot wounds to the chest, he died in her arms. Although the two shared his last earthly moments together in a heartfelt embrace, Mbatha faced the daunting task of reconciling her loss. Mbatha availed herself of what many Alexandrans did at a time when they could not honor the deceased with a public funeral: she shared the tragedy with other bereaved parents. She states, "I talked and talked. I talked to friends and I talked to you [(the author)] each time the pain lessens."[2] Heart wrenching as this story is, Mbatha recounted it several times, subtracting and adding embellishments where she saw fit. One recurring theme was Mbatha's belief that to express grief meant to defy apartheid. As tears welled up in her eyes, she exclaims, "they controlled our funerals and they disturbed us. All we wanted to do was to bury our children properly."[3]

In another lesser known case, 57-year-old Alexandran mother Margaret R. conducted an illegal funeral for her daughter during the 1976 student uprising. Margaret R. shares the horrific story of how her 22-year-old daughter, Nobuhle, died by hanging. When recounting the day she buried her daughter, Margaret R. laments, "My child died and I clung onto the grave."[4] In recalling a personal tragedy, Margaret R.'s behavior at the gravesite captures a subtle change in power. Margaret R.'s outburst defies and antagonizes an oppressive apartheid regime that regulated funerary practices and heavily monitored these rites.[5] "I never thought I would have to bury my child. I cried everyday for two years after her death. The only way I consoled myself was to read the Bible. Our children died so horribly."[6]

After sharing this, Margaret R. catches her breath and then confesses, "I clung to my child's grave because I didn't want to let her go. She was my last born. We were very close; oh how I hate what apartheid did to Black people. It destroyed our families."[7] Mrs. Mbatha shares her viewpoint when she states, "My family was never the same after my son died.[8] Our faces continue to show the pain even through our laughter."[9] In discussing death, these women bring forth ideas on how women played a role in the student uprising as mourners and interpreters of death. They explain how they felt during the process and long after it. With all of apartheid's restrictions, Mrs. Mbatha and Margaret R. and others similarly affected illustrate just how much they fought for a basic right to mourn. Because women challenged the authority of judicial laws, they refused to accept the state's language to define or constrain their emotional responses.[10]

These examples also illustrate the extent to which apartheid officials intruded into the private realm of Africans and policed every aspect of their inner and public lives.[11] Because government officials interfered with funerals,[12] Alexandrans found other ways to grieve—by reclaiming their loved ones' bodies and visiting the sites of death. Survivors created their own eulogies when they described their family member's or friend's fate. Most of the testimonies refer to how people remembered their deaths rather than their lives. They highlight the site of death, what they witnessed, and how the state handled the corpses by either scooping them up or piling them on top of each other in morgues with no regard for their family's or the corpses' dignity.

By telling how loved ones died, these survivors created a different type of obituary. Instead of the traditional written and published programs, containing the decedents' date of birth and death, names of parents, siblings, and other next of kin, marital status, education, employment, prayers and remembrances from loved ones or friends, survivors render different forms of lamentation. As a result of this change in tradition, obituaries no longer serve as just tributes, but rather, they became accounts of what people witnessed. Even state officials created their own obituaries in the way that they reported deaths or falsified their tallies.

How the State Depicted and Caused Death

Throughout her mourning, Mrs. Mbatha frequently hid her sorrow in public because in apartheid South Africa officials devalued Black life. Gary Kynoch makes this same point when discussing the Marashea gangs, as one informant explains, "white people were happy when we were fighting, as they did not take the deaths of black people seriously."[13] Even the Cillie Commission Report fell into this categorization, with its itemized accounts—it dehumanized the victims. The Cillie Report contains extensive details on how the police killed protesters and bystanders. The appendix lists personal particulars, including race, sex, age, date and place of death, the postmortem number, the cause of death, the finding for liability, and circumstances leading to death. For example, the entry in the Cillie Report describing the death of Jacob Ledwaba, read, "the deceased was accidentally shot dead when the motor car in which he was a passenger was fired at."[14] The report half-heartedly assigned culpability to the police, as this entry for Aubrey Van Rooyen, a Coloured, illustrates, "the deceased presumably died by the police."[15]

Another entry clearly attributes the death of an unknown female to the police; however, it blames her for her own death. The report read, "The deceased was killed by the police during looting and arson at a store—she disregarded an order to stand still."[16] The police only issued one warning and resorted to violence. It was evident from this and eye witness accounts that "[they]...went on a mission to kill in Alexandra."[17] Table 5.1 highlights in itemized form some of the fatalities that occurred:[18]

Table 5.1 Student uprising fatalities

Name	Age and sex	Method of death
Florence Magadani	16 years, Black female	Killed by police
Grace Masenya	46 years, Black female	Shot dead by police
Jacob Mathebula	32 years, Black male	Died from a gunshot wound
Sello Matsonyane	32 years, Black male	Gunshot wound
Sipho Mavimbela	17 years, Black male	Gunshot wound in the chest
Margaret Wilson	25 years, Coloured female	Gunshot wound

Table 5.1   (Continued)

Name	Age and sex	Method of death
Harry Ruiters	35 years, Coloured male	Gunshot wound
Aubrey Van Rooyen	13 years, Coloured male	Gunshot wound in the chest
Mangoene Vilankulu	23 years, Black male	Gunshot wound
Elizabeth Siklangu	36 years, Black female	Gunshot wound
Benjamin Sithole	34 years, Black male	Gunshot wound
Sikhati Sithole	29 years, Black male	Gunshot wound

In an attempt to project control, the state only documented 39 Alexandran deaths. Oral testimonies, however, reveal that authorities omitted countless others from their official tally. For example, Ramatsobane Masenya lost her mother when she left the house to look for her school-aged children. Masenya's mother was a traditional healer or *sangoma*, who had no political ties to any organizations; however, the police never gave her a chance to explain, and instead adopted "a shoot to kill" strategy based on the idea that any persons outside of their homes were part of the struggle. Her daughter shares what transpired:

When she was approaching between 129 and 123 she came across Caspers [sic] and they were just shooting randomly. The [police] shot her [in] the back. The bullet penetrated right through her left breast. She tried to walk. A lady called Elste told us that our mother has been shot. I wanted to know how...they sho[t] her. And I found her bending on the grass. She was praying that her ancestors and God must help her pull through. I managed to get a car in order to take my mother that she would be taken to the clinic and fortunately when we got to the clinic the nurses knew her well and they transferred her to the General Hospital and we did take her there and she did survive but she passed away on the 19th June, on the Saturday. It was 20 past 11 midnight.[19]

Days after her mother's death, the police harassed Masenya: "they kept on coming all the time, demanding to know who told us that she was shot by the police."[20] Masenya's mother had admitted as much before she died. It was important that the apartheid regime prevented this information from leaking out so that it could justify the killings by maintaining the perception that the police only shot people who ignored warnings to cease and desist, confiscated items from stores, threw stones, or hurled Molotov cocktails. State agents wanted to alter the private record and distort the public one even if it meant going through great lengths to intimidate the bereaved. In fact, authorities were so disrespectful that they held up the burial process for an agonizing three weeks, forcing the Masenyas to keep the remains in the morgue.[21] In each case, the state's agents behaved despicably but also consistently, as their history and reputation had preceded them. Masenya's story was not out of the ordinary, as many people mourned under stressful circumstances and government-imposed regulations.[22]

How the State Regulated Mourning

The state disrupted the farewell ceremonies because of the power they held, and also because they wanted to prevent Africans from using the funerary space to mobilize people.[23] Africans often circumvented government restrictions and conducted visually impressive funerals. Oftentimes, the ANC's black, green, and gold, and other political organization regalia draped wooden coffins.[24] These scripted, dramatized, and theatrical events symbolized the nation's freedom, but also the deceased's spiritual liberation.[25] Because these events often served as political rallies, officials regulated these rites by determining the order of burials, stipulating how pallbearers carried the corpses,[26] intruding onto the gravesite, controlling who attended[27] and restricting the entrances and exits into the country for burials. During the Alexandra Six Day's War, authorities also required that hearses carried corpses rather than pallbearers who traditionally transported them on their shoulders. An official mandate determined the mass burials' time and order. Families had only one hour to honor the fallen in assembly line fashion. The Honourable Minister of Law and Order stated, "...that Banda, his funeral will start at half past one to half past two. Colin Dothli, his service will start at two o'clock to three o'clock...and so on."[28]

Former steel firm employee, and husband and father of three Jabu James Malinga became involved in the student uprising when he joined a group of children singing freedom songs. The chorus went from avenue to avenue before they ended up near the beer hall next to the cinema on Third Avenue, and then on to Second Avenue where they began throwing stones and then running all the way to Sixth Avenue where they ducked for cover as the police fired shots. One bullet felled Malinga's friend Japie who stayed on Fourteenth Avenue and whose parents ran a dairy shop. When Malinga saw his body, it lay in a pool of blood. Malinga shared, "I could hardly see his head."[29]

With his friend gone, Malinga decided he had nothing to lose, so he fought back with the only arsenals available, stones and dustbin lids. Malinga landed up on Twelfth Avenue and unlike his friend, he only suffered a gunshot wound in the back when a bullet penetrated his left arm next to his ribs, causing him to spend two weeks in the hospital. When he recuperated, the police arrested and carted him off to a prison farm, where he performed hard labor three consecutive months. Malinga's family did not know his whereabouts and he resisted telling them after he resurfaced. "I was scared to tell my parents where I was and what I was doing because my parents didn't like the things that we did as the youth. They were religious people. I didn't want to tell them because they would beat me up and chase me out from the house."[30] That trip to the farm prevented Malinga from attending his friend's funeral. He offered these words following the shooting and his subsequent arrest, Malinga states, "I couldn't even see his face. And I couldn't even attend his burial. I was quite disturbed. I couldn't even attend the funeral."[31]

Authorities also sought to restrict the numbers of people who attended funerals.[32] When Jessie Busisiwe Moquae buried her fiancé poet Jingles Magoti, police stopped people from going to the graveyard. Only Moquae and Jingle's mother and sister participated in the ceremony.[33] Moquae asked Patience how she felt "as a Black person where [they] [had] to bury [their] family members in the absence of people."[34] After the burial of her Black Power activist son Philip, Irene Tukie March recalled, "the coming back [from the funeral] was not so nice because traditionally we cook food for people and then from there people were not at ease."[35] Lesoro Hilda Mohlimi also remarked how only family members returned to the decedent's home to eat, drink, and reminisce. As much as the Mohlimis wanted everyone to pay their respect, the police either prevented this from happening or made people feel so uncomfortable that they never showed up or in the case of Reuben's teachers, were told, after being questioned, to remain for a specific amount of time. As if that was not enough, the police had Reuben's aunt who lived in Rustenburg arrested just to prevent her from going to the house to mourn with everyone else.[36]

Restrictions not only precluded teachers,[37] family members, or comrades from attending funerals, the state's rules also impacted well-known celebrities.[38] In the case of world renowned vocalist Miriam Makeba, she experienced similar dissatisfaction when government officials prevented her from returning to South Africa to bury her mother when she passed away in 1960. Makeba's inability to return home did not prevent her from speaking before the United Nations in opposition to apartheid in 1963. From that point on officials revoked her passport and prevented her reentry into South Africa. As a consequence of her political convictions, Makeba spent almost 30 years in exile as a citizen of the world. As one of the first musicians to choose exile rather than live under an oppressive, racist regime, Makeba planted roots in Brussels, the United States, South America, London and Guinea among other places on Africa's vast continent and throughout the world. However, it was on American soil where she mourned her mother's and daughter's death. When her daughter died she oversaw the funeral arrangements and witnessed the corpse, two crucial aspects of grieving that had previously eluded the songstress.

Reclamation and Visiting the Sites of Death as Forms of Grieving

Grieving was so universal that it allowed Africans in a rare opportunity to achieve parity with the White minority because everyone lost loved ones. However, the uniqueness of African' loss signifies something different because it forced Alexandrans to redefine the terms of their mourning to include nontraditional activities and patterns of discernment. When the police added deaths into apartheid's solvent account, they forced people to grieve differently in public by becoming inventive in the ways that they honored decedents. Because people failed to have a "... socially recognized right, role or capacity to grieve" the state disenfranchised them.[39] As Kenneth Doka explains, people experience a sense of loss without possessing the opportunity to mourn publicly. While Doka's definition is applicable to Alexandra, he focuses primarily upon the subjects' ability to grieve at funerals. Such a definition limits the notion of public to one central location, which is problematic when considering the Alexandra case study. There, township residents transformed ordinary sites such as the streets, the government mortuary and the police station into spaces of personal reflection. Neighboring Botswana and South Africa's Northwest Province functioned in the same capacity. To only analyze what transpired at funerals negates how other sites serve a similar function.

Alexandrans had ideological and religious beliefs that they adhered to when paying homage to decedents. Bodies belonged to individual families and to community members at large, who acted as surrogate relatives. They carried out certain cultural practices as well that differed from other regions of the world.[40] For instance, relatives and friends traveled to the site where the deceased passed away. Knowing where a person passed away was as important as knowing how he/she died. As Dokkie Elias Mayisa explains, "... customarily ... if someone died in a particular place we have to go to where the person has been killed and . . . traditionally explain to the deceased's body that we are coming to pick you up and take you back home."[41]

Obtaining the decedents' bodies was so important that Alexandrans traveled for miles and went to neighboring countries to bring back their loved ones. Gardiner Majova whose son went missing in 1985 explains the significance of having the body.[42] "All you ask for are the remains of your child so that you can give him a proper burial."[43] When the state killed her husband Frank, nurse N. L. Rivers wanted to "reclaim" the body as she explained, "according to our culture and tradition, if a person had passed away we come together as a family . . . and pray and we see that we bury him."[44] When requested to leave the jail an adamant Rivers refused to move. "I am not going anywhere. I want to make sure. I want to know where you are taking these coffins."[45] Despite her determination, the police refused Rivers' request. In lieu of the body that Rivers so desired, she obtained a death certificate and a grave number.

Ntombidzudoa Sidzumo also engaged in *reclamation* to find and gain possession of her 14 year old brother's body after a police unit patrolling in a hippo, shot him three times during the height of the 1976 student uprising. Instead of allowing the survivors to take the body, the police took custody causing the family to wonder and worry about his whereabouts. "After he was taken away," the Sidzumos, like other bereaved people searched for loved ones[46] by going to, " . . . hospitals, . . . mortuaries; [because] [they] [didn't] know where his grave [was]."[47] From that day on, she never saw her brother again and no official ceremony occurred because as Mayisa explains without the corpses, survivors cannot carry out their burial practices and properly honor African customs.

In discussing her son Bongani, Margaret Madlana shares the story of what transpired at 5 A. M. on a summery February morning in 1986 when a group of youth came to her house and took away her 12 year old son. Hours elapsed and a worried Madlana wondered why her son had not returned home especially since he had not eaten breakfast. Fearing trouble, Madlana went to her sister's house on Fifth Avenue. There, along with a milling crowd, she noticed the police pulling a youngster whose head they later pummeled against a large rock. A curious Madlana tried to identify the child until the police chased the crowd away. Madlana then returned home to find an absent Bongani and relayed the account of what she witnessed. The following day, Madlana continued her search by going to the clinic, the police station and onto the government mortuary.[48] Upon finding Bongani lying on top of a government mortuary plank, a distraught Madlana uttered five heartfelt words, "Bongani you left me behind."[49]

Another bereaved mother Lesoro Hilda Mohlimi had a more extensive conversation when she found her son Reuben's body at the Alexandra Clinic. Mohlimi stated, "When I arrived there all the bodies were lying down the hall. I thought that he might still be alive and I tried to drag him out."[50] Not only did Mohlimi drag him, she also admonished him for going to the funeral because he had poor eyesight. She stated, "I tried to talk to him and I asked him where were you going Reuben because I told you not to go."[51] Then Mohlimi took off Reuben's shoes and emptied his pocket. Enclosed were the contents of a key and a letter written to Nelson Mandela.[52] Mohlimi pocketed the items and continued her activities only stopping when an approaching hospital staff member posed this question, "why are you looking and talking to this boy because he is dead."[53] Mohlimi then realized her son was dead. She went back home and with a priest's assistance recovered the body in five weeks.[54] For Madlana and Mohlimi, their experiences of viewing the bodies were tactile and visceral. As parents, they communicated with the deceased and touched their bodies as if they still possessed breath. Fortunately for these women, officials allowed them to recover the bodies unlike N. L. Rivers who "observed" her husband's coffin.

Other Alexandrans traveled further than these women to visit the site of death. Hilda Phahle, Esther Mthembu and Mamokete Malaza took a *kombi* (mini-van taxi) all the way to neighboring Botswana to see the site where the South African Defense Force (SADF) killed their children: George, Lindi and Joseph on June 14, 1985. The Gaborone Raid formed part of a larger government program called "Total Strategy," which officials first advanced in the 1977 Defence Force White Paper. Based on the premise that the state must face its enemies domestically and internationally, the SADF planned to flush out and kill exiled ANC activists. High on the list of activists was George Phahle, who had surfaced as a government target beginning in the 1970s. When, the police came to search the Phahle home, they detained his brother Levi to send his brother a message. After Levi's release, the Phahle brothers decided to skip the country. George's decision to leave the country as his mother put it, " . . . was the beginning of the rest of our beloved son'[s] life."[55] The day George died, Levi hid underneath the bed, and lived to tell the harrowing story to his mother and the other women who had traveled to Botswana to witness the site of death.

When Esther Mtembu heard the tragic news about "all the children dying in Botswana," she was at home sewing clothes for a wedding. She then asked the undertaker to bring back her son's body from Botswana. Instead of picking up the body himself and charging her a lot of money, the mortician loaned her a coffin and suggested that it would be cheaper to hire a kombi. When Mtembu made the return trip home and reached the border, she encountered harassment and an intrusion into her privacy. Border agents wanted to open the black coffin "soldered in copper,"[56] but when all efforts proved futile, they allowed them to pass. With Joseph's body on South African soil, family and friends had the opportunity of visiting the gravesite at their convenience. Margaret Madlana, whose son died at the police's hand after they pummeled it against a rock, shared the significance of this notion when she stated, " . . . I will never rest because I used to go . . . and sleep on top of his [Bongani's] grave . . . even today I still go there and pray [at] his grave."[57] Phahle echoes Madlana's sentiments, "It . . . [was] their right to rest in peace on the soil where they were born, the soil they died for. It [was] time they were brought home to be buried where we can visit them at our convenience."[58]

Even the silver screen depicts the significance of *reclamation*. *Amandla: A Revolution in Four Part Harmony* director Lee Hirsch portrays in his film on music and resistance, an exhumation of freedom fighter, song writer, vocal bassist, and father of six Vuyisile Mini. Mini penned the ever popular festive but highly inflammatory song, "Beware Verwoerd" which warned the White establishment that the Black man was coming. In 1998, 34 years after Mini's death, family and friends rescued his remains from a pauper's cemetery in Pretoria and reburied him in his native Port Elizabeth.[59] In another celebrated case, Sarah Baartman's highly televised funeral was almost a two-century old repatriation.[60] After spending years derisively labeled as the "Hottentot Venus," and on display for European consumption, interrogation and scrutiny, the nation finally rested when Baartman's remains returned in 2002. Mini's and Baartman's burials symbolized their reconciliation with South Africa and the ancestors that enveloped them.

COMMEMORATING DEATH THROUGH FUNERALS, BODIES, AND THE LANDSCAPE

Commemorating the lives lost in Alexandra during the student uprising and beyond took many forms. When survivors could celebrate, they honored decedents with funerals, tombstones, wreaths or by conducting prayer vigils. However, when authorities prohibited or interrupted funerals, Alexandrans internalized their pain, and in another unique way commemorated a loved one's passing by creating obituaries. Instead of the usual tribute given at funerals, Alexandrans paid homage years later by speaking before the Truth and Reconciliation Commission (TRC) or by allowing private interviews. Throughout their testimonies, informants recall how people died or how the state prevented them from grieving publicly at funerals.

During the death of a teenager named Mashudu following the student uprising, one unidentified preacher proclaimed amid deafening shouts of "Viva Mandela," "Viva Joe Slovo," "in her, as in hundreds of other black children who have died since this whole nightmare began, had been embodied the hope for a better Africa."[61] Mashudu was a heroine because her death, symbolized the apartheid regime's brutality. After this funeral, Mark Mathabane went home and reflected "...I shut myself in the bedroom and questioned a belief that I had long cherished: that there is a place in South Africa for the teachings of Mahatma Gandhi, that what Martin Luther King, Jr., had done for blacks in America could be done for blacks in South Africa."[62] Mathabane's account conveys how funerals allowed the living to question the status quo, to discuss world issues and to make parallels with other places. Comparing Alexandra to other sites around the world enabled Mathabane and others to understand that what happened in the township did not occur within a vacuum. This was extremely important given the fact that apartheid proponents banned books, and controlled the media to seal Mathabane and others from the outside world. In honoring Mashudu's memory in this fashion, Mathabane pays homage to the fallen in a less ceremonial and inconspicuous way, by offering his own form of commemoration: he thought.

Activist, philanthropist, and AmaAfrika burial owner Linda Twala provides a different and a more traditional example. Learning to take care of others from his mother, who lived to be 100 years old, Twala reached out to several elderly people, as his place Phutaditjaba, which means a "gathering of nations," continues to do. One elderly woman, Rosie Tshabalala, who was born in 1892, catapulted Twala on the road to philanthropy and care giving. He stated, "My mother used to look after an old lady who made me promise that I would arrange a respectable burial for her. When she died, I made her a coffin out of timber and arranged the church and the undertaker."[63] Not only did Twala make these arrangements, he also raised money to provide a tombstone in 1986.

Days after the state bombed his home, Twala held a tombstone unveiling ceremony. The tombstone pays tribute to Tshabalala's life, with this statement, "In Loving Memory," signed Twala and Alex residents, to indicate who erected the tombstone and held the unveiling ceremony. Aside from tombstones, as of today, no monuments stand in Alexandra, like they do in Soweto at the Hector Pietersen Memorial, or at the Arlington National Cemetery or the Holocaust Museums. These public monuments, which honor Soweto's fallen, war veterans and victims of Nazi persecution respectively, have as their recurrent motif a national ideology of sacrifice.[64] These places capture a dominant interpretation of death, with the landscape,[65] depicting huge stones and epitaphs that serve as landmarks historicizing the decedents' accomplishments. Under the radar, another form of commemoration existed and thrived. Bodies honored the fallen in much the same way as monuments on the landscape.

Because Alexandrans experienced trauma, their health declined.[66] N. L. Rivers' troubles were far from over after the stalemate that she had with the authorities who held her husband's corpse in their custody. She faced daily harassment. Police officers went so far as to tell her that if she wanted to erect a tombstone she had to visit the authorities and they would tell her what to inscribe. She also could not conduct a prayer service. Rivers commented on the effect this had upon her mental psyche and physical health. "I could not enjoy a normal life as usual … I became sick. There were a lot of complications and the police were doing a lot of strange things that affected my health."[67] Rivers was not the only one who "…had lost her health."[68] Maria Dimikatso Makajane suffered from heart ailments and high blood pressure following the death of her son David Mofokeng. Matsiliso Paulina Monageng also experienced hypertension when unknown people killed her Minerva high school son Jacob Mabizela. Hilda Phahle experienced insomnia following the death of her son George and daughter-in-law Lindi. Irene Tukie March also suffered health ailments:

I was very, very, very sick. Can you imagine in the morning you go away, before lunch time you get a report that your child is shot at. All of a sudden I became very sick. The police usually came to my house and say I must come and write a statement. I asked them what statement am I to give because I was not available. Let them do a statement and give it to me because they did their job, I was not available.[69]

Added to their personal pain and the physical reactions that they experienced, these women raised family members' children or managed one-parent households.[70] Rivers reared children without a male figure, Phahle raised her granddaughter Gaborone and Makajane raised her sister's and father's children. Makajane confesses:

...I am suffering from heart ailments and blood pressure;...I have got my child and my sister's and father's children. I have got a lot of responsibility. I cannot meet all my responsibilities because I am very short tempered I don't even know, my life doesn't have direction and I won't be happy until I know who the murderers of my child are.[71]

Insomnia, hypertension, heart ailments and other somatic complaints crippled these women, yet at the same time, these physical reactions allowed their bodies to memorialize death. Instead of wreaths and flowers, commemoration appeared in the form of physical ailments because "...the energy generated by grief...converted to physical symptomology."[72]

Not only did Alexandrans use their ingenuity and their personal space to defy apartheid, they also used the landscape to ascertain how people died. In analyzing Finnish memories of World War II and the ways in which they embody notions of nation, Petri Ravio examines monuments, battlefields, cemeteries and other inscriptions on the landscape to address death. He writes, "Finnish collective memory of World War II is most evidently inscribed on the landscape in the form of cemeteries for the fallen."[73] Ravio's examination focuses primarily upon history created from above rather than below, and not into delving into other forms of commemoration that appear on the landscape aside from monuments and grave markers, et cetera.

While Alexandrans adhere to the cultural practice of purchasing tombstones, and conducting tombstone unveiling ceremonies,[74] they also used the landscape in a fundamentally different way. Blood stains and remains of body parts served as markers. For instance, an indelible black mark highlighted the site where Philip March was fatally shot on June 18, 1976. Following African customs, Philip's friends took his mother Irene Tukie March to the Alexandran spot where he lay before being taken to the hospital. March described what happened:

Okay, I proceeded down. When I was opposite his school yard I found some of his friends and then they told me that Philip was shot. Then I wanted to know boys now where is he. They told me he was taken to hospital. Then I asked them why are they on their way—why are they lingering about when they see shots firing from left and right. Then they told me that they knew that I will come down home. They are actually waiting for me. So to show me where my son was shot at. They have shown me a black spot in the school yard and they told me that is Philip's blood there. The black spot was Philip's blood.[75]

After witnessing the spot, March walked to her house and did the following:

When I reached home I asked the eldest brother where is Philip, then he told me he didn't know where Philip went to because he rushed from school, the elder one rushed from school to the créche. So he doesn't know what happened to Philip. I told him that I learned that Philip went to hospital so that was that. Philip was going to hospital.[76]

On another occasion March witnessed the brains of her son Joseph scattered all over the ground inside a double up (short cut) near the family home.[77] These "monuments" on the landscape provided, "a sense of closure, and the satisfaction of appeasing the ancestors," commented Mrs. M. Reports indicated that her daughter held meetings throughout the township to garner support for the uprising, but upon returning from one of these events, an unidentified sniper fatally shot her, sending her mother into hysteria when she heard the news. Mrs. M. underwent reclamation to ascertain information and the corpse she so desired for a proper burial. When Alexandrans experienced death, they also endured trauma and redefined how they mourned.

CONCLUSION

By telling how loved ones died, these survivors created a different form of an obituary. They immortalized the gunshot wounds, the hippos, the poses, the smells, and the morgues. This type of obituary places the emphasis on the interpreter rather than the interpreted. It showcases what they revealed as important. Not only that, these obituaries reflect how the deceased passed away, and therefore explain the process under which they went to reclaim bodies, visited the sites of death, and found information about loved ones. In very telling ways, the women's bodies also manifested ways that Alexandrans commemorated death. Their experiences provide examples of network accounts of history. Networked accounts of history provide a holistic experience of Africans from one local to another by unifying space and place.[78] When Hilda Phahle and others went to Botswana, they meshed several stories. One story centered on how they arrived in Botswana, and another story focused upon the crime scene. A remaining narrative was Levi Phahle's survival. His story captures the deceased's last earthly moments and how the South African Defence Force policed beyond its national jurisdiction.

Other networked accounts also existed. For example, their children's deaths united Margaret Madlana, Mrs. Mbatha, Lesoro Hilda Mohlimi and Irene Tukie March into a single genealogy of violence and mourning. Each mother faced violence differently. Madlana unknowingly witnessed her son's death, Mbatha stood there helpless as a gunshot felled her son, while the other two parents, either witnessed body parts or came face to face with a rotting corpse. Each scenario showed women reacting instinctively as mothers. Mbatha held her son tightly, Madlana expressed guilt as a survivor, Mohlimi issued an admonishment and Irene Tukie March holds prayer meetings and candle light vigils.[79] Mothers, fathers, brothers, uncles, aunts, sisters, nieces, and cousins experienced and coped with their grief differently. For a state as embattled as South Africa, however, township residents needed catharsis, and while prayer, vigils, singing, and dancing, provided outlets, they never professionally resolved their pain.[80]

Chapter 6 "Conclusion: David's Story," explores the ways in which Alexandrans revealed how safety became an antidote for fixing and overlooking emotional problems.

C H A P T E R 6

C O N C L U S I O N : D A V I D ' S S T O R Y

Following the student uprising, concerned parents wanted to find something for students to do besides wander the streets, so they, along with the Alexandra Liaison Committee (ALC), founded the Thusong Youth Centre in 1979, the year of Alexandra's reprieve.[1] Therapy was needed because according to Thusong employee Beauty More, "We didn't know a person was traumatized.... In the olden days we viewed things such as counseling, as a white thing. We as Blacks, we didn't have those skills of saying if a child was chased by the police there must be a trauma on that child."[2] Parents took physically unhurt children to mean that they had no problems or suffered from any ailment because "the children were safe."[3] One parent who asked for anonymity; explained;

My child was fifteen years old at the time of the uprising, and suffered from nightmares and barely slept after he saw one of his friends shot. He would wake up trembling. I didn't pay attention to this at first so I sent him to Thusong, because his grades got bad, and he started acted funny and doing those things that children do. So, they got him drawing pictures of what he saw. He drew pictures showing how his friend died. Most of the pictures showed hippos. This taught me a lot about what he was going through. In the beginning, all I cared about was that he was safe.[4]

Another mother, Refilwe S. proclaimed, "my child was alive, he was safe, but he wasn't the same and I didn't understand why."[5]

When she recounted the horrific story of her son David, who suffered from posttraumatic stress following the student uprising, Refilwe S. lamented how she failed to understand or recognize the symptoms. This daughter of a factory worker and a domestic revealed her anguish in a telling way. Surrounded by loved ones, and amid photographs, Refilwe S. explained how the student uprising impacted her. "My son committed suicide and I don't know why."[6] Preferring to use the name David, he was 12 years old when the student uprising swept the nation. Standing at almost 6'4 inches tall, and with a medium build and with finely coiffed goatee, David towered over everyone. When he was a youth, David, just as most Alexandran children, loved playing in the yards. He knew little about politics; however, David understood the significance of the government's decision to teach all subjects in Afrikaans. David commented, "Even though I had a lot of Coloured friends, and speaking Afrikaans was second nature to me, I understood the people's plight."[7]

That plight was the ability of residents to use the enclosed space that they inherited to affect change. Alexandra's Black isle stood amid a swath of White residential areas, yet David and other township dwellers appearing in this book converted their liminal space into a site of political contestation. David recalls, "We turned Alexandra into a geographical hotbed by using the barriers that the government established to our advantage."[8] The same 23 avenues and seven perpendicular streets that demarcated the township, and created a grid-iron pattern that authorities easily monitored, became places that residents used for defensive and offensive maneuvers. Dwellers used the "double-ups" or shortcuts to navigate throughout the township without using the main thoroughfares.[9] By using these routes, Alexandrans eluded the police and allowed insiders' knowledge to provide an avenue for continuing their resistance. Inhabitants also constructed "earthen traps" so that when state vehicles crossed a particular area, they fell below the surface, giving uprising participants time to hurl Molotov cocktails.

David was one of the students who participated in this resistance. "I would light the Molotov cocktail and jump with glee when we struck the police. I thought this was fun until I saw one of my friends shot and killed."[10] David's friend Thomas, who ran alongside him, tumbled to the ground, and his brains splattered all over the street. He left his friend's body at Seventh Avenue because the police inundated the streets and with their instructions shoot to kill, he ran as fast as he could to a two-roomed shack that he and his mother called home. From that day on David started having nightmares, sweating profusely, and not eating. His lack of an appetite worried his mother, who commented that David never missed a meal, especially his favorite deep fried bread snack *amagwinya*.

David's story puts into perspective how much apartheid affected everyday existence. The constant need to know where children were, making sure that the passbooks stayed in order, having money to bribe police officers, and feeling that apartheid consumed their lives, weighed heavy on all Alexandrans. Many prayed. Some left the township altogether. During the forced removal process, Topsy Piliso, rather than give up her property, left Johannesburg and went to live in the Eastern Cape with her daughter. There, as Chapter 1 discusses, she lived out her remaining days under a self-imposed exile.

Other Alexandrans resisted removal, for example, Carol Britz's father, who refused to move even when offered the opportunity to live in the Coloured only area of Eldorado Park. Because he spurned Peri-Urban's offer, Britz's father went to the local authority's offices and discussed his refusal.[11] In this regard, the movement centers on what Britz and others did within the home and the township. By carrying out their normal duties, going to the grocery shops, and visiting friends and families that remained, Alexandrans also engaged in a wider struggle, survival. They took an intrusion into their everyday lives and normalized it, and by doing this, they won the moral battle even if they lost the political war. Normalcy,[12] became a way for residents to reclaim their lives.

Insurgents also practiced everyday normalcy to disguise the work that they engaged in. Their movement centered on excursions within and outside Alexandra; however, their ability to go to other places involved peril. With their bodies and cars serving as arsenals, people such as Richard Ngculu treaded the permeable boundaries of legality to support the liberation struggle. Operatives transported recruits, money, weaponry, and seasoned activists. By engaging in political mobility, insurgents established new cells, united Alexandra with other regions, engaged in avenue to avenue travel, and ran an alternate ferrying arrangement that appeared, to the uninitiated, as a regular taxi company with its multiple vehicles.

When mothers, and other concerned individuals scoured the neighborhood for friends and family, they too utilized mobility and defied authorities who sought to contain them. In that respect, their movement involved explorations to the morgue, the police station, and the streets. Survivors transformed Alexandra's streets into a crime lab or forensics scene where they looked for clues either by asking people questions or by examining the landscape for blood stains to ascertain how decedents experienced their lastly earthly moments. Bodies not only served as vessels used to walk throughout the township, they also explained how people carried around their grief. Many residents highlighted and examined in *Apartheid on a Black Isle* revealed how psychosomatic symptoms and ailments identified their internal pain and hindered their everyday activities.

David's story also revealed the significance of moving. When he describes going from avenue to avenue running from the police, David uses movement to escape and to elude. He also disguises his grief. Panting and out of breath when he reached home, David immediately went to bed, with his mother innocently thinking that he needed rest, and that in the morning, "[he] would be himself."[13] Days went by. Finally, David confessed to his mother that "I was one of the children fighting the police the other day. That's when I saw Thomas killed."[14] David's narrative symbolizes the loss that the entire township felt during the forced removals, and the student uprising. David, like Jabu James Malinga, whom the police arrested and sentenced to conscript labor on a farm, never attended his friend's funeral and this added to his bereavement and his personal anguish.

Even years after the historic event, David's face embodied the pain of his forefathers and foremothers who fought against racial injustices in Alexandra. Former businessman R. G. Baloyi, and anti-pass women's activists Virginia Thoko Mngoma[15] and Dorothy Morwesi Pitso, to name a few of Alexandra's illustrious pioneers, figured prominently in his political education. Just as operatives received history and political lessons near Alexandra's only waterway, the Jukskei River, so did David—even though things, as by his own admission, failed to click until years later. "That's when I started being politicized and angry about apartheid and the poverty that we lived under. I knew why we said no to Afrikaans but I just didn't understand why we lived under apartheid."[16] David lived to see the township's nineti-eth anniversary. Never able to reconcile his friend's death, and the experience of living under apartheid, David took his own life in 2002. When many Africans lost their lives while under police custody, with the authorities ruling many of their deaths as suicides, David left nei-ther a note nor any information behind to explain the decision to end his life. His mother lamented, "After that day he saw Thomas die, David was never the same, no matter how much he went to Thusong for cultural therapy, he never laughed like he used to."[17]

Still in mourning, Refilwe takes solace in the fact that her son helped to make not only Alexandran history but also South African. Though he never joined the ANC or any other political organization, David stood up for his rights. His mother had long thought he would assume a position as a lawyer, considering that he loved to argue, rarely lost a debate, or was ever speechless. "That boy would liven up the atmosphere with his constant questioning,"[18] says his mother who commemorates her son's life by keeping the clothes that he last wore.

When David passed away on June 12, 2002, four days before the twenty sixth anniversary of the student uprising, the ancestors welcomed another one of apartheid's fallen soldiers. To date, thousands have lost their lives to an inhumane system that imprisoned both the exploited and the exploiter. Although many victims and perpetrators appeared before the TRC to discuss missing or murdered individuals, the official count that apartheid created is not really known. Some victims lie in unmarked graves. David, thank goodness, was not one of the unidentified or unclaimed. His mother, unlike some during the seventies, held a respectable funeral replete with song, anecdotes, and friends and family. Different from N. L. Rivers whom the police prevented from having a last rite and from inscribing something personal and meaningful on the tombstone, Refilwe S., allowed these words to capture and encapsulate David's life, when she stated, "David was a dear son, and friend of the struggle, may you rest in peace and remember me when I come to join you. Always love you, your adoring mother."[19] If David could respond, perhaps he would have relieved his mother of the guilt that she now carries because he opted for suicide rather than living. His pain, as was endured by all Alexandrans who lost loved ones, was a lot to bear for many, but for David it was beyond his comprehension and his emotional stamina.

David's story, like others told in this book, speaks to Alexandra's resilience as a township. Alexandra played a pivotal role in defying the widely held belief that resistance wavered until the student uprising. During the seventies, inhabitants used their agency to create cells, to oppose the forced removal process, and to participate in the student uprising. The 1970s marked a turning point in Alexandran lives as that decade challenged their sensibilities and their resolve. For all these reasons, Alexandrans stood, and continue to stand, at the vanguard of protest. David knew this firsthand.

Notes

Introduction

1. Richard Ngculu (pseudonym), interview, tape recording, Alexandra Township, June 11, 2002.
2. Ngculu, interview.
3. Ngculu, interview.
4. Personal communication with Sarah Ngculu, Alexandra Township, June 11, 2002.
5. This part was revised with suggestions from Dr. Seanna Sumalee Oakley.
6. Gregory Houston and Bernard Magubane, "The ANC Political Underground in the 1970s," in *The Road to Democracy in South Africa, Volume 2, 1970–1980*, South African Democracy Education Trust (Cape Town: Zebra Press, 2004).
7. Raymond Suttner, *The ANC and the Underground* (Auckland Park: Jacana Media, 2008).
8. Belinda Bozzoli, "Ritual and Transition,: The Truth Commission in Alexandra, Township, South Africa 1996." University of the Witwatersrand Institute for the Advanced Social Research, Seminar Paper No. 435, 1998, 10–11, 17–18.
9. Bozzoli, "Ritual and Transition."
10. Belinda Bozzoli, *Theatres of Struggle and the End of Apartheid* (Athens: Ohio University Press, 2004).
11. Raymond Suttner, *The ANC and the Underground* (Auckland Park: Jacana Media, 2008).
12. Gregory Houston and Bernard Magubane, "The ANC Political Underground in the 1970s," in *The Road to Democracy in South Africa, Volume 2, 1970–1980*, South African Democracy Education Trust (Cape Town: Zebra Press, 2004), 402.
13. Houston and Magubane, "The ANC Political Underground in the 1970s."
14. Alfred Stadler, "A Long Way to Walk: Bus Boycotts in Alexandra, 1940–1945," in Phil Bonner (ed). *Working Papers in Southern African Studies* (Johannesburg: Ravan Press, 1981) 228–257.
15. See John Nauright, "An Experiment in Native Self-Government: The Alexandra Health Committee, the State and Local Politics," *South African Historical Journal*, 43 (2001): 223–243, David

Duncan, "Liberals and Local Administration in South Africa: Alfred Hoernle and the Alexandra Health Committee, 1933–1943," *International Journal of African Historical Studies* 23, 3 (1990): 475–493.

16. See Philip Bonner and Noor Nieftagodien, *Alexandra: A History* (Johannesburg: Witwatersrand University Press, 2008), Alan Brooks and Jeremy Brickhill, *Whirlwind before the Storm: The Origins and Development of the Uprising in Soweto and the Rest of South Africa from June to December 1976* (London: International Defence and Aid Fund for Southern Africa, 1980), Pat Hopkins and Helen Grange, *The Rocky Rioter Teargas Show: The Inside Story of the 1976 Soweto Uprising* (Cape Town: Zebra, 2001).

17. See Justine Lucas, "Space, Domesticity and People's Power: Civic Organisations in Alexandra in the 1990s," *African Studies*, 54, 1 (1995): 89–113, Bozzoli, *Theatres of Struggle and the End of Apartheid* (Athens: Ohio University Press, 2004).

18. Tony Buti, "The Systematic Removal of Indigenous Children from Their Families in Australia and Canada: The History-Similarities and Differences," 8, http://www.newcastle.edu.au/centre/cispr/conferences/land/butipaper.pdf, date assessed June 5, 2010.

19. Solidarity Peace Trust, "Discarding the Filth, Operation Murambatsvina," June 27, 2005, http://www.solidaritypeacetrust.org/180/discarding-the-filth-operation-murambatsvina/ date assessed June 3, 2010.

20. Bradley Skelcher, "Apartheid and the Removal of Black Spots from Lake Bhangazi in KwaZulu/Natal South Africa," *Journal of Black Studies*, 33, 6 (July 2003): 761–765.

21. J. Dunston, *Alexandra, I Love You* (Alexandra: Alexandra Liaison Committee, 1998), 39.

22. Dunston, *Alexandra, I Love You.*

23. Dunston, *Alexandra, I Love You*, 33–39.

24. The Save Alexandra Party members participated voluntarily and operated without administrative staff or office equipment. The group comprised Lepile Taunyane, Lucas Khoza, and Roger Sishi.

25. Reverend Sam Buti, interview, Alexandra, South Africa, July 22, 2002.

26. Mike Sarakinsky, "From 'Freehold' to 'Model Township' A Political History of Alexandra 1905–1983," (unpublished honours, University of the Witwatersrand 1984), 61.

27. Dawne Y. Curry, "Community, Culture and Resistance in Alexandria, South Africa," Phd dissertation, Michigan State University, East Lansing, Michigan, 2006, 107.

28. Sarakinsky, "From 'Freehold' to 'Model Township.' "

29. Bonner and Nieftagodien, *Alexandra: A History.*

30. Bonner and Nieftagodien, *Alexandra: A History*, 171–196.

31. "Bantu Education Act," http://en.wikipedia.org/wiki/Bantu_Education_Act, date assessed November 9, 2010.

32. Rose Innes Phahle, interview, tape recording, Illovo, Johannesburg, February 4, 2002. His mother, Hilda Phahle, founded the Pholosho School located on Twelfth Avenue near London Street, sometime in the 1940s.

33. Samuel Mabolle Ramagaga, "The Contributions of the Holy Cross Sisters to Black Schooling in Alexandra, Johannesburg, with Particular Reference to the Period 1950–1970," A Research Report submitted to the Faculty of Education, University of the Witwatersrand, Johannesburg, in partial fulfillment of the requirements for the degree of Master of Education, January 1988, 62–65.

34. "Alexandra Teachers Arrested," *Bantu World*, December 3, 1955 and, "Police Raid School in Alexandra," *Bantu World*, December 10, 1955.

35. Mongane Wally Serote, "Post-Sharpeville Poetry: A Poet's View," *Third World Quarterly*, 10, 4 (1988): 1600–1606.

36. Dawne Y. Curry, "Community, Culture and Resistance in Alexandria, South Africa 1912–1985," Phd Dissertation, Michigan State University, East Lansing, Michigan, 2006, 137.

37. Sipho Zungu, interview, tape recording, Parktown North, Johannesburg, April 22, 2002.

38. Bonner and Nieftagodien, *Alexandra: A History*.

39. Ben Mhlongo, interview, tape recording, Alexandra Township.

40. Coloureds are persons having Malaysian, European, African, Indian, Asian, and Khoisan ancestry.

41. Bonner and Nieftagodien. *Alexandra: A History*, 210.

42. Bonner and Nieftagodien. *Alexandra: A History*.

43. Hopkins and Grange.

44. Commission of Inquiry into the Riots at Soweto and other Places in South Africa, 1976–1977, hereafter referred to as the Cillie Report, appendix.

45. Helena Pohlandt-McCormick, "I Saw a Nightmare," Memory and Violence, Chapter 6," in 'I Saw a Nightmare': "Doing Violence to Memory, the Soweto Uprising, June 16, 1976" (New York: Columbia University Press, 2007), HEB http://www.gutenberg-e.org/pohlandt-mccormick/ date assessed March 18, 2012.

46. Bozzoli, "Ritual and Transition", 9–10.

47. Belinda Bozzoli, "Ritual and Transition: The Truth Commission in Alexandra Township, South Africa, 1996," University of the Witwatersrand Institute for Advanced Social Research, Seminar Paper No. 435, 1998, 10–11, 17–18.

48. Bozzoli, *Theatres of Struggle and the End of Apartheid* (Athens: Ohio University Press, 2004), 206–232. In the chapter entitled "Nationalism and Theatricality," Bozzoli discusses how funerals were opportunities to mobilize and create a national identity.

49. Belinda Bozzoli, "Ritual and Transition,": The Truth Commission in Alexandra, Township, South Africa 1996." University of the Witwatersrand Institute for the Advanced Social Research, Seminar Paper No. 435, 1998, 10–11.

50. Margaret Madlana, interview. October 28, 1996, Alexandra Township. Truth and Reconciliation Commission, http://www.doj.gov. za/trc/hrvtrans/index.htm., date assessed March 3, 2006.

51. Mrs. M. L. Mbatha. interview, tape recording, Alexandra, South Africa, May 10, 2002.

52. Irene Tukie March. interview, Alexandra Township, October 28, 1996, Truth and Reconciliation Commission, http://www.doj.gov. za/trc/hrvtrans/index.htm date assessed July 10, 2007.

53. Dawne Y. Curry, "When Apartheid Interfered with Funerals: We Still Found Ways to Grieve in Alexandra, South Africa," *International Journal of Interdisciplinary Social Sciences*: 22, 2 (2007): 245–252.

54. Somalia, Nigeria, Republic of the Congo (DRC), Cote d'Ivore (Ivory Coast), Madagascar, Benin, Senegal, Central African Republic, Gabon, Senegal, Burkina Faso (Upper Volta), Chad, Mali, Togo, Cameroon, and Mauritania.

55. David B. Coplan, *In Township Tonight!: South Africa's Black City Music and Theatre* (London: Longman, 1985), 165.

56. Born in Venda in 1909, Josias Madzunya arrived in Johannesburg in 1930, where he worked several jobs before selling Hessian and cardboard alongside the intersection of Troye and President Streets where he held court as a street corner speaker. This self-educated man, husband, and father had an alluring presence. Madzunya donned a well-groomed beard with a short coiffed Afro, which he accentuated with a cascading black trench coat. That trench coat became his trademark. John Mhlontlo, interview, tape recording, Alexandra Township, January 16, 2002. When questioned about Madzunya John Mhlontlo, smiled and stated, "I don't remember what he said at meetings, but I tell you he wore that black trench coat no matter how hot or cold." An article appearing in *Drum*, a widely read Black entertainment magazine that was launched in the early 1950s, had echoed the same sentiment as early as 1959.

57. See Kenneth Margo, *Underground Encounters: True Tales of an ANC Operative's Long Walk to Freedom*, Kindle edition, Padraig O'Malley, *Shades of Difference: Mac Maharaj and the Struggle for South Africa* (New York: Penguin, 2008), Elias Masilela, *Number 43 Trelawney Park: Kwa Magogo* (Cape Town: New Africa Books, 2011).

58. Raymond Suttner, *The ANC and the Underground* (Auckland Park: Jacana Media, 2008).

59. See Raymond Suttner, *The ANC and the Underground* (Auckland Park: Jacana Media, 2008), Philip Noyce, director. *Catch a Fire* Jacklyn Cock, *Colonels and Cadres: War and Gender in South Africa*

(Cape Town: Oxford, 1991), Robin Curnow, "Interview: Thandi Modise: A Woman at War," *Agenda* 43 (2000): 36–40.

60. Raymond Suttner, *The ANC and the Underground.*
61. Lynda Schuster, *A Burning Hunger.*
62. See Jacklyn Cock, *Colonels and Cadres: War and Gender in South Africa* (Cape Town: Oxford, 1991), Robin Curnow, "Interview: Thandi Modise: A Woman at War," *Agenda* 43 (2000): 36–40., *Amandla!. A Revolution in Four Part Harmony.* 108 min. Lions Gate Entertainment. United States, 2002. DVD.
63. *Amandla.*
64. Raymond Suttner, *The ANC and the Underground.* Houston and Magubane, "The ANC Political Underground in the 1970s."
65. Raymond Suttner, *The ANC and the Underground.* Houston and Magubane, "The ANC Political Underground in the 1970s."
66. Raymond Suttner, *The ANC and the Underground.*
67. See Jacklyn Cock, *Colonels and Cadres War and Gender in South Africa* (Cape Town: Oxford University Press, 1991), Robyn Curnow, interview, "Thandi Modise: A Woman at War," *Agenda* (2000), pp. 36–40, Elaine Unterhalter, "The Work of the Nation: Heroic Masculinity in South African Autobiographical Writing of the Anti-Apartheid Struggle," *The European Journal of Development Research*, 12, 2 (2000): 167–172, Natasha Erlank, "Gender and Masculinity in South African Nationalist Discourse 1912–1950," *Feminist Studies* 29 (2003): 653–671.
68. Raymond Suttner, *The ANC and the Underground*, 104–132.
69. Raymond Suttner, *The ANC Underground in South Africa* (Auckland Park, Jacana Media Press, 2008), 87.
70. Curry, "When Apartheid Interfered with Funerals," 245–252.
71. Curry, "When Apartheid Interfered with Funerals."
72. Mongane Wally Serote, *To Every Birth its Blood* (Johannesburg: Ravan Press, 1997).
73. Mark Mathabane, *Kaffir Boy: The True Story of a Black Youth's Coming of Age in Apartheid South Africa* (New York: New American Library), 1.
74. Dawne Y. Curry, "An African American Confronts and Constructs: The Social Construction of Race in Post Apartheid South Africa," *Safundi*, 22 (2006): 1–26.
75. See Gavin Lewis, *Between the Wire and the Wall: A History of South African Coloured Politics* (New York: St. Martin's Press, 1987), Ian Goldin, *Making Race: The Politics of Economics and Coloured Identity* (London: Longman, 1987), and Zimitri Erasmus, *Coloured by History, Shaped by Place: New Perspectives on Coloured Identities in Cape Town* (Cape Town: Kwela, 2001).
76. During the 1980s "ungovernability" campaign, residents led by Moses Mayekiso wanted to paralyze the government economically,

so they ordered people not to pay utilities and to erect homes on any vacant space. See Mzwanele Mayekiso, *Township Politics: Civic Struggles for a New South Africa* (New York: Monthly Review Press, 1996), Belinda Bozzoli, "From Governability to Ungovernability: Race, Class and Authority South Africa's Black Cities," University of the Witwatersrand, Institute for Advanced Social Research, no. 394, 1996.

77. Philip Bonner and Noor Nieftagodien, *Alexandra: A History* (Johannesburg: Wits University Press, 2008), 18–25.

78. Luli Callinicos, *Gold and Workers: a People's History of South Africa*, Volume 1 (Johannesburg: Ravan Press, 1985), 42.

79. Belinda Bozzoli, "Interviewing the Women of Phokeng," in Robert Perks and Alistair Thomson (eds). *The Oral History Reader* (New York: Routledge, 1998), 145–156. Even when they knew the language or grew up in the same area, age and education often distanced them from the informants they chose to record. When South African born Mmantho Nkotsoe conducted interviews for Belinda Bozzoli's work, she stood at the crossroads between familiarity and discovery, as she knew the ins and outs of this village near her birthplace in the former Bantustan homeland, Bophuthatswana, lying near Rustenburg. Nkotsoe spoke the same indigenous language, was reared in the same Tswana culture, and with her familiarity of the terrain, she understood the landscape's complexity, and the people it nourished and resuscitated. Despite having this knowledge and intimacy, Nkotsoe's education and age also made her an outsider to the mothers, activists, daughters, nieces, grandmothers, and wives that she interviewed. She was after all a minor, and in true African custom, her interviewees exercised reticence when discussing childbirth and other issues deemed suitable only for adults.

80. Alexandra maintained this status, like Sophiatown, Newclare, Martindale, and other freeholds even after the government enacted the 1913 Natives Land Act.

81. Callinicos, *Gold and Workers*, 42.

82. John Nauright, "I am With You as Never Before": Women in Urban Protest Movements, Alexandra Township, South Africa, 1912–1945, in Kathleen Sheldon (ed) *Courtyards, Markets, City Streets: Urban Women in Africa*, (Boulder: Westview Press, 1996), 260–262.

83. Philip Bonner and Noor Nieftagodien, *Alexandra: A History* (Johannesburg: University of Witwatersrand Press, 2008, 390.

84. James Giblin, "Passages in a Struggle Over the Past: Stories of Maji Maji in Njombe, Tanzania," in Toyin Falola and Christian Jennings (eds). Sources and Methods in African History: Spoken, Written, Unearthed (Rochester: University of Rochester, 2003), 296–297.

85. Sarah Mthembu, interview, tape recording, Alexandra, South Africa, April 30, 2002.

86. The original street names appear first with their new name in parenthesis: Vasco da Gama (Florence Moposho), Hofmeyr (Richard Baloyi), Rooseveld (Alfred Nzo), Selbourne (Reverend Sam Buti), London (Vincent Tshabalala), and Rooth (Josias Madzunya). John Brandt retains its original nomenclature.

87. "Mbaqanga," http://en.wikipedia.org/wiki/Mbaqanga date assessed 10 June 2005.

88. Isaac Zakes Nkosi, "South African History Online," http://www.sahistory.org.za/people/isaac-zakes-nkosi, date assessed November 22, 2011.

89. Pohlandt-McCormick, "I Saw a Nightmare," The Participants, Shifting the Point of View, Chapter 4.

90. Titus Mathebidi, interview, tape recording, Wynberg, South Africa, March 14, 2002.

91. Mhlongo, interview, tape recording, Alexandra, South Africa, January 8, 2002.

92. Belinda Bozzoli, "Ritual and Transition."

93. Tente Mngoma, interview, tape recording, Alexandra Township, April 15, 2002.

94. Ibid.

95. Ibid.

96. "Shosholoza," http://en.wikipedia.org/wiki/Shosholoza date assessed 18 July 2011.

97. Simon Noge, interview, tape recording, Alexandra, South Africa, March 9, 2002.

98. Dan Mokoyane, *Lessons of Azikwelwa* (Johannesburg: Nakong Ya Rena, 1994), 15–17.

99. "Chocho Had Yen for Bagging Goals: Deadly Striker Wasted Few Opportunities," Sowetan, April 11, 2002, p. 12. Isaac Chocho granted an interview to the *Sowetan* in which he discussed his abilities on the field and the lack of documentation regarding athletes' statistics. Chocho stated, "I was too fast and always at the right place at the right time. I would have won the top goal scorer award every year if there were such awards during our time."

100. "Mogoai's Seventh Title," *The World*, December 17, 1960.

101. "Alexandra Soccer Attracts Big Crowd," *Bantu World*, September 17, 1949. This article captured plays and allowed the reader to visualize what transpired and those in attendance to relive worthy scoring feats. The unidentified correspondent also provided readers with a capsule of the culture that sports bred in Alexandra.

102. "Fighters Sink Gunners," *The World*, January 18, 1965.

103. Doreen Mashonte, interview, tape recording, Alexandra Township, April 23, 2002.

104. "Daughters of Africa Morning Market," *Alexandra News Bulletin* February-March, No. 41, 2. Topsie Piliso chaired the Marketing

Committee, which consisted of five other members: Johannah Eland, Edith Masedi, Elizabeth Msimanga, treasurer, Albina Salanyaneland, Julia Nzonza, secretary. See Brandel-Syrier, "Daughters of Africa News," *Ilanga laseNatal*, July 14, 1945.

105. Caroline Nkosi, interview, tape recording, Alexandra Township, December 9, 2001.

Chapter 1

1. John Nauright, "An Experiment in Native Self-Government: The Alexandra Health Committee, the State and Local Politics," *South African Historical Journal*, 43 (2001): 225.The Health Committee consisted of Herbert Papenfus, Christian Frederick Wienand (The Alexandra Township Company), Ernest Powys Adams (Department of Native Affairs), Jesse Mahabuke Makhothe (Africans), and Canral Cacelhaus (Coloured). Papenfus served as the chair and business owner Lulius Campbell served as secretary. While the Health Committee lacked the statutory and financial power to make concrete changes, such as creating a public transit corporation, the body did carry out specific functions. Dawne Y. Curry, "Community, Culture and Resistance in Alexandria, South Africa 1912–1985," Phd dissertation, Michigan State University, East Lansing, Michigan, 2006, 30. Health Committee officials established building regulations, provided sewage removal, purchased land for burial, issued passes, and created a system of taxation. Health Committee officials imposed taxes on dog licenses, property holdings, business certificates, water, bicycles, ambulances, and sanitation removal. In 1934, taxes generated approximately £13,000 from which the body earned £500 from the two shillings it had charged for sanitation. With that money the Health Committee enclosed the cemetery, planted trees, and purchased a cart along with 20 oxen.

2. The Msomi gang formed to rid the community of the Spoilers, a gang formed in the 1940s, which harassed Alexandran residents and stole their money. First seen as community protectors, the Msomis emerged more fearful and ruthless than their predecessor and with their protection rackets, rapes, and murders held the community hostage. In 1957, the Msomis' reign ended. An undercover police officer, Sergeant Gilbert Sibeko, who worked for Msomi boss Shadrack Matthews, helped to arrest the gangsters.

3. Passes were identity documents that Africans carried on their person at all times, containing employer and residential history.

4. Dawne Y. Curry, "Community, Culture and Resistance in Alexandria, South Africa," Phd dissertation, Michigan State University, East Lansing, MI, 2006, 109.

5. "Alexandra in Danger-Unite Against Peri-Urban," issued by the United Anti-Peri-Urban Areas Action Committee, Putuma

Printers, 103rd Avenue, Alexandra, Johannesburg, File No. 80 (313).

6. Dawne Y. Curry, "Community, Culture and Resistance," 109–110.

7. Named after a Durban axe murder, the Msomi gang was led by business owner Shaddrack Matthews. It was originally established to help the community to defeat the Spoilers who instituted a protection racket and harassed residents and even killed them.

8. Interviews with Thomas Sipho Piliso, Caroline Nkosi and Patricia Mokoae respectively on March 3, 2002, December 9, 2001, and April 10, 2002; Dawne Y. Curry, "Community, Culture and Resistance," 109.

9. Alexandra in Danger: Unite Against Peri-Urban.

10. Todd Lethatha, interview, tape recording, Melville, Johannesburg, January 2, 2002.

11. Lethatha, interview.

12. Dawne Y. Curry, "Community, Culture and Resistance," 122.

13. Ibid.

14. Luli Callinicos, *A Place in the City: The Rand on the Eve of Apartheid* (Johannesburg: Ravan Press, 1983), 40–44.

15. Mateu Nonyane, "I Won't Go Said 42-yr Resident," *Rand Daily Mail,* September 18, 1975.

16. Mateu Nonyane, "Alex Barber Shorn of R30 for Staying," *Rand Daily Mail, extra,* October 3, 1971.

17. Philip Bonner and Noor Nieftagodien, *AleXandra: A History,* 195. Mateu Nonyane, "Lonely Christmas for Jailed Barber's Wife," *Rand Daily Mail,* December 10, 1975. His wife mentioned in an interview when she faced an uncertain future without him the following, "It's a pity there was no fine. I would not hesitate to release him. I have done that before."

18. Mateu Nonyane, "Jail for Man Who Will Not Quit His Site," *Rand Daily Mail,* December 6, 1975.

19. Philip Bonner and Noor Nieftagodien, *AleXandra: A History,* 171.

20. "Changes go on at Alexandra: This Township Not for Married Folk," *Star,* October 8, 1964.

21. "Who Qualifies for Alex?" *Izwi laseBantu* (June/July 1982), 10.

22. Bonner and Nieftagodien, *AleXandra: A History,* 193. This was not anything new, because, historically, other townships had incorporated Alexandra's influx of people. "Squatters Reject Nazi Rules," Inkululeko, May 1947. Going back to 1947, when the squatters left the township, the government created an emergency camp whose established rules included "No Dogs," "No Agitators," "No Hawkers," "No Democracy," and "No Bachelors."

23. Bonner and Nieftagodien, *AleXandra: A History,* 192.

24. Mike Sarakinsky, "from 'Freehold' to 'Model Township' A Political History of Alexandra 1905–1983," (unpublished honours diss., University of the Witwatersrand 1984), 23.

25. Changes go on at Alexandra: This Township Not for Married Folk," *Star*, October 8, 1964.
26. "Alex Push to Get Out and Live in Diepkloof," *The World*, May 4, 1965.
27. Bonner and Nieftagodien, *ALEXandra: A History*, 176.
28. Mateu Nonyane, "Churchman Thrown Out in Street," *Rand Daily Mail Extra*, no date provided.
29. 'Home or Hope,' *Weekend World*, September 18, 1977.
30. Fleur De Villiers, " 'Half-Value' Property Scandal," *Sunday Times*, May 4, 1975.
31. Mohammed Asif, "Why Displaced Person Reject Project Resettlement Colonies," *Economic and Political Weekly*, 35, 24 (June 10, 2000): 2005.
32. Terri L. Orbuch, "People's Accounts Count: The Sociology of Accounts," *Annual Review of Sociology*, 23 (1997): 455.
33. Barbara H. Fiese, Karen A. Hooker, Lisa Kotary, Janet Schwagler, and Meredith Rimmer, "Family Stories in the Early Stages of Parenthood," *Journal of Marriage and Family* 57, 3 (August 1995): 763–764.
34. Doreen Mashonte, interview. Her mother also participated in the Helping Hand Society, a mutual aid organization that visited clinics, held baked goods bazaars and singing competitions for impoverished children.
35. Mateu Nonyane, "9 held in Alex Land grab row," *Rand Daily Mail*, September 14, 1973.
36. Mateu Nonyane, "9 held in Alex Land grab row." Malinga estimated his damages at R4000 for his demolished home and belongings.
37. Mashonte, interview.
38. Bonner and Nieftagodien, *AleXandra: A History*, 226.
39. Ibid.
40. In the 1940s, a similar set of criteria for weeding out squatters also existed. Elandsdoorn, for example, only inhabited elderly people while other places, such as Moroka, Hammanskraal, and Klipspruit, incorporated established Johannesburg workers, unemployed residents, and people employed in Alexandra.
41. "General News: We Won't Budge, say Alex Families," *Rand Daily Mail*, May 25, 1979.
42. Tshediso Buti, interview, tape recording, Alexandra Township, January 17, 2002.
43. Villiers, 'Half-Value Property Scandal,' Sunday *Times*, May 4, 1975.
44. Philip Bonner and Noor Nieftagodien, AleXandra: A History, 194.
45. Other freeholds included Sophiatown, Martindale and Newclare.
46. Lillian Tshabalala founded the Daughters of Africa in 1931. Following her 18-year tenure in the United States, where Tshabalala attended Hampton University before heading to an unknown Hartford Connecticut institution, the DOA founder returned to

South Africa in 1930. While in the United States, Tshabalala attended the Chautauqua conferences and performed social work in African American churches. She often wrote articles in the Women's Section of *Bantu World*, which discussed the importance of clubs and women's roles in society. The DOA maintained branches throughout the country, stretching from Soweto to Durban. She used the editorials in the women's supplement of the *Bantu World* to discuss female empowerment and nation-building. Tshabalala believed that women had unique roles in building and sustaining the nation. In her editorials, she outlines the ways in which women could create alternative and parallel political spaces that differed from or were similar to male-dominated organizations.

47. Topsie Pilliso's husband worked for the Native Affairs Department for 25 years.
48. Thomas Sipho Piliso, interview, tape recording, Alexandra Township, February 22, 2002.
49. Mateu Nonyane, "Board Move to Evict Last Alex Landowners," *Rand Daily Mail* November 11, 1975.
50. Dawne Y. Curry, "Community, Culture and Resistance, "123.
51. Nicholas Blomley, "Law, Property, and the Geography of Violence: The Frontier, the Survey and the Grid," *Annals of the Association of American Geographers*, 93, 1 (March 2003): 122.
52. Noge followed a long tradition of entrepreneurs in Alexandra. One of the most noted was bus owner R. G. Baloyi, whose "mighty six" offered transport from the township to Noord Street in Johannesburg before offering excursions to the rural areas. More successful businessmen assumed control over the main routes, forcing Baloyi out of business in the 1940s.
53. Nzo was born in Alexandra while Mandela lived there in the early 1940s.
54. Mateu Nonyane, "Board to Evict Last Alex Landowners," *Rand Daily Mail*, November 11, 1975.
55. "Families Split as Slums are Wrecked," *Rand Daily Mail*, October 16, 1975.
56. These homelands were Lebowa (North Sotho, also referred to as Pedi), QwaQwa (South Sotho), Bophuthatswana (Tswana), KwaZulu (Zulu), KaNgwane (Swazi), Transkei and Ciskei (Xhosa), Gazankulu (Tsonga), Venda (Venda), and KwaNdebele (Ndebele).
57. See Roger Omond, *The Apartheid Handbook* (London: Penguin Books, 1985).
58. Staff Reporter, "Families Split as Slums are Wrecked," *Rand Daily Mail*, January 10, 1975.
59. Philip Bonner and Noor Nieftagodien, AleXandra: A History, 188.
60. "Changes go on at Alexandra."
61. Municipal Reporter, "Africans 'may be told to Go Home for Sex,'" *Rand Daily Mail*, April 22, 1974.

62. Philip Bonner and Noor Nieftagodien, AleXandra: A History, 194.
63. "Law, Property, and the Geography of Violence," 122.
64. Belinda Bozzoli, "Public Ritual and Private Transition," 177–178.
65. Bozzoli, "Public Ritual and Private Transition."
66. Mateu Nonyane, "New House, No Home for Mrs. Banyini," *Rand Daily Mail T. E.*, December 12, 1975.
67. Mateu Nonyane, "Lonely Christmas."
68. Ibid.
69. Mateu Nonyane, "Untitled," *Rand Daily Mail Times Extra*, December 12, 1975.
70. Mateu Nonyane, "New House, No Home for Mrs. Banyini," *Rand Daily Mail Times Extra*, December 13, 1975.
71. Nonyane, "New House."
72. Mashonte, interview.
73. Doreen Mashonte, interview, Alexandra, South Africa.
74. Doreen Mashonte, interview.
75. Ibid.
76. Ibid.
77. Piliso, interview. In 1998, Piliso reacquired his family's property. Before Piliso moved back into the house he evicted tenants who occupied the space there. Piliso confessed, "It was dangerous. They were staying in this sitting room and the back bedroom there. They even made a shack out front. You couldn't see the house or the veranda." The property also changed, becoming two separate pieces of land rather than one. Piliso's story relays the significance of loss, but also gain. He regained his family's property for R9000; he had to refurbish the home and learn to resettle in his childhood home with his wife and family.
78. Belinda Bozzoli, "Ritual and Transition," 10–11.

CHAPTER 2

1. Hereafter referred to as Bafana.
2. S v Mosima Sexwale and 11 Others, Case Number: CC. 431/77, Volume 48, Pretoria, April 5, 1978 Judgment, 2306–2307.
3. Ibid.
4. Annie Staten and Susan Roach, Take me to the Water: African American River Baptism, http://www.louisianafolklife.org/LT/Articles_Essays/creole_art_river_baptism.html date assessed January 1, 2010.
5. "Tokyo Sexwale," http://en.wikipedia.org/wiki/Tokyo _Sexwale date assessed November 29, 2010. Sexwale received his nickname because he enjoyed karate as a youth. There was a second trial because the first judge passed away. S V Mosima Sexwale, Judgment, 2306–2307. Twelve defendants, six of them involved themselves directly with Alexandra, pleaded not guilty to the main count enumerated

here: to conspire with the African National Congress, the Communist Party of South Africa, and Umkhonto weSizwe, banned or unlawful organizations that sought to endanger the maintenance of South Africa's law and order; to distribute propaganda material that supported a movement seeking to overthrow the government violently; recruit or attempt to recruit persons to join the aforementioned movements; train persons in war tactics and maneuvers and subversive activities; engage in secret expeditions outside the country to train people; to return military trainees secretly back to South Africa and have them struggle arms, ammunition, and explosives into the country; to establish arm caches and hideouts or safe houses in South Africa; to commit acts of sabotage; infiltrate associations; seek to establish and/or extend an underground organization in South Africa by creating secret groups or cells and arrange finance to support the cells. Five additional counts followed the main one or "the alleged conspiracy", however, only the first, second and fifth count, participation in terrorist activities and unlawful or banned organizations, applied to all the accused. The other counts applied as follows. Count three, which was possession of firearms, explosives, weapons and ammunition, were registered against Simon Bafana Mohlanyaneng (hereafter referred to as Bafana) and Jacob Seathlolo. Seathlolo and Bafana faced another charge under count four, along with Sexwale, Tseto and Motaung. For harboring, concealing and providing assistance to alleged terrorists. Prosecuting attorneys had hundreds of exhibits ranging from identifiable fingerprints on glycerin bottles to earthen concealed bagged weapons. Witnesses included the defendants' friends, spouses, siblings, and other relatives, police officers and informants. Another person who also faced arrest was Freddie "One-Night" Motaung S v Mosima Sexwale, 2259. Police officials captured him on December 31, 1976. At his residence the police found these items: 5 scorpion machine guns, loaded with bullets in the barrel; a plastic bag; one Tokarev pistol; one magazine with 7 by 7, 62 bullets; 2 sets of cleaning material and a packet of 75 pamphlets entitled, "Message to the workers from the South African Communist Party" dated December 14, 1976, and certain newspapers.

6. Nelson Mandela, *Long Walk to Freedom: The Autobiography of Nelson Mandela* (Boston: Little, Brown and Company, 1994), 144.

7. Mandela, *Long Walk to Freedom*, 145. See also Raymond Suttner, *ANC and the Underground* (Johannesburg: Jacana Media), 25.

8. Suttner, *ANC and the Underground*, 26.

9. In Algeria, Morocco and Kenya, insurgents used cells to liberate their countries from French and British rule respectively. In Morocco, Algeria and South Africa cells range from 3–4 people, while in Kenya they reached into the hundreds.

10. Gregory Houston and Bernard Magubane, "The ANC Political Underground," in *The Road to Democracy in South Africa, Volume 2,*

1970–1980, South African Democracy Education Trust (Cape Town: Zebra Press, 2004), 402.

11. Naledi Tsiki, interview conducted by Howard Barrell, University of Witwatersrand Cullen Library, Karis-Gerhart Collection, Political Trials A2675, Part I. Interview, Folder 39, 1263.

12. Freddy Lekiso Kumalo, interview, tape recording, Alexandra Township, March 3, 2002. Prior to 1992, only a semi-mentally challenged young lady ever questioned Kumalo about a bag containing weapons. Kumalo repositioned this bag every day so that people would not inquire about its contents.

13. Kumalo, interview.

14. Ibid.

15. Kumalo used this phrase to explain the activity of the underground movement and the services that insurgents rendered.

16. Kumalo, interview.

17. Suttner, *ANC and the Underground*, 8.

18. Michael Dingake, *My Fight against Apartheid*, (London: Kliptown Books, 1987), 61.

19. Fran Lisa Buntman, *Robben Island and Prisoner Resistance to Apartheid*, (Cambridge: Cambridge University Press, 2003). Political prisoners used their incarceration to reconcile differences between political organizations, to teach the youth about resistance, to forward information to the outside world, to take correspondence courses, and to remake the environment in which they lived.

20. South African History Online, http://www.sahistory.org.za/topic/segregationist-legislation-timeline-1960–1969, date assessed March 5, 2012.

21. Dingake, *My Fight against Apartheid*, 60.

22. Dingake, *My Fight against Apartheid*, 61.

23. Suttner, *The ANC and the Underground*, 2–7, 11, 20–21, 40, 44–8.

24. Kumalo, interview.

25. Suttner, *The ANC and the Underground*, 20.

26. Thabo Mnisi, interview, tape recording, Alexandra, South Africa, May 7, 2002. Mnisi died from cancer in 2007.

27. Kumalo, interview.

28. Beauty More, interview, tape recording, Alexandra Township, May 27, 2002.

29. Allen Feldman, *Formations of Violence: The Narrative of the Body and Political Terror in Northern Ireland* (Chicago: University of Chicago Press, 1991), 44.

30. Sipho Zungu, interview, tape recording, Parktown North, Johannesburg, April 22, 2002.

31. Zungu, interview.

32. Elias Masilela, *Number 43 Trelawney Park: Kwa Magogo* (Cape Town: New Africa Books, 2011), 99.

33. Dingake, *My Fight against Apartheid* 76.

34. Tsiki, interview.

35. George Ritzer and Douglas J. Goodman, *Sociological Theory*, 6th edition (Boston: McGraw Hill, 2004), 176–177.

36. Ritzer and Goodman, *Sociological Theory*.

37. Ritzer and Goodman, *Sociological Theory*, 179.

38. Ritzer and Goodman, *Sociological Theory*, 179.

39. S v Mosima Sexwale, testimony of Johannes Baloyi, 448.

40. Richard Ngculu, interview.

41. Deposition to South African Police of Naledi Tsiki, February 3, 1977, AK 2675 Karis-Gerhart Collection, Political Documents, Folder 26.

42. His concocted story fell on deaf ears as police officials, possessing knowledge of his involvement in an underground cell and other alleged subversive activities, carted him off to jail. When his case reached the court docket, the judge sentenced Sexwale to an 18-year prison sentence of which he served 13 years, all on Cape Town's Robben Island.

43. S v Mosima Sexwale, Judgment, 2306–2307.

44. S v Mosima Sexwale, testimony of Victor Sithole, 386.

45. S v Mosima Sexwale, testimony of Victor Sithole.

46. Deposition to South African Police of Naledi Tsiki, , Folder 26, February 3, 1977, AK 2675 Karis-Gerhart Collection, Political Documents, Folder 26, Historical Papers, Cullen Library, University of Witwatersrand, 26.

47. Naledi Tsiki, Deposition to South African Police, 16.

48. Tsiki, Deposition.

49. Tsiki, Deposition, 13.

50. Antonio Gramsci, *Selections from the Prison Notebooks of Antonio Gramsci* (New York: International Publishers Company, 1971).

51. Frantz Fanon, *The Wretched of the Earth* (New York: Grove Press, 2005).

52. Karl Marx, *Das Kapital* (London: Synergy International Publishers, 2007).

53. Suttner, *The ANC and the Underground*, 95.

54. Ibid., 70.

55. The Voice of the A. N. C., The War is on, undated.

56. Kumalo, interview.

57. James Ngculu, "The Role of Umkhonto we Sizwe in the Creation of a Democratic Civil-Military Relations Tradition," www.iss.co.za/pubs/Books/OurselvesToKnow/Ngculu2.pdf, November 2, 2010, 244.

58. Mnisi, interview.

59. Ngculu, "The Role of Umkhonto we Sizwe," 244.

60. Tsiki, Deposition, 16.

61. Ndaba revealed during the trial that he burnt these notes.

62. Naledi Tsiki, Deposition, Other weapons existed such as the Tokarev-a Soviet caliber, semiautomatic rifle, a USSR made pistol with eight rounds of magazine having a range of 50 meters, Mokarev-9mm

USSR made with a 50 meter range, and the AK47-a Soviet constructed submachine gun having a 10–50 meter range.

63. Sexwale Trial Record, Ndaba, v. 13, Box 61, 2292.

64. Donald L. Barnett and Karari Njama, *Mau Mau from Within: An Analysis of Kenya's Peasant Revolt* (New York: Modern Reader Paperbacks, 1966), 117–118.

65. Ibid.

66. Kumalo, interview.

67. Ngculu, interview.

68. Caroline Nkosi, interview.

69. "Cholera Found in Alexandra's Jukskei River," *Daily Dispatch*, January 19, 2001, http://www.queensu.ca/msp/pages/In_The_News/2001/January/jukskei.htm, date assessed June 22, 2008.

70. Then, Dutch leader Jan van Riebeeck planted an almond hedge bush to separate his colony, in what later became Cape Town, from the indigenous people, and presented South Africa with its first incarnation of apartheid.

71. European settlers had originally stopped at the Cape to replenish supplies before they journeyed to Asia in search of spices and other commodities. Eventually, they settled in Cape Town. Following years of colonization, the Dutch migrated inland to escape the British who had arrived in South Africa in 1789 with guns blaring. That was not the only way that the British, with their trademark redcoats, fired on all cylinders. They also challenged the Boers' rugged individualism and their relationship with the indigenous Khoisan, a group of hunter-gathers and farmers, whom they had enslaved. The British would have nothing of it, and in 1808, they issued the Hottentot Code, which granted some protective measures for slaves. This move went totally against the Boers' sensibilities. In fact, the Dutch descendants, who would later assume the name, Afrikaners, detested the British and their laws so much that they left the Cape and went on Great Treks into the interior to escape their political hold in 1834 and 1835; This began years of acrimony between the Afrikaners and the British that would later erupt during the South African War from 1899–1902; Bafana's rendition and my extrapolation of this well rehearsed story explores the different ways in which hegemony or domination by consent reared its ugly head. The topic of subjugation frames this story, as Bafana was careful to discuss the evolution of power and how a system of apartheid ultimately dictated how all South Africans lived. For information on the Boers' expansion, see Norman Etherington, The Great Treks: The Transformation of Southern Africa, 1815–1854 (New York: Pearson, 2001), for early Cape history see Richard Elphick and Hermann Giliomee, (eds) The Shaping of South African Society, 1652–1840 (Cape Town: Maskew Miller Longman, 1979) for research on the South African War see

Peter Warwick, Black People and the South African War 1899–1902 (Cambridge: Cambridge University Press, 1983), Bill Nasson, The South African War 1899–1902, (London: Arnold, 1999), Thomas Pakenham, The Boer War (New York: Random House, 1999).

72. Jackson Ngubane (pseudonym) interview, tape recording, Alexandra, South Africa, June 15, 2006.

73. Bheki R., (pseudonym) interview, tape recording, Alexandra, South Africa, June 10, 2006.

74. "Moyaha," Sexwale Trial Record, v. 12, January 27, 1978, 507.

75. Air rifles, which work either with compressed air or gas, release projectiles and differ from firearms which burn a repellant.

76. "Moyaha," Sexwale Trial Record, 516.

77. Tsiki, interview, 1255.

78. Tsiki, Deposition, 15.

79. Bheki, interview.

80. Raymond Suttner, *The ANC and the Underground.*

81. Ibid.

82. "Nighttime," interview, tape recording, Alexandra, South Africa, February 2, 2002.

83. "Nighttime," interview.

84. Ngubane, interview.

85. Chimurenga is a Shona word that means uprising.

86. David Martin and Phyllis Johnson, *The Struggle for Zimbabwe: The Chimurenga War* (New York: Monthly Review Press, 1981), 77–78. See also David Lan, *Guns and Rains: Spirit Mediums in Zimbabwe* (Berkeley: University of California Press, 1985).

87. "Nighttime," interview.

88. Ibid.

89. "Radio: Freedom: Voice of the African National Congress and the People's Army Umkhonto weSizwe," by Bill Nowlin, Rounder Records, 1996.

90. "Follow the Drinking Gourd," Owen Sound's Black History, http://www.osblackhistory.com/drinkinggourd.php date assessed 6 June 2009.

91. Ngubane, interview.

92. Bheki, interview.

Chapter 3

1. The State Versus: Mosima Sexwale and 11 Others, Case Number: CC. 431/77, Volume 48, Pretoria, April 5, 1978 (hereafter referred to as S v Mosima Sexwale, v. 49, Sexwale, 2381. Sexwale was no stranger to the police that he eluded. As a child, teenager, and young adult, he witnessed units patrolling his beloved Soweto in southwestern Johannesburg. Sexwale also experienced his family's stark poverty,

and when his father assumed responsibility of his brother's children, a family of six doubled in size. Added to the dire poverty that the family experienced, Sexwale witnessed a landscape littered with matchbox houses and walls inundated with political slogans; 425. Then, when the future business tycoon went to the restricted Whites-only area, he observed palatial homes and other forms of ostentation, confirming the stark reality of a Black and White South Africa. All of these conditions seared an indelible impression; however, despite Sexwale's inauspicious beginnings, his determination to succeed skyrocketed. Part of his transformation involved political education, and familiarizing himself with the policies and goals of the ANC and PAC and other leading political organizations. Sexwale argued that the ANC, which ran on a platform of multiracialism, refused to blame unlike the more militant PAC, the white minority or to declare race as the primary problem encumbering Africans. After learning more about the ANC and the Black Consciousness Movement, Sexwale concluded "that the methods [the ANC] had chosen could not be questioned, because there was no alternative: the nonviolent struggle seemed like a relic of the past, a myth which was suicidal in the 1960s and 1970s."

2. S v Mosima Sexwale, Judgment, 2278–2282. The other parties were David Charles Ramusi, Alois Manci and Amos Lubisi, 2302.

3. S v Mosima Sexwale, Judgment, 2278–2282.

4. Ibid.

5. Lynda Schuster, *A Burning Hunger: One Family's Struggle against Apartheid* (Athens: Ohio University, 2007). Nomkhita Mashinini visited her sons Dee and Tsietsi on separate occasions in jail.

6. Tim Cresswell, "Mobility as Resistance: Geographical Reading of Kerouac on the Road," *Transactions of the Institute of British Geographers*, 18, 2 (1993): 254. In his analysis of *On the Road*, Cresswell argues that moving from place to place signifies a form of resistance. Cresswell bases his interpretation on the main characters Sal and Dean who travel across America to escape hegemonic constructions of family and home. Cresswell writes, "as the story develops, it becomes clear the non-stop 'going' for its own sake is the main joy of the two friends."

7. Belinda Bozzoli, "Public Ritual and Private Transition: The Truth Commission in Alexandra Township, South Africa, 1996," 177.

8. Bozzoli, "Public Ritual and Private Transition."

9. Ibid.

10. Gregory Houston and Bernard Magubane, "The ANC Political Underground in the 1970s," in *The Road to Democracy in South Africa, Volume 2, 1970–1980*, South African Democracy Education Trust (Cape Town: Zebra Press, 2004), 395–396.

11. Victor Mogale, interview, tape recording, Wynberg, Johannesburg, April 15, 2002.

12. Mogale, interview.

13. Hilda Phahle, Mamokete Malaza, Esther Mtembu, interview, transcript, Truth and Reconciliation Commission, October 30, 1996, http://www.justice.gov.za/trc/hrvtrans/alex/phahle.htm date assessed May 4, 2006.

14. Schuster, *A Burning Hunger*, 129.

15. Anthony W. Marx, *Lessons of Struggle: South African Internal Opposition, 1960–1990* (New York: Oxford, 1992), 67.

16. Philip Bonner and Noor Nieftagodien, *Alexandra: A History*, (Johannesburg: Witwatersrand University Press, 2008), 180.

17. Fran Lisa Buntman, *Robben Island and Prisoner Resistance to Apartheid* (Cambridge: Cambridge University Press, 2003). In this work, Buntman discusses how Mandela and other prisoners fought for equality within the prison walls. The government instituted apartheid within its prison system by originally allowing Indians longer trousers, sugar with their tea, and some other privileges. Buntman also distinguishes between detainees and political prisoners while also discussing how the different political organizations, the ANC, the PAC, BC and others united and taught each other. See book review, Dawne Y. Curry, *Peace and Change* 31, July 3, 2006.

18. Anthony Marx, *Lessons of Struggle: South African Internal Opposition, 1960–1990* (New York: Oxford University Press, 1992), 67.

19. S v Mosima Sexwale, Judgment, 2278–2282.

20. S v Mosima Sexwale, testimony of Martin Ramokgadi 2330.

21. Elias Masilela, *Number 43, Kwa Magogo* (Cape Town: New Africa Books, 2011) 85.

22. Gregory Houston and Bernard Magubane, "The ANC Political Underground," in *The Road to Democracy in South Africa, Volume 2, 1970–1980*, South African Democracy Education Trust (Cape Town: Zebra Press, 2004), 425.

23. S v Mosima Sexwale, Judgment, 2330.

24. Darlene Clark Hine, William C. Hine and Stanley Harrold, *The African American Odyssey: Combined Volume*, Second Edition, (New Jersey: Prentice Hall, 2005), 201. During the American slavery era, abolitionists turned their homes, barns and haylofts into stations along the Underground Railroad in Washington, D. C., Michigan, Pennsylvania, and Ohio among other states and regions.

25. S v Mosima Sexwale, testimony of Martin Ramokgadi, 2330.

26. "Analysis of the Evidence of Carl Stephen Rabotho Whose Evidence Appears at p. 706," Vol. 18 to p. 731, Vol. 19, 1–3.

27. Masilela, *Number 43*, 99.

28. S v Mosima Sexwale, testimony of Victor Sithole, 382.

29. Ibid.

30. S v Mosima Sexwale, testimony of Victor Sithole, 384.

31. Ibid.

32. S v Mosima Sexwale, testimony of Martin Ramokgadi, 2245. Located on the N4, Malelane had served as the first rest stop between present-day Maputo, Mozambique (formerly Lourenco Marques, Mozambique), and Pretoria, South Africa. In the seventies, it formed part of Alexandra's extension as an underground network, as the court records and A. R.'s testimony indicated.

33. S v Mosima Sexwale, testimony of Martin Ramokgadi.

34. Richard Ngculu, interview.

35. Kumalo, interview.

36. Marx, *Lessons of Struggle*, 93.

37. Naledi Tsiki, Deposition to South African Police, 16.

38. Operatives used plastic and military explosives.

39. Tsiki, Deposition to South African Police, 17.

40. "Kaapmuiden," http://en.wikipedia.org/wiki/Kaapmuiden, date assessed June 17, 2011.

41. Naledi Tsiki, interview, 1259–1260.

42. "Polokwane," http://en.wikipedia.org/wiki/Polokwane date assessed August 4, 2011.

43. "Polokwane," http://en.wikipedia.org/wiki/Polokwane.

44. Personal communication with Todd Lethata, August 22, 2011.

45. Ibid.

46. Marx, *Lessons of Struggle*, 93.

47. Richard Ngculu, interview.

48. Werner Zips, *Black Rebels: African Caribbean Freedom Fighters in Jamaica* (Princeton: Marcus Weiner Publishers, 1999), 86–87.

49. Patrick Deer, *Culture in Camouflage: War, Empire, and Modern British Literature* (Oxford: Oxford University Press, 2009), 44.

50. "The Women Freedom Fighters of Zimbabwe," National Public Radio, 60 minutes, 1982.

51. Tsiki, "Deposition to South Africa Police," 13.

52. Ibid.

53. Tsiki, "Deposition to South Africa Police," 27.

54. Shana Penn, *Solidarity's Secret: the Women Who Defeated Communism in Poland* (Ann Arbor: University of Michigan, 2005), 183. Because women fell under the radar, Polish women successfully published anti-government sentiment, camouflaged their bodies, and helped to play a large role in changing the country's political climate.

55. Richard Ngculu, interview.

56. Lynda Schuster, *A Burning Hunger: One Family's Struggle Against Apartheid* (Athens: Ohio University Press, 2006).

57. Tsiki, "Deposition to South Africa Police," 13.

58. "Hope Themba Jamda" Sexwale Trial Record, July 14, 1977, v. 2, 776.

59. S v Mosima Sexwale, testimony of Hope Themba Jamda,777.
60. Tsiki, "Deposition to South Africa Police," 16.
61. S v Mosima Sexwale, testimony of Khoza, January 27, 1978, 537.
62. Tsiki, "Deposition to South Africa Police," 16.
63. S v Mosima Sexwale, testimony of Moyaha, 510–511.
64. Penn, *Solidarity's Secret*, 181.
65. S v Mosima Sexwale, testimony of Martin Ramokgadi, Emily Seane, Judgment, 2323.
66. S v Mosima Sexwale, Summary of Evidence of Alpheus Ramokgadi (in so far as it relates to Accused No. 11), 1366–67.
67. Raymond Suttner, *The ANC and the Underground*, 93.
68. Raymond Suttner, *ANC and the Underground* (Auckland Park: Jacana Media, 2008), 20–24.
69. Masilela, *Number 43*, 99. In his narrative about personal family history and its contribution to the liberation struggle, Elias Masilela explains some of the perils involved with maintaining a safe house. Swazi police often worked in concert with South African officials or occupants had to keep up the appearance of normality. *Catch a Fire.* This definitely held true for Patrick Chamusso and the Mozambican compound where he hides, enjoys camaraderie, sings Bob Marley's "Is this love," chooses a code name and conducts military drills. During a routine perusal of identity papers, the Mozambican police along with White South Africans stage a raid. On this somber occasion he witnesses his comrades dying when an all-white South African Defense Force, with the help of local Mozambicans, dons black faces, storms the lair and engages in a killing orgy.
70. Raymond Suttner, *The ANC Underground in South Africa* (Auckland Park, Jacana Media Press, 2008), 5.

Chapter 4

1. Sometimes uprising participants had butcher knives, knobkerries, guns and other weapons.
2. Cillie Commission Report, 31.
3. "Statement by Mr. T. Maboela, Supreme Court of South Africa (Witwatersrand Local Division) in the Case between the West Rand Administration Board and Santam Insurance Company Limited, April 22, 1981, 24, University of South Africa Archives, Pretoria, South Africa.
4. Irene Tukie March, interview, Alexandra Township, October 28, 1996, Truth and Reconciliation Commission, http://www.doj.gov.za/trc/hrvtrans/index.htm date assessed July 10, 2007.
5. Abie Mo, interview, tape recording, Alexandra, South Africa, May 5, 2002.
6. President-General African National Congress Memorandum to the Commission Appointed to Enquire into the Operation of Bus Services for Non-Europeans on the Witwatersrand and in the

Districts of Pretoria and Vereeniging, Xuma Papers ABX 430711d, 2. Xuma cited 87 instances of bus operators overloading. Over a four day period, his observations included jotting down bus numbers, license plates, tabulation of trips made and passengers per bus. The chart shows how the bus drivers exceeded the regulated capacity limit by 21, 13 and 15 people.
Bus No. Date Total Trips People Per Trip Avg.
T. J. 25777 26th August 1943 56 (all buses) 77
T. J. 53652 26th August 1943 56 (all buses) 70
T. J. 25777 26th August 1943 56 (all buses) 72

7. Belinda Bozzoli, *Theatres of Struggle and the End of Apartheid* (Athens: Ohio University Press, 2004).

8. Belinda Bozzoli, "Space, Identity in Rebellion: Power, Target, Resource," University of the Witwatersrand, Institute for Advanced Social Research, 1999. In this work, Bozzoli puts forth that bus boycotts and other protests in Alexandra, were defined by the use of space within the township. This was very evident during the 1976 student uprising when dwellers used the confined space to destroy symbols of apartheid. Belinda Bozzoli, Theatres of Struggle and the End of Apartheid, (Athens: Ohio University, 2004), 20–36.

9. Alan Brooks and Jeremy Brickhill, *Whirlwind Before the Storm: The Origins and Development of the Uprising in Soweto and the Rest of South Africa from June to December* 1976 (Johannesburg: International Defence and Aid Fund for Southern Africa, 1980), 24.

10. March, interview.

11. Miriam Sekele, interview, tape recording, Alexandra Township, April 24, 2002.

12. Mrs. M. (pseudonym) interview, tape recording, Alexandra, South Africa, May 5, 2002.

13. Philip Bonner and Noor Nieftagodien, *AleXandra: A History* (Johannesburg: University of Witwatersrand Press, 2008), 205.

14. Brooks and Brickhill, *Whirlwind before the Storm*, 20.

15. Pat Hopkins and Helen Grange, The Rocky Rioter Teargas Show: The Inside Story of the 1976 Soweto Uprising. (Cape Town: Zebra, 2001), 108.

16. Hopkins and Grange, The Rocky Rioter Teargas Show, 193–194. While on assignment in Alexandra, renowned photographer Peter Magubane shared, "I saw a man [Peter Jones] shot dead while he was on the toilet." Peter Magubane, Soweto: Fruit of Fear Apparently, Magubane was not the only witness as journalist Maria Shinn captured the scene with this description, "A stray bullet meant for the beer hall looters, hit him in the head. He lay crumpled at the door of the corrugated iron shack, his trousers around his ankles." The victim's friend also stood nearby weeping. "That's my best friend they shot in the lavatory. They shot him for nothing. He did nothing.

He was going to relieve himself." Hopkins and Grange, 193–194 Magubane also faced the police's wrath when one bludgeoned his nose. While Magubane suffered physical abuse, the worst injustice, the photographer believed, concerned his camera and its contents, which the police destroyed.

17. SADET, Noor Nieftagodien, "Alexandra and Kathorous," in *The Road to Democracy in South Africa* Volume 2 [1970–1980], South African Democracy Education Trust, (Pretoria: Unisa Press, 2006), 355.

18. Cillie Commission Report, 120.

19. Mark Mathabane, *Kaffir Boy* (New York: Free Press, 1986), 264.

20. Salani Sithole, interview, tape recording, Alexandra, South Africa, May 18, 2002.

21. Posters: Vorster and Kruger are Rubbish, Alexandra, June 1976, SAB K345, National Archives of South Africa, Pretoria, South Africa.

22. Cillie Commission Report, 33.

23. Mathabane, *Kaffir Boy*, 63.

24. Cillie Commission Report, 46.

25. "Alexandra Traders Protest Against Indian Traders," *Bantu World*, April 9, 1949. "Africans Wage "War" Against Indians," The *World*, November 10, 1956.

26. Mathabane, *Kaffir Boy*, 4.

27. Mathabane, *Kaffir Boy*.

28. Mathabane, *Kaffir Boy*, 67.

29. Mathabane, *Kaffir Boy*.

30. Ibid.

31. Rees, *Commission of Inquiry into the Riots at Soweto and other Places in South Africa held on 24 September 1976*, volume 14, 544–547.

32. Maria Shinn, *When Alexandra Went Up in Flames* in Peter Magubane, *Soweto: The Fruit of Fear* (Trenton: Africa World Press, 1986), no page numbers given.

33. Shinn, *When Alexandra Went Up in Flames*.

34. Mo, interview.

35. Cillie Commission Report, 32.

36. Rees, *Commission of Inquiry*, 548.

37. Abbey X., interview.

38. Ibid.

39. Fah-fee was a local lottery game whose numbers corresponded to different characters.

40. Mathabane, *Kaffir Boy*, 264.

41. Mathabane, *Kaffir Boy*.

42. Mathabane, *Kaffir Boy*, 265.

43. Mathabane, *Kaffir Boy*, 264.

44. Mathabane, *Kaffir Boy*.

45. Personal communication with Linda Twala in Alexandra Township, 2010.

46. "Jack Lerole," http://en.wikipedia.org/wiki/Jack_Lerole date assessed May 17, 2010. In 1958, Aaron "Big Voice" Jack Lerole and the Alexandra Shamba Boys recorded the song *Tom Hark*. The song was originally called tomahawk but record producers spelled it wrong. The song also became a theme to a British TV show called the Killing Stones. *Tom Hark* grossed over £250,000 but Lerole never saw any of the royalties. In 2003, Lerole died from cancer.

47. Susan Piliso, interview, tape recording, Alexandra, South Africa, March 15, 2002.

48. Piliso, interview.

49. Ben Mhlongo, interview, Alexandra, South Africa, January 8, 2002.

50. John Mhlontlo, interview, tape recording, Alexandra, South Africa, January 16, 2002.

51. Piliso, interview.

52. Godfrey Tshabalala, interview, tape recording, Alexandra, South Africa, May 28, 2002. Not long after my interview with Tshabalala he was killed by unknown assailants.

53. Titus Mathebidi, interview, tape recording, Wynberg, South Africa, March 14, 2002.

54. The Cillie Report, appendix.

55. Mo, interview.

56. Mathabane, *Kaffir Boy*, 52.

57. The Voice of the A. N. C. (Spear of the Nation) "The War is on," August 1976.

58. The Voice of the A. N. C.

59. Biko became not only a major proponent of the Black Consciousness Movement; he was also one of its chief theorists and practitioners. His *I Write what I like*, for example, details his thoughts on apartheid, his adherence to "Black is Beautiful," and his ideas on the meaning of Black. Borrowing and enhancing theory professed by African American theologians and by Caribbean Francophone poet and politician Aime Cesaire and Senegalese President Leopold Senghor with their concept of Negritude, Biko tried to instill pride.

60. Bonner and Nieftagodien, *AleXandra: A History*, 215. The same thing happened in the United States where natural locks replaced straightened hair and African garb superseded western style dress.

61. The Voice of the A. N. C.

62. Ibid.

63. Cillie Commission Report, 33.

64. Cillie Commission Report, 47.

65. "Statement by Mr. T. Maboela," 10.

66. "Statement by Mr. T. Maboela," 11.

67. "Statement by Mr. T. Maboela."

68. Shinn, *When Alexandra Went Up in Flames*.

69. Helena Pohlandt-McCormick, *"I Saw a Nightmare,": Doing Violence to Memory, June 16, 1976* (New York: Columbia University Press, 2006), 250.

70. Pohlandt-McCormick, *"I Saw a Nightmare,"* Essays on Beer Halls and Bottle Stores.

71. Shinn, *When Alexandra Went Up in Flames.*

72. James C. Scott, *Weapons of the Weak* (New Haven: Yale University, 1985).

73. Bonner and Nieftagodien. *Alexandra: A History,* 205.

74. Mhlongo, interview.

75. Mhlongo, interview.

76. Nancy L. Clark and William H. Worger, *South Africa-The Rise and Fall of Apartheid.* Seminar Studies in History, (New York: Pearson Education Limited, 48—52).

77. Bantu of Alexandra, III Folder 794 Political, SSRC, August 25, 1976.

78. Bonner and Nieftagodien, *Alexandra,* 201–202.

79. "Bantu of Alexandra."

80. Pohlandt-McCormick, "I Saw a Nightmare," Essays on Beer Halls and Bottle Stores.

81. Sithole, interview, tape recording, Alexandra, South Africa, May 18, 2002.

82. Memorandum for the City Boundaries Commission submitted by the Alexandra Coloured Associations representing the Coloured community of Alexandra Township, AD843/RJ Nal.2 File, Historical Papers, Cullen Library, University of Witwatersrand, Johannesburg, South Africa. Members earned their positions by appointment (Europeans), nominations or votes (Africans and Coloureds). Europeans occupied the largest number of positions, followed by Africans and then Coloureds. African and Coloured males aged 21 and above voted if they met the qualifications as explained in Proclamation No. 23 of 1921: maintained residence in Alexandra for three consecutive months, or attained status as a registered owner of immovable property.

83. Memorandum of Matters to be Discussed.

84. Ibid.

85. See Gavin Lewis, *Between the Wire and the Wall: A History of South African Coloured Politics* (New York: St. Martin's Press, 1987), Ian Goldin, *Making Race: The Politics of Economics and Coloured Identity* (London: Longman, 1987), and Zimitri Erasmus, *Coloured by History, Shaped by Place: New Perspectives on Coloured Identities in Cape Town* (Cape Town: Kwela, 2001), Mohammed Adhikari, *Not Black Enough, Not White Enough: Racial Identity in the South African Coloured Community* (Athens: Ohio University Press, 2005).

86. When the African Methodist Episcopal Church merged with the Apostolic Church, the educational center became known as the Alexandra Amalgamated School in 1936. The institution offered classes from Sub-Standard A to Standard Six. Its first principal was Mr. Ngubeni, but Mr. E. Noge, son of soccer star Simon Noge,

later succeeded him. In 1944, Noge left the school while his wife succeeded him at the Alexandra Amalgamated School. With the assistance of Reverend B. M. Sechaba of the AME, Noge established another institution called the Ithuthe Primary School which was divided into junior and senior sections; Belinda Bozzoli, "Space, Identity in Rebellion: Power, Target, Resource," University of the Witwatersrand, Institute for Advanced Social Research, 1999. In this work, Bozzoli puts forth that bus boycotts and other protests in Alexandra, were defined by the use of space within the township. This was very evident during the 1976 student uprising when dwellers used the confined space to destroy symbols of apartheid. Noge headed the school until his death in 1959, at which point, Mr. Ramaisa succeeded him.

87. Carol Britz, interview, tape recording, Alexandra, South Africa, April 16, 2002.

88. Britz, interview.

89. Dorah Molepo, interview, tape recording, Alexandra, South Africa, February 26, 2002. Women from diverse educational, occupational, and social backgrounds harnessed their power to teach females sewing, welding, gardening, catering, baking, candle making, computer technology, and furniture making.

90. Alinah Serote, interview, tape recording, Alexandra, South Africa, February 9, 2002. The group also differed from the Alexandra Interim Committee and Soweto's Black Parent Council (BPC), a coed group founded by Manas Buthelezi; both formed in the uprising's wake, which founders created to help parents who grieved the loss of loved ones, obtain legal fees.

91. Serote, interview, tape recording, Alexandra, South Africa, February 9, 2002.

92. Serote, interview.

93. John Carter, *Ray: A Memoir of Ray Carter* (Cape Town: Pretext, 1997), 39. Oppenheimer explained the rationale for establishing Women for Peace, "women were not bound as men [were] by politics of convention. We're free to operate."

94. Serote, interview.

95. March, interview.

96. Sipho Zungu, interview, tape recording, Parktown North, Johannesburg April 22, 2002.

97. Cillie Commission Report, 303.

98. Cillie Commission Report, 288.

99. Scott, *Weapons of the Weak*, 29.

100. Cillie Commission Report, 47.

101. Cllie Commission Report, 1–300.

102. Cllie Commission Report, 129. There were also arson attempts at the Pholosho School and the Gordon School.

103. Tshabalala, interview.
104. Mrs. M. L. Mbatha, interview, tape recording, Alexandra, South Africa, May 10, 2002.
105. K345 Exhibit 34: Alexandra and Soweto, Alexandra Skade Geboue [Damage to Buildings] opp cited Pohlandt-McCormick, "I Saw a Nightmare."
106. Pohlandt-McCormick, *"I Saw a Nightmare,"* Essays on Beer Halls and Bottle Stores.

Chapter 5

1. M. L. Mbatha, interview. Portions of this chapter originally appeared in Dawne Y. Curry, "When Apartheid Interfered with Funerals": We Still Found Ways to Grieve in Alexandra, South Africa, *International Journal of Interdisciplinary Social Sciences,* 2, 22 (2007): 245–252.
2. Mbatha, interview.
3. Ibid.
4. R. Margaret, interview, tape recording, Alexandra, South Africa, November 12, 2001.
5. Dawne Y. Curry, "When Apartheid Interfered with Funerals, We Still Found Ways to Grieve in Alexandra, South Africa," *International Journal of Interdisciplinary Social Studies,* 2, 22 (2007): 245.
6. Margaret, interview.
7. Ibid.
8. Mbatha, interview.
9. Ibid.
10. ibid.
11. Belinda Bozzoli, "Ritual and Transition,": The Truth Commission in Alexandra, Township, South Africa 1996." University of the Witwatersrand Institute for the Advanced Social Research, Seminar Paper No. 435, 1998, 10–11.
12. Belinda Bozzoli, Ritual and Transition, 10–11.
13. Gary Kynoch. *We are Fighting the World: A History of the Marashea Gangs in South Africa, 1947–1999* (Athens: Ohio University Press, 2005), 139.
14. Cillie Commission Report, 109.
15. Ibid., 115.
16. Cillie Commission Report.
17. Pat Hopkins and Helen Grange, The Rocky Rioter Teargas Show: The Inside Story of the 1976 Soweto Uprising. (Cape Town: Zebra, 2001), 108.
18. Cillie Report, "Appendix," 105–120.
19. Ramatsobane Masenya, interview, October 28, 1996, Alexandra Township. Truth and Reconciliation Commission, http://www.

doj.gov.za/trc/hrvtrans/index.htm., date assessed March 28, 2010.

20. Masenya, interview. Belinda Bozzoli, "Ritual and Transition," 11.
21. Ibid.
22. Bozzoli, "Ritual and Transition," 10–11.
23. Belinda Bozzoli, *Theatres of Struggle and the End of Apartheid* (Athens: Ohio University, 2004), 206–232.
24. Belinda Bozzoli, "Ritual and Transition," 10-11.
25. Bozzoli, *Theatres of Struggle and the End of Apartheid* (Athens: Ohio University, 2004), 213–219. Portions of this section originally appeared in Dawne Y. Curry book review, H-SAfrica http:www.h-net.org, 2005.
26. Reverend Snoekie Mzambu, interview, Alexandra Township, October 28, 1996. Truth and Reconciliation Commission, http://www.doj.gov.za/trc/hrvtrans/index.htm.
27. Mzambu, interview.
28. Snoekie Mzambu, interview. October 28, 1996, Alexandra Township. Truth and Reconciliation Commission, http://www.doj.gov.za/trc/hrvtrans/index.htm., date assessed April 4, 2006.
29. Jabu James Malinga, interview. 28 October. Alexandra Township. Truth and Reconciliation Commission, http://www.doj.gov.za/trc/hrvtrans/index.htm, date assessed March 5, 2008.
30. Malinga, interview.
31. Ibid.
32. Bozzoli, "Ritual and Transition," 10–11.
33. Ibid., 10.
34. Jessie Busisiwe Moquae, interview. October 28, 1996, Alexandra Township. Truth and Reconciliation Commission, http://www.doj.gov.za/trc/hrvtrans/index.htm., date assessed August 8, 2006.
35. Irene Tukie March, interview, Alexandra Township, October 28, 1996, Truth and Reconciliation Commission, http://www.doj.gov.za/trc/hrvtrans/index.htm date assessed July 10, 2007.
36. Lesoro Mohlimi, interview, October 29, 1996, Alexandra Township. Truth and Reconciliation Commission, http://www.doj.gov.za/trc/hrvtrans/index.htm., date assessed February 3, 2005.
37. Bozzoli, "Ritual and Transition, 10.
38. Bozzoli, "Ritual and Transition."
39. Kenneth J. Doka, *Disenfranchised Grief: Recognizing Hidden Sorrow* (Maryland: Lexington Books, 1989), 3.
40. Farah Gilanshah. "Islamic Customs Regarding Death," in Donald P. Irish, Kathleen F. Lundquist and Vivian Jenkins Nelson (eds). *Ethnic Variations in Dying, Death and Grief: Diversity in Universality.* Washington, D. C.: Taylor and Francis, 1993), 141. In Islamic culture, for example, in preparation for the funeral relatives take the deceased to the place where they bathe the corpse.

41. Dokkie Elias Mayisa, interview. October 30, 1996, Alexandra Township. Truth and Reconciliation Commission, http://www.doj.gov.za/trc/hrvtrans/index.htm., date assessed March 18, 2006.

42. Belinda Bozzoli, "Ritual and Transition," 12. Obtaining the corpses was so important that Ntombizodwa Sidzumo waited until fire died down to get the corpses of her family. Fortunately for her, they had hidden in the bushes. Bozzoli's discussion not only analyzes the loss of Alexandran life, she also explores the abuse of the bodies. I, on the other hand, discuss in greater depth, the need to reclaim bodies to further African customs that included the importance of visiting the sites of death.

43. Richard A. Wilson, *The Politics of Truth and Reconciliation in South Africa: Legitimizing the Post-Apartheid State* (Cambridge: Cambridge University Press, 2001), 120.

44. N. L. Rivers, interview. October 30, 1996, Alexandra Township. Truth and Reconciliation Commission, http://www.doj.gov.za/trc/hrvtrans/index.htm., date assessed February 2, 2006.

45. Rivers, interview.

46. Bozzoli, "Ritual and Transition," 10.

47. Ntombidzudoa Sidzumo, interview October 28, 1996, Alexandra Township. Truth and Reconciliation Commission, http://www.doj.gov.za/trc/hrvtrans/index.htm date assessed March 28, 2010.

48. Bozzoli, "Ritual and Transition," 10.

49. Ibid. Margaret Madlana, interview. October 28, 1996, Alexandra Township. Truth and Reconciliation Commission, http://www.doj.gov.za/trc/hrvtrans/index.htm., date assessed March 3, 2006.

50. Mohlimi, interview.

51. Ibid.

52. Belinda Bozzoli, "Ritual and Transition," 10.

53. Ibid.

54. Bozzoli, "Ritual and Transition," 10.

55. Hilda Phahle, interview. October 30, 1996, Alexandra Township. Truth and Reconciliation Commission, http://www.doj.gov.za/trc/hrvtrans/index.htm., date assessed January 2, 2006.

56. Esther Mtembu, interview. October 30, 1996, Alexandra Township. Truth and Reconciliation Commission, http://www.doj.gov.za/trc/hrvtrans/index.htm., date assessed January 2, 2006.

57. Madlana, interview.

58. Phahle, interview.

59. *Amandla: A Revolution in Four Part Harmony.* 108 min. Lions Gate Entertainment. United States, 2002. DVD.

60. See Clifton Crais and Pamela Scully, *Sara Baartman and the Hottentot Venus: A Ghost Story and a Biography* (Princeton: Princeton University Press, 2010).Rachel Holmes, African Queen: The Real Life of the Hottentot Venus (New York: Random House, 2007).

Natasha-Gordon Chipembere, *Representation and Black Womanhood: The Legacy of Sarah Baartman* (New York: Palgrave, 2011).

61. Mark Mathabane, *Kaffir Boy* (New York: Free Press, 1986) 267.
62. Mathabane, *Kaffir Boy*.
63. A Gathering of Nations: Linda Twala, http://www.sandtonmag.co.za/pages/421483389/Articles/2008/November/hero-linda-twala.asp date assessed August 2, 2010.
64. Meira Weiss, "Bereavement, Commemoration, and Collective Identity in Contemporary Israeli Society," *Anthropological Quarterly* 70, 2 (April 1997): 97.
65. Dawne Y. Curry, "When Apartheid Interfered with Funerals," 246–250.
66. Bozzoli, "Ritual and Transition," 11.
67. Rivers, interview.
68. Bozzoli, "Ritual and Transition," 11.
69. March, interview.
70. Bozzoli, "Ritual and Transition," 11.
71. Dimikatso Makajane, interview, October 28, 1996. Alexandra Township. Truth and Reconciliation Commission, http://www.doj.gov.za/trc/hrvtrans/index.htm, date assessed June 9, 2006.
72. Terry L. Martin and Kenneth J. Doka, *Men Don't Cry, Women Do: Transcending Gender Stereotypes of Grief* (Philadelphia: Brunner/Mazel, 2000), 12.
73. Petri Ravio. "This is Where they Fought': Finnish War Landscape as a National Heritage," in T. G. Ashplant et al. *The Politics of War Memory and Commemoration*, (London: Routledge, 2000), 149–150.
74. In African customs, they have a ceremony to unveil the tombstone.
75. March, interview.
76. Ibid.
77. Ibid.
78. Alan Lester, "Introduction: Historical Geographies of Southern Africa," *Journal of Southern African Studies*, 29, 3 (September 2003): 606.
79. March, interview.
80. Dawne Y. Curry, "Community, Culture and Resistance in Alexandra, South Africa 1912–1985," PhD dissertation, Michigan State University, East Lansing, Michigan, 2006, 152–153.

CONCLUSION: DAVID'S STORY

1. Beauty More, interview, Alexandra, South Africa, May 27, 2002.
2. Ibid, 153.
3. Ibid.

4. Anonymous, interview, tape recording, Alexandra, South Africa, May 3, 2002.

5. S. Refilwe, interview, tape recording, Alexandra, South Africa May 3, 2002.

6. S. Refilwe, interview.

7. "David," (pseudonym), interview, Alexandra, South Africa, May 22, 2002.

8. David, interview.

9. Veli Mahopa, interview, Alexandra, South Africa, March 5, 2002.

10. Ibid.

11. Carol Britz, interview, Alexandra, South Africa, April 16, 2002.

12. Belinda Bozzoli, *Theatres of Struggle and the End of Apartheid* (Athens: Ohio University, 2004), Throughout this work, Bozzoli discusses how until the 1986 Alexandra Six Day's War how township exercised normal relations, in other words, that war disrupted everyday patterns of existence.

13. S. Refilwe, interview.

14. David, interview.

15. Thoko Mngoma influenced many people in Alexandra; one of them was Zithulele Msimang. During my interview with him, he explained and refuted notions that a leadership vacuum existed from the 1960s to the 1970s. He was one of the few men who paid homage to a female leader and attributed her influence on a younger generation. Sue Gordon features Mngoma in her work, *A Talent for Tomorrow: Life Stories of South African Servants* (Johannesburg: Ravan Press, 1985), 95–105.

16. David, interview.

17. S. Refilwe, interview

18. Ibid.

19. Ibid.

BIBLIOGRAPHY

PRIMARY SOURCES

Newspapers

African Drum
Bantu Forum
Bantu World
Cape Standard
Drum Magazine
Guardian
Ilanga Lase Natal (Natal Sun)
Inkululeko (Freedom)
Inkundla ya Bantu
Izwi Lase Township
Rand Daily Mail
Sechaba
Sowetan
Star (Johannesburg)
UmAfrika
Umsebenzi (The Worker)
Umteteli wa Bantu (The African Mouthpiece)
World
Workers Voice

INTERVIEWS

Abi Mo, Twelfth Avenue, Alexandra, South Africa, May 5, 2002.
Anonymous, Alexandra, South Africa, 2 June 2008.
Carol Britz, Fourth Avenue, Alexandra, South Africa, April 16, 2002.
Reverend Sam Buti, Alexandra, South Africa, July 22, 2002.
Tshediso Buti, Alexandra, South Africa, January 17, 2002.
Lucas Cele, Alexandra, South Africa, May 10, 2002.
"David," Alexandra, South Africa, May 22, 2002.
Peter Fox, Alexandra, South Africa, May 12, 2002.
Ethel Germaine, Eighth Avenue, Alexandra, South Africa, April 26, 2002.
H. Bopape (pseudonym), Alexandra, South Africa, June 11, 2008.
Josiah Jele, Sunnyside, Pretoria, April 2, 2002.

Dennis Johnstone, Alexandra, South Africa, March 10, 2002.
Freddy Lekiso Kumalo, Alexandra, South Africa.
Tsietsi Kungoane, Alexandra, South Africa, March 21, 2002.
Todd Lethata, Melville, Johannesburg, January 20, 2002.
Freddy Lekiso Kumalo, Alexandra, South Africa, March 3, 2002.
Mrs. M. Alexandra, South Africa, May 5, 2002.
Sheila Maabe, Alexandra, South Africa, April 26, 2002.
Arthur Magerman, Alexandra, South Africa, January 29, 2002.
Veli Mahopa, Alexandra, South Africa, March 5, 2002.
Margaret R., Alexandra, South Africa, November 12, 2001.
Doreen Mashonte, Second Visit, Alexandra, South Africa, April 23, 2002.
Titus Mathibedi, Wynberg, Johannesburg, March 14, 2002.
Reginald Matthews, Alexandra, South Africa, April 31, 2002.
Mrs. M. L. Mbatha, Alexandra, South Africa, May 4, 2002.
Inhlanhla Mgenge, Alexandra Township, April 10, 2002.
Ben Mhlongo, Alexandra, South Africa, January 8, 2002.
John Mhlontlo, Alexandra, South Africa, January 16, 2002.
Thabo Mnisi, Alexandra, South Africa, May 7, 2002.
Abi Mo, Alexandra, South Africa, May 5, 2002.
Minah Moche, Alexandra, South Africa, June 19, 2002.
Victor Mogale, Wynberg, Johannesburg, April 15, 2002
Martha Mokgatle, Alexandra, South Africa, March 21, 2002.
Patricia Mokoae, Alexandra, South Africa, April 10, 2002.
Bennet Mokoena, Alexandra Township, May 21, 2002.
Dorah Molepo, Alexandra, South Africa, February 26, 2002.
Beauty More, Alexandra, South Africa, May 27, 2002.
P. Mphahlele, Alexandra, South Africa, July 2, 2002.
Zithulele Msimang, Alexandra, South Africa, April 18, 2002.
J. Ngcobo (pseudonym), Alexandra, South Africa, March 3, 2002.
Beauty Nhlapo, Alexandra, South Africa, June 13, 1998.
Richard Ngculu, (pseudonym), Alexandra, South Africa, June 11, 2006.
Jackson Ngubane, Alexandra, South Africa, June 10, 2006.
Ben Nkosi, Alexandra, South Africa, June 10, 2007.
Caroline Nkosi, Alexandra, South Africa, December 9, 2001.
Simon Noge, Alexandra, South Africa, March 9, 2002.
Susan Noge, Alexandra, South Africa, March 23, 2002.
Katie Oleni, Alexandra, South Africa, March 3, 2002.
Rose Innes Phahle, Illovo, Johannesburg, February 4, 2002.
Susan Piliso, Third Avenue, Alexandra, South Africa, March 15, 2002.
Thomas Sipho Piliso, Alexandra Township, March 3, 2002.
Dorothy Morwesi Pitso, Alexandra, South Africa, February 15, 2001.
Mr. Q, Alexandra, South Africa, May 22, 2002.
Jan Sekele, Alexandra, South Africa, April 24, 2002
Miriam Sekele, Alexandra, South Africa, April 24, 2002.
Refilwe S., Alexandra, South Africa.

Simon Selepe, Alexandra, South Africa, February 9, 2002.
Alinah Serote, Alexandra, South Africa, February 9, 2002.
Salani Sithole, Alexandra, South Africa, May 18, 2002.
Godfrey "Ginger" Tshabalala, Alexandra, South Africa, May 28, 2002.
Jika Twala, Alexandra, South Africa December 9, 2001.
Linda Twala, Alexandra, South Africa, July 31, 2010.
Mrs. X., Alexandra, South Africa, March 9, 2002.
Sipho Zungu, Parktown North, Johannesburg, April 22, 2002.

ARCHIVES CONSULTED

Historical Papers, Cullen Library, University of Witwatersrand.
Institute of Commonwealth Studies, London, England.
Killie Campbell Library, Durban South Africa.
National Archives of South Africa, Pretoria, South Africa.

COMMISSION REPORTS

Transvaal Province. T. P. 6-'37 Report of the Johannesburg and Germiston Boundaries Commission Part Three. (Feetham Commission), Pretoria: Government Printer, 1937.

Union Government (UG). Report of the Native Affairs Commission Appointed to Enquire into the Workings of the Provisions of the Native (Urban Areas) Act Relating to the Use and Supply of Kaffir beer. Pretoria: Government Printer, 1925.

UG. 39'25 Report of the Native Affairs Commission. Pretoria: Government Printer, 1925.

UG. Report of the Inter-Departmental Committee on the Social, Health and Economic Conditions of Urban Natives (Smit Committee). Pretoria: Government Printer, 1942.

UG. 42-'41 Report of the Native Affairs Commission 1939–40. Pretoria: Government Printer, 1932.

UG. 31-'44 Report of the Commission Appointed to Inquire into the Operation of Bus Services For Services for Non-Europeans on the Witwatersrand and in the Districts of Pretoria and Vereeniging, 1944. Pretoria: Government Printer, 1944.

University of Witwatersrand, Historical and Literary Papers and Government Publications Libraries.

Alfred B. Xuma Papers.

Alexandra Youth Civic Organisation.

Alexandra Residents Association.

Alexandra Treason Trial.

Commission of Inquiry into the Riots at Soweto and other Places in South Africa (Cillie Report).

Ellen Hellman Papers.

John David Rheinallt Papers.
Karis/Gerhart Political Trials.
Mayekiso Trial.
Sexwale Trial and Eleven Others.
South African Institute of Race Relations, Records.
Treason Trial.
Institute of Commonwealth Studies, London, England.
Hyman Basner Papers.
Josie Palmer Papers.
South Africa Truth and Reconciliation Commission (online archive of oral testimonies on 1960s-1994) http://www.justice.gov.za/trc/

SECONDARY SOURCES

Abbink, Jon and Ineke van Kessel (eds.). *Vanguard or Vandals: Youth, Politics and Conflict in Africa.* Leiden: Brill, 2005.

Adam, H. *Modernizing Racial Domination: The Dynamics of South African Politics.* Berkeley: University of California Press, 1971.

Alexandra, Peter. *War and the Origins of Apartheid: Labour and Politics in South Africa, 1939–48.* Athens: Ohio University Press, 2000.

Allman, Jean (ed.). *Fashioning Africa: Power and Politics of Dress.* Bloomington: Indiana University Press, 2004.

Anderson, Benedict. *Imagined Communities.* London: Verso Books, 1988.

Anderson, P. "The Antimonies of Antonio Gramsci." *New Left Review*, 100, (November 1976-January 1977): 76–89.

Ashforth, Adam. *The Politics of Official Discourse in Twentieth Century South Africa.* Oxford: Oxford University Press, 1992.

Baines, G. "The Origins of Urban Segregation: Local Government and the Residence of Port Elizabeth c. 1835–1865." *South African Historical Journal*, 22, 6 (1990): 61–81.

Baldwin, Alan. "Mass Removals and Separate Development." *Journal of Southern African Studies*, 1 (1974): 32–46.

Ballentine, Christopher. "Music and Emancipation: The Social Role of Black Jazz and Vaudeville in South Africa between the 1910s and the Early 1940s." *Journal of Southern African Studies*, 17, 1 (March 1991): 25–36.

Ballinger, Mary. *From Union to Apartheid: A Trek to Isolation.* Johannesburg: Witwatersrand University Press, 1969.

Beinart, William. *Twentieth-Century South Africa.* 2nd ed. Oxford: Oxford University Press, 2001.

Benjamin, A. "Kings of Alexandra." *Africa South*, 3, 3 (1959): 29–34.

Benson, Mary. *South Africa: The Struggle for a Birthright.* New York: Funk & Wagnalls, 1969.

Berger, Iris. *Threads of Solidarity: Women in South African Industry 1900–1980.* Indianapolis: Indiana University Press, 1992.

——. "Sources of Class Consciousness: South African Women in Recent Labour Struggles." *International Journal of African Historical Studies*, 16, 1 (1993): 49–66.

Bernstein, Hilda. *For Their Triumphs and for Their Tears: Women in Apartheid South Africa*. London: International Defence Fund, 1975.

Blackwell, Basil. *Unfairly Structured Cities*. Oxford: Oxford University Press, 1994.

Bloch, R., P. Wilkinson. "Urban Control and Popular Struggle: A Survey of State Urban Policy, 1920–1970." *Africa Perspective*, 20 (1982): 23–37.

Blomley, Nicholas. "Law, Property, and the Geography of Violence: The Frontier, the Survey, and the Grid." *Annals of the Association of American Geographers*, 93, 1 (March 2003): 121–141.

Bloom, H. "The South African Police: Laws and Powers." *Africa South*, 2, 2 (1958): 63–74.

Bonin, Debby. "Claiming Spaces, Changing Places: Political Violence and Women's Protests in Kwa-Zulu-Natal," *Journal of Southern African Studies*, 26, 2 (June 2000): 301–317.

Bonner, Philip, Noor Nieftagodien. *Alexandra, A History*. Johannesburg: University of Witwatersrand Press, 2008.

—— et al., (eds.). *Holding Their Ground: Class, Locality and Culture in 19th and 20th Century South Africa*. Johannesburg: Ravan and University of the Witwatersrand Press, 1989.

Bonner, Philip. "The Politics of Black Squatter Movements on the Rand, 1944–1952," *Radical History Review* (Winter 1990): 46–47.

——. "Family, Crime and Political Consciousness on the East Rand, 1939–1955," *Journal of Southern African Studies*, 14, 3 (April 1988): 393–420.

Bozzoli, Belinda. *Theatres of Struggle and the End of Apartheid*. Athens: Ohio University Press, 2004.

——. "Space and Identity in Rebellion: Power, Target, Resource." Seminar Paper. Institute for Advanced Social Research 446, 24 May 1999.

——. "From Ungovernability to Ungovernability: Race, Class and Authority in South Africa's Black Cities." Seminar Paper. Institute for Advanced Social Research. 18 May 1996.

——. "Public Ritual and Private Transition: The Truth Commission in Alexandra Township, South Africa, 1996." *African Studies*, 57, 2 (1998): 96–108.

——. *Women of Phokeng*. Johannesburg: Ravan Press, 1991.

—— (ed.). *Class, Community and Conflict: South African Perspectives*. Johannesburg: Ravan Press, 1987.

—— (ed.). *Town and Countryside in the Transvaal: Capitalist Penetration and Popular Response*. Johannesburg: Ravan Press, 1983.

—— (ed.). *Labour, Townships and Protest: Studies in the Social History of the Witwatersrand*. Johannesburg: Ravan Press, 1979.

Borstelmann, Thomas. *Apartheid's Reluctant Uncle: The United States and Southern Africa in the Early Cold War.* Oxford: Oxford University Press, 1993.

Bradford, Helen. *A Taste of Freedom: The ICU in Rural South Africa, 1924–1930.* Johannesburg: Ravan Press, 1988.

Brewer, J. *Black and Blue: Policing in South Africa.* Oxford: Oxford University Press, 1994.

Brooks, Pamela E. *Boycotts, Buses, and Passes: Black Women's Resistance in the U. S. South and South Africa.* Amherst: University of Massachusetts, 2008.

Bundy, Colin. "Street Sociology and Pavement Politics: Some Aspects of Student/Youth Consciousness during the 1985 Schools Crisis in Greater Cape Town," *Journal of Southern African Studies,* 13, 3 (1987): 52–68.

Buntman, Fran Lisa. *Robben Island and Prisoner Resistance to Apartheid.* Cambridge: Cambridge University Press, 2003.

Buti, Tony. "The Systematic Removal of Indigenous Children from Their Families in Australia and Canada: The History-Similarities and Differences, 8, http://www.newcastle.edu.au/centre/cispr/conferences/land/butipaper.pdf.

Butler, Kim D. *Freedoms Given, Freedoms Won: Afro-Brazilians in Post Abolition Sao Paulo and Salvador.* New Brunswick: Rutgers, 1998.

Callinicos, Luli. *Gold and Workers 1886–1940: Factories, Townships and Popular Culture on the Rand.* Volume II. *A People's History of South Africa.* Johannesburg: Ravan Press, 1987.

——. *A Place in the City: The Rand on the Eve of Apartheid: A People's History of South Africa.* Johannesburg: Ravan Press, 1987.

Carter, Charles. "We are the Progressives:" Alexandra Youth Congress Activists Charter, 1983–85." *Journal of Southern African Studies,* 17, 2 (June 1991): 197–220.

Carter, John. *Ray: A Memoir of Ray Carter.* Cape Town: Pretext, 1997.

Cell, John W. *The Highest Stage of White Supremacy: The Origins of Segregation in SouthAfrica and the American South.* Cambridge: Cambridge University Press, 1982.

Christopher, A. J. "Race and Residence in Colonial Port Elizabeth," *South African GeographicalSociety,* 69, 1 (1987): 3–20.

——. "Segregation Levels in South African Cities, 1911–1985," *International Journal of African Historical Studies,* 25, 3 (1992): 561–582.

——. "The Roots of Urban Segregation: South Africa at Union, 1910." *The Journal of Historical Geography,* 14, 2 (1988): 151–169.

Cobley, Alan Gregor. *Class and Consciousness: The Black Petty Bourgeoisie in South Africa, 1924 to 1950.* New York: Greenwood Press, 1990.

Cock, Jacklyn. *Maids and Madams: A Study of the Politics of Exploitation.* Johannesburg: Ravan Press, 1980.

——. *Colonels and Cadres: War and Gender in South Africa.* Cape Town: Oxford, 1991.

Cole, Josette. *Crossroads: The Politics of Reform and Repression, 1976–1986.* Johannesburg: Ravan Press, 1987.

Coplan, David. *In Township Tonight!.* London: Longman, 1985.

Crankshaw, Owen. "Apartheid and Economic Growth: Craft Unions, Capital and The State in the South African Building Industry, 1945–1975." *Journal of Southern African Studies,* September 16, 3 (1990): 167–178.

——. *Race, Class and the Changing Division of Labor Under Apartheid.* 1994.

Curry, Dawne Y. "When Apartheid Interfered With Funerals: We Still Found Ways to Grieve in Alexandra, South Africa." *International Journal of Interdisciplinary Social Sciences,* 2, 22 (2007): 245–252.

Damoyi, Pascal. "We Must Ensure Houses for All: Dispute in Alexandra Township," *Work in Progress,* 44, (September/October 1986): 12–14.

Davenport, T. R. H. "African Townsmen? South African Natives (Urban Areas) Legislation through the Years." *African Affairs,* 68, 271 (1969): 450–462.

——. "The Triumph of Colonel Stallard: The Transformation of the Natives (Urban Areas) Act between 1923 and 1937." *South African Historical Journal,* 2 (1970): 320–335.

——. (1971) "The Beginnings of Urban Segregation in South Africa: The Natives (Urban Areas) Act of 1923 and Its Background." Occasional Paper 15, Institute for Social and Economic Research, Rhodes University.

Deer, Patrick. *Culture in Camouflage: War, Empire, and Modern British Literature.* Oxford: Oxford University Press, 2009.

De Kiewet, C. W. *A History of South Africa: Social and Economic.* New York: Oxford University Press, 1991.

Diani, Mario. "The Concept of the Social Movement," *The Sociological Review,* 40, 1 (February 1992): 64–78.

Dikobe, Modikwe. *Dispossessed.* Johannesburg: Ravan Press, 1983.

Dingake, Michael. *My Fight Against Apartheid.* London: Kliptown, 1987.

Diseko, N. "Origins and the Development of the South African Students Movement," *Journal of Southern African Studies,* 1 (March 1991): 40–62.

Dreyer, Peter. *Martyrs and Fanatics: South Africa and Human Destiny.* New York: Simon and Schuster, 1980.

Dubow, Saul. *The African National Congress.* Johannesburg: Jonathan Ball Publishers, 2000.

——. "Holding a Just Balance Between White and Black': The Native Affairs Department in South Africa, c. 1920–33." *Journal of Southern African Studies,* 12, 2 (April 1986): 217–239.

——. *Racial Segregation and the Origins of Apartheid in South Africa, 1919–1936.* Oxford: Oxford University Press, 1989.

——. "Afrikaner Nationalism, Apartheid and the Conceptualization of 'Race'" *The Journal of African History,* 33, 2 (1992): 209–237.

——. *Scientific Racism in Modern South Africa.* Cambridge: Cambridge University Press, 1995.

———. "Ethnic Euphemisms and Racial Echoes," *Journal of Southern African Studies*, 20, 3 (September 1994): 50–63.

Duncan, David. "Liberals and Local Administration in South Africa: Alfred Hoernle' and The Alexandra Health Committee, 1933–1943," *International Journal of African Historical Studies*, 23, 2 (1990): 475–493.

Dunston, J. *Alexandra, I Love You: A Record of Seventy Years.* Johannesburg: Alexandra Liaison Committee, 1984.

Du Toit, Brian M. "Afrikaners, Nationalists, and Apartheid," *Journal of Southern African Studies*, 8, 4 (December 1970): 531–551.

Edgar, Robert (ed.). *An African American in South Africa: The Travel Notes of Ralph Bunche.* Athens: Ohio University Press, 1992.

———. *Freedom in Our Lifetime: The Collected Writings of Anton Muziwakhe Lembede.* Athens: Ohio University Press, 1996.

——— and Hilary Sapire. *African Apocalypse: The Story of Nontetha Nkwenkwe, a Twentieth-Century South African Prophet.* Athens: Ohio University, 2000.

Eggars, Dave. *What is the What.* New York: Vintage, 2007.

Erlmann, Veit. "Black Political Song in South Africa: Some Research Perspectives," in International Association for the Study of Popular Music, *Popular Music Perspectives* 2, Goteborg: IASPM, 1985.

Evans, Ivan. "Racial Domination, Capitalist Hegemony and the State Review Essay of *Legitimating the Illegitimate* by Stanley Greenberg." *South African Sociological Review*, 1, 1 (1988): 220–235.

———. *Bureaucracy and Race: Native Administration in South Africa.* Berkeley: University of California Press, 1997.

Everett, David. "Alliance Politics of a Special Type: The Roots of the ANC/SACP Alliance, 1950–1954," *Journal of Southern African Studies*, 18, 1 (March 1991): 19–39.

Fair, J. J. D., Manfred Shaffer. "Population Patterns and Policies in South Africa, 1951–1960," *Economic Geography*, 40, 3 (July 1964): 261–274.

——— and C. F. Schmidt. "Contained Urbanisation: A Case Study," *South African Geographical Journal*, 56, 2 (1974): 155–166.

Fanon, Frantz. *A Dying Colonialism.* New York: Grove Press, 1994.

Fatton, Robert. *Black Consciousness in South Africa: The Dialectics of Ideological Resistance to White Supremacy.* Albany: State University of New York Press, 1986.

Feit, Edward. *African Opposition in South Africa: The Failure of Passive Resistance.* Stanford: The Hoover Institution on War, Revolution and Peace, 1967.

———. *Urban Revolt in South Africa, 1960–1964.* Evanston: Northwestern University Press, 1971.

Field, Sean (ed.). *Lost Communities, Living Memories: Remembering Forced Removals in Cape Town.* Cape Town: David Philip, 2001.

Fine, Robert, Dennis Davis. *Beyond Apartheid: Labour and Liberation in South Africa.* London: Pluto Press, 1990.

First, Ruth. "The Bus Boycott." *Africa South*, 2, 3 (1957): 63–72.

Floyd, T. B. *Township Layout*. Pietermaritzburg: Shuter and Shooter, 1951.

Fortescue, Domenic. "The Communist Party of South Africa and the African Working Class in the 1940's," *International Journal of African Historical Studies*, 24, 3 (1991): 481–512.

Frankel, Philip. "The Politics of Passes: Control and Change in South Africa," *Journal of Modern African Studies*, 17, 2 (June 1979): 199–217.

Fredrickson, George. *White Supremacy: A Comparative Study on American and South African History*. New York: Oxford University Press, 1981.

———. *Black Liberation*. New York: Oxford University Press, 1995.

Friedland, Elaine A. "The South African Freedom Movement: Factors Influencing Its Ideological Development 1912–1980s," *Journal of Black Studies*, 13, 3 (March 1983): 337–354.

Furlong, Patrick. *Between the Sword and Swastika: The Impact of the Radical Right on the Afrikaner Nationalist Movement in the Fascist Era*. Middletown: Wesleyan University Press, 1991.

Gerhart, Gail M. *Black Power in South Africa: The Evolution of an Ideology*. Berkeley: University of California Press, 1978.

Giddens, A. and D. Held. (eds.). *Classes, Power and Conflict*. London: Cambridge University Press, 1982.

Gilanshah, Farah. "Islamic Customs Regarding Death." in Donald P. Irish, Kathleen F. Lundquist and V. Nelson (eds). *Ethnic Variations in Dying, Death and Grief: Diversity in Universality*. Washington, D. C.: Taylor and Francis, 1993.

Giliomee, H. and L. Schlemmer. (eds.). *Up Against the Fences: Poverty, Passes, and Privilege in South Africa*. Cape Town: Juta Press, 1985.

Gillepsie, James A. "Class in Urban History: A Review Article," *Comparative Studies in Society and History*, 26 (January 1984): 167–173.

Glaser, Clive. *Bo-Tsotsi: The Youth Gangs of Soweto, 1935–1976*. Portsmouth: Heinemann, 2000.

———. 'We must Infiltrate the Tsotsis': School Politics and Youth Gangs in Soweto 1968–1976,' *Journal of Southern African Studies*, 24, 2 (1998): 301–323.

———. 'When are They Going to Fight? Tsotsis, Youth Politics and the PAC,' in P. Bonner, P. Delius and D. Posel (eds.). *Apartheid's Genesis 1935–1962*. Johannesburg: Ravan Press, 1993.

———. "Swines, Hazels, and the Dirty Dozen: Masculinity, Territoriality and the Youth Gangs of Soweto, 1960–1976," *Journal of Southern African Studies*, 24, 4 (December 1988): 719–736.

Gordon, Suzanne. *A Talent for Tomorrow: Life Stories of South African Servants*. Johannesburg: Ravan Press, 1985.

Greenberg, Steven. *Legitimating the Illegitimate: State, Markets and Resistance in South Africa*. Berkeley: University of California Press, 1989.

Grinker, D. *Inside Soweto*. Johannesburg: Ravan Press, 1986.

Grundlingh, Albert. *Fighting Their Own War: South African Blacks and the First World War*. Johannesburg: Ravan Press, 1987.

Guenter, Lewy. *False Consciousness: An Essay of Mystification*. New Brunswick: Transaction Books, 1982.

Habermas, Jurgen. "New Social Movements." *Telos*, 49 (Fall 1981): 43–57.

——. *The Structural Transformation of the Public Sphere*. Cambridge: MIT Press, 1989.

Hallet, R. "Revolution on the Veld: Forced Removals in South Africa." *African Affairs*, 83 (1984): 301–320.

Harries, D. (pseudonym). "Daniel Koza: A Working Class Leader," *Africa Perspective*, 19 (1981): 2–38.

Hart, D. M. "Political Manipulation of Urban Space: The Razing of District Six, Cape Town," *Urban Geography*, 9 (1990): 603–628.

Harvey, David. *Consciousness and the Urban Experience*. Oxford: Blackwells, 1985.

Hellmann, Ellen. *Rooiyard: A Sociological Survey of an Urban Native Slumyard*. Oxford: University Press, 1948.

Hepple, Alex MP. "Bus Boycott and African Wages," *The Forum* (April 1957): 7–11.

——. *Pass Controls and the Urban African Proletariat*. Johannesburg: Ravan Press, 1987.

Herdt, Gilbert. *Secrecy and Cultural Reality: Utopian Ideologies of the New Guinea Men's House*. Ann Arbor: University of Michigan, 2006.

Hine, Darlene Clark. "Rape and the Inner Lives of Black Women in the Middle West: Preliminary Thoughts on the Culture of Dissemblance," *Signs: Journal of Women and Culture in Society*, 14 (Summer 1989): 912–920.

Hirschmann, David. "The Black Consciousness Movement in South Africa," *Journal of Modern African Studies*, 28, 1 (March 1990): 1–22.

Hirson, Baruch. *Yours for the Union: Class and Community Struggles in South Africa, 1930–1947*. Johannesburg: University of the Witwatersrand, 1989.

——. *Year of Fire, Year of Ash*. London: Zed, 1979.

Hoare, Quinten and Geoffrey Novell (eds.). *Selections from the Prison Notebooks of Antonio Gramsci*. New York: International Publishers, 1971.

Hobart, Houghton D. "Men of Two Worlds: Some Aspects of Migratory Labour in South Africa," *South Africa Journal of Economics*, 28, 3 (1960): 20–32.

Hoernle, R. F. *South African Native Policy and the Liberal Spirit*. Johannesburg: Ravan Press, 1945.

Holland, Heidi. *The Struggle: A History of the African National Congress*. London: Grafton Books, 1989 & 1990.

Horrell, Muriel. *The Pass Laws*. Johannesburg: South African Institute of Race Relations, 1960.

——. *A Survey of Race Relations, 1959–60*. Johannesburg: South African Institute of Race Relations, 1961.

——. *A Survey of Race Relations, 1962*. Johannesburg: South African Institute of Race Relations, 1963.

——. *Bantu Education to 1968.* Johannesburg: South African Institute of Race Relations, 1968.

——. *Legislation and Race Relations.* Natal: University of Natal Press, 1971.

——. *Group Areas: The Emerging Pattern with Illustrative Examples from the Transvaal.* Johannesburg: South African Institute of Race Relations, 1966.

Houston, Gregory F. *The National Liberation Struggle in South Africa: A Case Study of the United Democratic Front, 1983–1987.* Ashgate: Aldershot, 1999.

Huddleston, Trevor. *Naught for Your Comfort.* Johannesburg: Hardingham and Donaldson, 1956.

Hyslop, Johnathan. "Teacher Resistance in African Education from the 1940s to the 1980s." in Mokubung Nkomo, ed. *Pedagogy of Domination: Toward a Democratic Education in South Africa.* Trenton: Africa World Press, 1990.

——. "State Education Policy and the Social Representation of the Urban Working Class: The Case of the Southern Transvaal 1955–1976," *Journal of Southern African Studies,* 14, 3 (April 1988): 446–476.

Jacobs, Margaret. *White Mother to a Dark Race: Settler Colonialism, Maternalism, and the Removal of Indigenous Children in the American West and Australia, 1880–1940.* Lincoln: University of Nebraska Press, 2008.

Jenkins, Tim. Talking to Vula: The Story of the Secret Underground Communication Network of Operation Vula, 1995. Articles from Mayibuye, reproduced on www.anc.org.za/ancdocs/history/vula.html.

Jochelson, Karen. "Reform, Repression and Resistance in South Africa: A Case Study of Alexandra Township, 1979–1989," *Journal of Southern African Studies,* 16, 1 (March 1990): 1–32.

Johnson, Shaun. "The Soldiers of Luthuli: Youth Politics of Resistance in South Africa," in Shaun Johnson (ed.). *South Africa No Turning Back.* Basingstoke: Macmillan, 1989, 345–362.

Johnstone, F. A. *Class, Race and Gold: A Study of Class Relations and Racial Discrimination in South Africa.* London: Routledge & Kegan Paul, 1976.

Jones, Emrys. *Readings in Social Geography.* Athens: Ohio University Press, 1975.

Joseph, Helen. *If This Be Treason.* London: Andre Deutsch, 1963.

Kane-Berman, Jane. *Soweto: Black Revolt: White Reaction.* Johannesburg: Ravan Press, 1978.

Karis, Thomas, Gwendolyn Carter. *From Protest to challenge: Documents in South African Politics, 1882–1964.* Vols. 1–3. Berkeley: University of California Press, 1977.

Kelley, Robin D. G. . "We are Not What We Seem: Rethinking Black Working Class Opposition in the Jim Crow South," *Journal of American History,* 80 (June 1993): 75–112.

——. *Race Rebel: Culture and Politics of the Black Working Class.* New York: Free Press, 1994.

Khosa, Meshack M. "Changing Patterns of 'Black' Bus Subsidies in the Apartheid City, 1944–1986." *Geo Journal,* 22 (1990): 251–259.

——. "Routes, Ranks and Rebels: Feuding in the Taxi Revolution," *Journal of Southern African Studies*, 18, 1 (March 1992): 232–251.

Kirk, Joyce F. "A 'Native' Free State at Korsten: Challenge to Segregation in Port Elizabeth, 1901–1905." *International Journal of African Historical Studies*, 17, 2 (June 1991): 309–336.

——. *Making a Voice: African Resistance to Segregation in South Africa.* Boulder: Westview Press, 1988.

Kuper, Leo. *An African Bourgeoisie: Race, Class and Politics in South Africa.* New Haven: Yale University Press, 1967.

——. *Passive Resistance in South Africa.* New Haven: Yale University Press, 1957.

Kuumba, M. Bahati. "You've Struck a Rock:! Comparing Gender, Social Movements, and Transformation in the United States and South Africa." *Gender and Society*, 4, 16 (August 2002): 503–523.

Kynoch, Gary. *We are Fighting the World: A History of the Marashea Gangs in South Africa, 1947–1999.* Athens: Ohio University Press, 2005.

Lacy, M. *Working for Boroko: The Origins of a Coercive Labour System in South Africa.* Johannesburg: Ravan Press, 1981.

La Hausse, Paul. *Brewers, Beerhalls and Boycotts: A History of Liquor in South Africa.* History Workshop Topics Series 2, Johannesburg: Ravan Press, 1988.

Lefebvre, Henri. *The Production of Space*, Translated by Donald Nicholson-Smith. Massachusetts: Blackwell Publishing, 1974, 1984.

Legassick, Martin. *Class and Nationalism in South African Protest: The South African Communist Party and the 'Native Republic', 1928–1934.* Syracuse: Syracuse University Press, 1973.

——. "Legislation, Ideology and Economy in Post-1948 South Africa." *Journal of Southern African Studies*, 1, 1 (1974): 52–65.

Lerumo, A. (pseudonym for Michael Harmel). *Fifty Fighting Years: The Communist Party of South Africa, 1921–1971.* London: Inkululeko Publications, 1971.

Levine, Carole. *Dreaming the English Renaissance: The Politics of Desire in Court and Culture.* New York: Palgrave Macmillan, 2008.

Lewis, P. R. B. "A City within a City: The Creation of Soweto." in E. Hellman (ed.). *Soweto: Johannesburg's African City.* Johannesburg: Ravan Press, 1971.

Lloyd, Fran and Catherine O'Brien, (eds). *Secret Spaces, Forbidden Places: Rethinking Culture.* New York: Berghahn Books, 2000.

Lodge, Tom. *Black Politics in South Africa since 1945.* London: Longman, 1983.

——. "We Are Being Punished Because We Are Poor: The Bus Boycott of Evaton and Alexandra, 1955–1957." in Phil Bonner (ed.). *Working Papers in Southern Africa*, (Johannesburg: Ravan Press) 1981. 258–303.

——. "The Destruction of Sophiatown." *Journal of Modern African Studies*, 19, 1 (March 1991): 107–132.

Love, Janice, Peter C. Sederberg. "Black Education and the Dialectics of Transformation in South Africa, 1982–8." *Journal of Modern African Studies*, 28, 2 (June 1990): 299–326.

Luthuli, Albert. *Let My People Go*. New York: McGraw Hill, 1962. Reprint ed. New York:Meridian Books, 1969.

Mabin, Alan. "Comprehensive Segregation: The Origins of the Group Areas Act and Its Planning Initiatives," *Journal of Southern African Studies*, 18, 2 (June 1992): 405–429.

Magubane, Bernard Makhosezwe. *The Political Economy of Race and Class in South Africa*. New York: Monthly Review Press, 1979.

——. *From Soweto to Uitenhage*. Trenton: African World Press, 1990.

Magubane, Bernard, Nzomgola Ntalaja. "Proletarianization and Class Struggle in Africa," *International Journal of African Historical Studies*, 17, 2 (1984): 323–355.

Mandela, Nelson. *The Long Walk to Freedom*. Johannesburg: Ravan Press, 1994.

Mandela, Winnie. *Part of My Soul*, Edited by Anne Benjamin. Harmondsworth: Penguin Books, 1985.

Mare, Gerhard. *Ethnicity and Politics in South Africa*. London: Zed Books, 1993.

Marks, Shula. *The Ambiguities of Dependence in South Africa: Class, Nationalism, And the State in Twentieth Century Natal*. London: Longman, 1986.

Marks, Shula & Richard Rathbone (eds.). *Industrialisation and Social Change in South Africa: African Class Formation, Culture and Consciousness*. London: Longman, 1985.

Martin, David, Phyllis Johnson. *The Struggle for Zimbabwe: The Chimurenga War*. New York: Monthly Review Press, 1981.

Marx, Anthony. *Making Race and Nation: A Comparison of South Africa, the United States and Brazil*. Cambridge: Cambridge University Press, 1998.

——. *Lessons of Struggle: South African Internal Opposition, 1960–1990*. New York: Oxford University Press, 1992.

Mathabane, Mark. *Kaffir Boy: The True Story of A Black Youth's Coming of Age in Apartheid South Africa*. New York: Free Press, 1986.

Mather, C. T. "Racial Segregation and Johannesburg's 'Location in the sky,' " *South African Geographical Journal*, 69 (1987): 119–128.

Mattera, Don. *Gone with the Twilight: A Story of Sophiatown*. London: Zed Books, 1987.

McCarthy, Jeff, Mark Swilling. "Transport and Political Resistance." *South African Review*, 2 (1984): 26–44.

——. " 'SA's Emerging Pattern of Bus Transportation." *Political Geography Quarterly*, 5 (1985): 235–249.

Merrett, Christopher. *A Culture of Censorship: Secrecy and Intellectual Repression in South Africa*. Macon: Mercer University Press, 1995.

—— and Roger Granvil. "Comparing Human Rights: South Africa and Argentina, 1976–1989." *Comparative Studies in Society and History*, 33, 2 (April 1981): 255–287.

Mokonyane, Dan. *Lessons of Azikwelwa*. London: Nakong ya Rena, 1994.

Moodie, Dunbar. *The Rise of Afrikanerdom: Power, Apartheid and Afrikaner Civil Religion*. Berkeley: University of California Press, 1975.

Morrell, Robert. "Of Boys and Men: Masculinity and Gender in South African Society." *Journal of Southern African Studies*, 24, 4 (December 1988): 605–630.

Mthetwa, Themba. "Urban Community, Migrant Workers and Popular Protests: Alexandra Case Study from 1984 to 1987." University of the Witwatersrand, Industrial Sociology, 1990.

Mufson, Stephen. *Fighting Years: Black Resistance and the Struggle for a New South Africa*. Boston: Beacon Press, 1990.

Munger, Edwin S. *Afrikaner and African Nationalism, South African Parallels and Parameters*. London: Oxford University Press, 1967.

Mzamane, Mbuleo Vizikhungo. *The Children of Soweto*. London: Longman, 1982.

Ngculu, James. "The Role of Umkhonto we Sizwe in the Creation of a Democratic Civil-Military Relations Tradition," www.iss.co.za/pubs/Books/OurselvesToKnow/Ngculu2.pdf,

Ngubane, Jordan K. *An African Explains Apartheid*. London: Pall Mall, 1963.

Odendaal, Andre. *Vukani Bantu! The Beginnings of Black Protest Politics in South Africa to 1912*. Cape Town and Johannesburg: David Phillip, 1984.

O'Meara, Dan. *Vokskapitalism, Class, Capital and Ideology in the Development of Afrikaner Nationalism 1934–1948*. Johannesburg: Ravan Press, 1983.

Parnell, Susan. "Public Housing as a Device for White Residential Segregation in Johannesburg, 1934–1953." *Urban Geography*, 9, 6 (November-December 1988): 345–360.

——. "Creating Racial Privilege: The Origins of South Africa Public Health and Town Planning Legislation," *Journal of Southern African Studies*, 19, 3 (September 1993): 471–488.

——. "Sanitation, Segregation and the Natives (Urban Areas) Act: African Exclusion from Johannesburg's Malay Location, 1897–1925." *Journal of African Historical Geography*, 17 (July 1991): 271–288.

——. "Racial Segregation in Johannesburg: The Slums Act 1934–1939 " *South African Geographical Journal*, 70 (1986): 112–126.

Penn, Shana. *Solidarity's Secret: The Women Who Defeated Communism in Poland*. Ann Arbor: University of Michigan, 2005.

Perlan, John. "Bus Boycotts, Monopolies and the State," *Work in Progress*, 31 (May 1984): 23–37.

Pile, Steve, Michael Keith. *Geographies of Resistance*. London: Routledge, 1997.

Pirie, G. H. "Ethno-linguistic Zoning in South African Black Townships." *Area*, 16, 4 (1988): 462–523.

———. "Rolling Segregation into Apartheid: South African Railways, 1948–1953." *Journal of Contemporary History*, 27 (October 1992): 671–693.

———. "The Transformation of Johannesburg's Western Areas." *Journal of Urban History*, 11 (August 1985): 387–410.

———. "Urban Population Removals in South Africa," *Geography*, 68 (1983): 347–349.

Pirie, G. H., D. Hart. "The Transformation of Johannesburg's Black Western Areas." *Journal of Urban History*, 11, 4 (August 1985): 220–235.

Piven, Frances Fox. *Poor People's Movements: Why They Succeed, How They Fail.* New York: Vintage, 1979.

Plaatje, Solomon T. *Native Life in South Africa Before and Since the European War And the Boer Rebellion.* London: P. S. King and Sons, Ltd, 1920.

Platzky, L., Cherryl Walker. *The Surplus People: Forced Removals in South Africa.* Johannesburg: Surplus Peoples Project, 1985.

———. "The Meaning of Apartheid before 1948: Conflicts of Interests and Powers Within the Afrikaner Nationalist Alliance." *Journal of Southern African Studies*, 14, 1 (1987): 154–166.

———. *The Making of Apartheid.* Oxford: Oxford University Press, 1991.

Price, R. *The Apartheid State in Crisis: Political Transformation in South Africa, 1975–1990.* Berkeley: University of California Press, 1990.

Reagan, Timothy A. "The Politics of Linguistic Apartheid: Language Politics in Black Education in South Africa," *Journal of Negro Education*, 56, 3 (Summer 1983): 299–312.

Rees, Rob. "Urban Movements in South African Black Townships: A Case-Study." *International Journal of Urban and Regional Research*, 14, 1 (March 1990): 109–134.

Rich, Paul. "Ministering to the White Man's Needs: The Development of Urban Segregation in South Africa, 1913–1923." *African Studies*, 37, 2 (1978): 444–465.

———. "Apartheid Theory, 1930–1939." *Journal of Southern African Studies*, 7, 2 (Summer 1980): 120–134.

Ritzer, George, Douglas J. Goodman. *Sociological Theory.* 6th ed. Boston: McGraw Hill, 2004.

Robinson, David. *Paths of Accommodation: Muslim Societies and French Colonial Authorities in Senegal and Mauritania, 1880–1920.* Athens: Ohio University Press, 2000.

Robinson, Jennifer. "A Perfect System of Control? State Power and 'Native Locations' in South Africa; *Environment and Planning Changing Society and Space*, 8 (1990): 135–162.

———. *The Power of Apartheid: State, Power, and Space in South African Cities.* Oxford: Heinemann, 1996.

Rogaly, Joe. "The Bus Boycott," *The Forum* (March 1957): 11–15.

Roux, Edward. *The Native Reserves in Post-War Reconstruction*. South African Race Relations Institute, 1944.

———. *Time Longer than Rope: A History of the Black Man's Struggle for Freedom in South Africa*. Madison: University of Wisconsin Press, 1966.

Rude, George. *Ideology and Popular Protest*. New York: Pantheon Books, 1980.

Lynn., Saffery, A. "A Colour Bar Question: Native Bus and Taxi Drivers." *Race Relations Journal*, 1, 2 (January-February 1934): 17–18.

Sampson, Anthony. *The Treason Cage: The Opposition on Trial in South Africa*. London: Heinemann, 1958.

Sapire, Hilary. "Apartheid's Testing Ground: Urban 'Native Policy' and African Politics in Brakpan, South Africa, 1943–1948." *Journal of African History*, 35, 1 (1994): 99–123.

Savage, Michael. "The Imposition of the Pass Laws on the South African Population in South Africa." *African Affairs*, 85, 339 (April 1986): 181–205.

———. "Social Mobility and Class Analysis: A New Agenda for Social History." *Social History*, 19 (January 1994): 69–79.

Scott, James C. *Weapons of the Weak*. New Haven: Yale University Press, 1985.

———. *Domination and the Arts of Resistance: Hidden Transcripts*. New Haven: Yale University Press, 1990.

———. *Seeing Like a State: How Certain Schemes Have Failed*. New Haven: Yale University, 1999.

Seidman, Gay. "Guerrillas in the Midst: Armed Struggle in the South African Anti-Apartheid Movement," *Mobilization: An International Journal*, 6, 2 (1992): 111–127.

Seekings, Jeremy. " Workers and the Politics of Consumer Boycotts." *South African Labour Bulletin*, 11, 6 (June/July 1986): 20–34.

———. "People's Courts and Popular Critics," in SARS (ed.). *South African Review*, 5 (Johannesburg: Ravan Press, 1989): 119–135.

———. *Heroes or Villains? Youth Politics in the 1980s*. Johannesburg: Ravan Press, 1993.

Simons, H. J. *African Women: Their Legal Status in South Africa*. London: Hurst, 1968.

—— & R. E. Simons. *Class and Colour in South Africa 1850–1950*. Baltimore: Penguin Books, 1969.

Sitas, Ari. "The Making of the Comrades Movement in Natal, 1985–1991." *Journal of Southern African Studies*, 18, 3 (1992): 45–62.

Skelcher, Bradley. "Apartheid and the Removal of Black Spots from Lake Bhangazi in KwaZulu/Natal South Africa," *Journal of Black Studies*, 33, 6 (July 2003): 761–783.

Southworth, Hamilton. "Strangling South Africa's Cities: Resistance to Group Areas in Durban During the 1950's," *International Journal of African Historical Studies*, 23, 1 (1990): 1–34.

Stadler, Alfred. "Birds in the Cornfield: Squatter Movements in Johannesburg, 1944–47." *Journal of Southern African Studies*, 6, 1 (1979): 360–372.

——. "A Long Way to Walk: Bus Boycotts in Alexandra, 1940–1945." in Phil Bonner (ed). *Working Papers in Southern African Studies*, 1981. 228–257.

Strydom, C. J. S. *Black and White Africans: A Factual Account of South African Race Policies in the Verwoerd Era*. Cape Town: Juta Press, 1967.

Suttles, G. D. *The Social Order of the Slum*. Chicago: University of Chicago Press, 1979.

Suttner, Raymond. *The ANC Underground in South Africa*. Auckland Park: Jacana Media, 2008.

——. "The African National Congress (ANC) Underground: From the M-Plan to Rivonia," *South African Historical Journal*, 49 (November 2003): 123–146.

Swanson, M. "The Sanitation Syndrome: Bubonic Plague and Urban Native Policy in the Cape Colony, 1900–1909." *Journal of African History*, 18 (1977): 44–56.

——. "The Politics of Subsistence: Community Struggles in War-time Johannesburg." in D. Hindson (ed.). *Working Papers in Southern African Studies*. Johannesburg: Ravan Press, 1983.

Swilling, M. "The Buses Smell of Blood: The East London Boycott," *South Africa Labour Bulletin*, 9, 5 (March 1995): 22–41.

Switzer, Les. "The Ambiguities of Protest in South Africa: Rural Politics and the Press During the 1920's." *International Journal of African Historical Studies*, 23, 1 (1990): 87–109.

——. "Bantu World and the Origins of a Captive African Commercial Press in South Africa," *Journal of Southern African Studies*, 14, 3 (April 1988): 352–370.

—— (ed.). *South Africa's Alternative Press: Voices of Protest and Resistance, 1880's-1960's*. Cambridge: Cambridge University Press, 1997.

—— and Mohamed Adhikari (eds.). *South Africa's Resistance Press: Alternative Voices in The Last Generation Under Apartheid*. Athens: Ohio University Center for International Studies, Research in Regional Studies Africa Series no.74, 2000.

Taylor, Maureen. "The 1913 Natal Indian Strike." *Journal of Southern African Studies*, 10, 2 (April 1984): 56–72.

Thompson, Leonard. *The Unification of South Africa 1902–1910*. Oxford: Clarendon Press, 1960.

——. *The Political Mythology of Apartheid*. New Haven: Yale University Press, 1985.

Unterhalter, Elaine. *Forced Removal: The Division, Segregation and Control of the People of South Africa*. London: International Defence Fund, 1987.

Van der Ross, R. E. *The Rise and Decline of Apartheid: A Study of Political Movements Among the Coloured People in South Africa, 1880–1985*. Cape Town: Talberg, 1986.

Van Onselen, Charles. *Studies in the Social and Economic History of the Witwatersrand 1886–1914.* Vol I, New Babylon and Vol II, New Ninevah. Johannesburg: Ravan Press, 1983.

Walker, Cherryl (ed). *Women and Gender in Southern Africa to 1945.* Cape Town: David Philip and London, 1990.

——. *Women and Resistance in South Africa.* New York: Monthly Review Press, 1982.

Walshe, Peter. *The Rise of African Nationalism in South Africa: The African National Congress, 1912–1952.* London: C. Hurst & Co, 1970.

Webster, Eddie (ed.). *Essays in Southern African Labour History.* Johannesburg: Ravan Press, 1981.

Wells, Julia C. *We Now Demand! The History of Women's Resistance to Pass Laws in South Africa.* Johannesburg: University of the Witwatersrand Press, 1993.

——. "Why Women Rebel: Women's Resistance in Bloemfontein (1913) and Johannesburg (1956)," *Journal of Southern African Studies,* 10, 1 (1983): 55–70.

Welsh, A. S. *Natives in Urban Areas.* Johannesburg: Radford & Addlington, 1942.

Welsh, David. *The Roots of Segregation: Native Policy in Colonial Natal, 1854.* Cape Town: Juta Press, 1971.

Yawitch, J. "Natal 1959-The Women's Protests." Paper presented at the Conference on the History of Opposition in South Africa, University of the Witwatersrand, January 1978.

Zips, Werner. *Black Rebels: African Caribbean Freedom Fighters in Jamaica.* Princeton: Marcus Weiner Publishers, 1999.

THESES AND DISSERTATIONS

Brooks, Alan K. "From Class Struggle to National Liberation: The Communist Party of South Africa, 1940–1950." MA thesis, Sussex University, 1967.

Carter, Charles E. "Comrades and Community: Politics and the Construction of Hegemony in Alexandra Township, South Africa 1984–7," unpublished PhD thesis, Oxford University, 1991.

Curry, Dawne Y. "Class, Community, Culture and Resistance in Alexandria, South Africa, 1912–1985." PhD Dissertation, Michigan State University, 2006.

French, Kevin J. "James Mpanza and the Sofasonke Party in the Development of Local Politics in Soweto," MA Dissertation, University of the Witwatersrand, 1983.

Glaser, Clive. "Anti-Social Bandits, Juvenile Delinquency and the Tsotsis: Youth Gang Subculture on the Witwatersrand 1936–1960," unpublished MA dissertation, University of the Witwatersrand 1995.

Hindson, Doug. "The Pass System and the Formation of an Urban African Proletariat: A Critique of the Cheap Labour Thesis." Ph. D. dissertation, University of Sussex, 1983.

Jeffrey, Ian. "Cultural Trends and Community Formation in a South African Township: Sharpeville1943–1985," MA Dissertation, University of the Witwatersrand 1991.

Jochelson, Karen. "Urban Crisis, State Reform and Popular Reaction: A Case Study of Alexandra," unpublished Honours dissertation, University of the Witwatersrand 1988.

Kramer, J. "Self Help in Soweto: Mutual Aid Societies in A South African City" MA dissertation, University of Bergen, Norway, 1976.

Kros, Cynthia. "Urban African Women's Organizations and Protests on the Rand from the Years 1939 to 1956," unpublished BA Honours thesis, 1978.

Lucas, Justine. "Space, Society and Culture: Housing and local Level Politics in a Section of Alexandra Township 1991–1992," unpublished MA thesis, University of the Witwatersrand 1995.

Manoim, I. "The Black Press 1945–63," MA dissertation, University of the Witwatersrand, 1983.

Mariotti, Amelia Marte. "The Incorporation of African Wage into Wage Employment in South Africa, 1920–1970," PhD Thesis, University of Connecticut, 1980.

Nauright, John. "Black Island in a White Sea," Ph. D. Thesis, Kingston: Queens University,1992.

Ramagaga, Samuel Mabolle. "The Contributions of the Holy Cross Sisters to Black Schooling in Alexandra, Johannesburg, With Particular Reference to the Period 1950–1970, MA thesis, University of the Witwatersrand, Johannesburg, January 1988.

Sarakinsky, Mike. "From Freehold Township to Model Township: A Political History of Alexandra 1905–1983," unpublished honours dissertation, University of the Witwatersrand 1984.

Seekings, Jeremy. "Quiescence and the Transition to Confrontation: South African Townships, 1978–1984." Ph. D. Phil. Thesis, University of Oxford (November 1990), 326.

Tourikis, P. "The Political Economy of Alexandra Township, 1905–1958," BA Honours Dissertation, Sociology, University of Witwatersrand, Johannesburg, 1981.

Works, Brendan. Popular Opposition to Apartheid, 1950–1990, Ph.D. dissertation, University of California at Berkeley, 1990.

Index